Nietzsche's
Legacy for Education

Critical Studies in Education and Culture Series

Racial Categorization of Multiracial Children in Schools
Jane Ayers Chiong

bell hooks' Engaged Pedagogy: Education for Critical Consciousness
Namulundah Florence

Wittgenstein: Philosophy, Postmodernism, Pedagogy
Michael Peters and James Marshall

Policy, Pedagogy, and Social Inequality: Community College Student Realities in Post-Industrial America
Penelope E. Herideen

Psychoanalysis and Pedagogy
Stephen Appel, editor

The Rhetoric of Diversity and the Traditions of American Literary Study: Critical Multiculturalism in English
Lesliee Antonette

Becoming and Unbecoming White: Owning and Disowning a Racial Identity
Christine Clark and James O'Donnell

Critical Pedagogy: An Introduction, 2nd Edition
Barry Kanpol

Michel Foucault: Materialism and Education
Mark Olssen

Revolutionary Social Transformation: Democratic Hopes, Political Possibilities, and Critical Education
Paula Allman

Critical Reflection and the Foreign Language Classroom
Terry A. Osborn

Community in Motion: Theatre for Development in Africa
L. Dale Byam

Nietzsche's Legacy for Education

Past and Present Values

Edited by Michael Peters, James Marshall and Paul Smeyers

CRITICAL STUDIES IN EDUCATION
AND CULTURE SERIES
Edited by Henry A. Giroux

BERGIN & GARVEY
Westport, Connecticut • London

Library of Congress Cataloging-in-Publication Data

Nietzsche's legacy for education : past and present values / edited by Michael Peters,
   James Marshall, and Paul Smeyers.
      p.   cm.—(Critical studies in education and culture series, ISSN 1064-8615)
   Includes bibliographical references and index.
   ISBN 0-89789-656-4 (alk. paper)
      1. Nietzsche, Friedrich Wilhelm, 1844-1900—Contributions in education.   2.
   Education—Philosophy.   I. Peters, Michael (Michael A.), 1948-   II. Marshall, James
   (James D.)   III. Smeyers, Paul.   IV. Series.
   LB675.N636N54   2001
   370'.1—dc21   00-036056

British Library Cataloguing in Publication Data is available.

Library of Congress Catalog Card Number: 00-036056
ISBN: 0-89789-656-4
ISSN: 1064-8615

First published in 2001

Bergin & Garvey, 88 Post Road West, Westport, CT 06881
An imprint of Greenwood Publishing Group, Inc.
www.greenwood.com

Printed in the United States of America

(∞)™

The paper used in this book complies with the
Permanent Paper Standard issued by the National
Information Standards Organization (Z39.48-1984).

10 9 8 7 6 5 4 3 2 1

Copyright Acknowledgment

The author and publisher gratefully acknowledge permission to reprint material from the
following copyrighted source:

"Thus Spake Zarathustra" by Friedrich Nietzsche and "Beyond Good and Evil" by Friedrich
Nietzsche, from THE PORTABLE NIETZSCHE, edited by Walter Kaufmann, translated by
Walter Kaufmann, copyright 1954 by The Viking Press, renewed © 1982 by Viking Penguin
Inc. Used by permission of Viking Penguin, a division of Penguin-Putnam Inc.

Contents

Series Foreword

Educational reform has fallen upon hard times. The traditional assumption that schooling is fundamentally tied to the imperatives of citizenship designed to educate students to exercise civic leadership and public service has been eroded. The schools are now the key institution for producing professional, technically trained, credentialized workers for whom the demands of citizenship are subordinated to the vicissitudes of the marketplace and the commercial public sphere. Given the current corporate and right wing assault on public and higher education, coupled with the emergence of a moral and political climate that has shifted to a new Social Darwinism, the issues which framed the democratic meaning, purpose, and use to which education might aspire have been displaced by more vocational and narrowly ideological considerations.

The war waged against the possibilities of an education wedded to the precepts of a real democracy is not merely ideological. Against the backdrop of reduced funding for public schooling, the call for privatization, vouchers, cultural uniformity, and choice, there are the often ignored larger social realities of material power and oppression. On the national level, there has been a vast resurgence of racism. This is evident in the passing of anti-immigration laws such as Proposition 187 in California, the dismantling of the welfare state, the demonization of black youth that is taking place in the popular media, and the remarkable attention provided by the media to forms of race talk that argue for the intellectual inferiority of blacks or dismiss calls for racial justice as simply a holdover from the "morally bankrupt" legacy of the 1960s.

Poverty is on the rise among children in the United States, with 20 percent of all children under the age of eighteen living below the poverty line.

Unemployment is growing at an alarming rate for poor youth of color, especially in the urban centers. While black youth are policed and disciplined in and out of the nation's schools, conservative and liberal educators define education through the ethically limp discourses of privatization, national standards, and global competitiveness.

Many writers in the critical education tradition have attempted to challenge the right wing fundamentalism behind educational and social reform in both the United States and abroad while simultaneously providing ethical signposts for a public discourse about education and democracy that is both prophetic and transformative. Eschewing traditional categories, a diverse number of critical theorists and educators have successfully exposed the political and ethical implications of the cynicism and despair that has become endemic to the discourse of schooling and civic life. In its place, such educators strive to provide a language of hope that inextricably links the struggle over schooling to understanding and transforming our present social and cultural dangers.

At the risk of overgeneralizing, both cultural studies theorists and critical educators have emphasized the importance of understanding theory as the grounded basis for "intervening into contexts and power . . . in order to enable people to act more strategically in ways that may change their context for the better."[1] Moreover, theorists in both fields have argued for the primacy of the political by calling for and struggling to produce critical public spaces, regardless of how fleeting they may be, in which "popular cultural resistance is explored as a form of political resistance."[2] Such writers have analyzed the challenges that teachers will have to face in redefining a new mission for education, one that is linked to honoring the experiences, concerns, and diverse histories and languages that give expression to the multiple narratives that engage and challenge the legacy of democracy.

Equally significant is the insight of recent critical educational work that connects the politics of difference with concrete strategies for addressing the crucial relationships between schooling and the economy, and citizenship and the politics of meaning in communities of multicultural, multiracial, and multilingual schools.

Critical Studies in Education and Culture attempts to address and demonstrate how scholars working in the fields of cultural studies and critical pedagogy might join together in a radical project and practice informed by theoretically rigorous discourses that affirm the critical but refuse the cynical, and establish hope as central to a critical pedagogical and political practice but eschew a romantic utopianism. Central to such a project is the issue of how pedagogy might provide cultural studies theorists and educators with an opportunity to engage pedagogical practices that are not only transdisciplinary, transgressive, and oppositional, but also connected to a wider project designed to further racial, economic, and political democracy.[3] By taking seriously the relations between culture and power, we further the possibilities of resistance, struggle, and change.

Critical Studies in Education and Culture is committed to publishing work that opens a narrative space that affirms the contextual and the specific while simultaneously recognizing the ways in which such spaces are shot through with issues of power. The series attempts to continue an important legacy of theoretical work in cultural studies in which related debates on pedagogy are understood and addressed within the larger context of social responsibility, civic courage, and the reconstruction of democratic public life. We must keep in mind Raymond Williams's insight that the "deepest impulse (informing cultural politics) is the desire to make learning part of the process of social change itself."[4] Education as a cultural pedagogical practice takes place across multiple sites, which include not only schools and universities but also the mass media, popular culture, and other public spheres, and signals how within diverse contexts, education makes us both subjects of and subject to relations of power.

This series challenges the current return to the primacy of market values and simultaneous retreat from politics so evident in the recent work of educational theorists, legislators, and policy analysts. Professional relegitimation in a troubled time seems to be the order of the day as an increasing number of academics both refuse to recognize public and higher education as critical public spheres and offer little or no resistance to the ongoing vocationalization of schooling, the continuing evisceration of the intellectual labor force, and the current assaults on the working poor, the elderly, and women and children.[5]

Emphasizing the centrality of politics, culture, and power, *Critical Studies in Education and Culture* will deal with pedagogical issues that contribute in imaginative and transformative ways to our understanding of how critical knowledge, democratic values, and social practices can provide a basis for teachers, students, and other cultural workers to redefine their role as engaged and public intellectuals. Each volume will attempt to rethink the relationship between language and experience, pedagogy and human agency, and ethics and social responsibility as part of a larger project for engaging and deepening the prospects of democratic schooling in a multiracial and multicultural society. *Critical Studies in Education and Culture* takes on the responsibility of witnessing and addressing the most pressing problems of public schooling and civic life, and engages culture as a crucial site and strategic force for productive social change.

Henry A. Giroux

NOTES

1. Lawrence Grossberg, "Toward a Genealogy of the State of Cultural Studies," in *Disciplinarity and Dissent in Cultural Studies*, ed. Cary Nelson and Dilip Parameshwar Gaonkar (New York: Routledge, 1996), 143.

2. David Bailey and Stuart Hall, "The Vertigo of Displacement," *Ten* 8 (2:3) (1992), 19.

3. My notion of transdisciplinary comes from Mas'ud Zavarzadeh and Donald Morton, "Theory, Pedagogy, Politics. The Crisis of the 'Subject' in the Humanities," in *Theory/Pedagogy/Politics: Texts for Change*, ed. Mas'ud Zavarzadeh and Donald Morton (Urbana University of Illinois Press, 1992), 10. At issue here is neither ignoring the boundaries of discipline-based knowledge nor simply fusing different disciplines, but creating theoretical paradigms, questions, and knowledge that cannot be taken up within the policed boundaries of the existing disciplines.

4. Raymond Williams, "Adult Education and Social Change," in *What I Came to Say* (London: Hutchinson-Radus, 1989), 158.

5. The term "professional legitimation" comes from a personal correspondence with Professor Jeff Williams of East Carolina University.

Preface and Acknowledgments

The works of Friedrich Nietzsche are enjoying perhaps the most sustained study and engagement by scholars and philosophers in the English-speaking world since his death in 1900. Certainly, there has been a huge increase of scholarly interest, activity and publishing on Nietzsche during the last decade. This degree of activity in the English-speaking world was preceded, by and large, with a few exceptions including Walter Kaufmann and R. J. Hollingdale, by the work of French philosophers. Jacques Derrida, Gilles Deleuze, Michel Foucault, Sarah Kofmann, Maurice Blanchot, Jean-François Lyotard, Pierre Klossowski, and many others—drawing upon the interpretations, in particular, of Martin Heidegger, but also Georges Bataille—began to read, translate and publish on the works of Nietzsche from the late 1950s. Their combined work provided an influential set of interpretations and laid the groundwork for the revival of interest in Nietzsche in the English-speaking world during the 1980s, although Walter Kaufmann's important translations and interpretation date also from the early 1950s.

Little work on Nietzsche's educational philosophy and writings had been written before David Cooper's book *Authenticity and Learning* appeared in 1983. While there has been some scholarship engaging his educational writings published in the journals of philosophy of education during the intervening period, notably by scholars from Israel, there have been very few book-length engagements with his educational philosophy and writings. This volume, then, is designed to fill the vacuum. We see it as only a first step in beginning to encourage greater scholarship and engagement with Nietzsche's works from an educational perspective. After all, Nietzsche was a classical scholar, though not a great one. As someone trained in philology, he understood in great detail the cultural importance of a classical humanist education, even though he would also want to question the figure of "man" underlying forms of humanism and what he regarded as the sterility of "technical" scholarship pursued for its own sake. In an obvious sense education was central to Nietzsche's cultural concerns. What also should make him of considerable interest to educationalists is his troubled legacy, his appropriation by various political and cultural groups and his uncanny ability to project the future on the basis of his analysis of the past. No one in education can afford to ignore his challenge to contemporary values; his diagnosis of Western modernity in terms of the question of nihilism; nor his positive philosophical and ethical response to present cultural phenomena of "homelessness," cultural dissolution and fragmentation and the disintegration of self.

Edited collections of this kind, involving the participation of scholars from New Zealand, the United States and Belgium, always require patience and cooperation to bring to fruition. Our thanks, as editors, first, go out to all contributors. Michael Peters and James Marshall would also like to acknowledge and thank the University of Auckland for providing some research funds to enable them to make a trip to Belgium in 1999 for an editorial meeting with Paul Smeyers.

Abbreviations

For this collection Nietzsche's works are abbreviated as follows (textual references are in section numbers):

BOOKS

A	*The Anti-Christ*
BGE	*Beyond Good and Evil*
BT	*The Birth of Tragedy*
CW	*The Case of Wagner*
D	*Dawn (Daybreak)*
EH	*Ecce Homo*
GM	*On the Genealogy of Morals*
GS	*The Gay Science*
HH	*Human, All Too Human*
HH1	*Assorted Opinions and Maxims*
HH2	*The Wanderer and His Shadow*
KSA	*Friedrich Nietzsche: Sämtliche Werke*
NCW	*Nietzsche Contra Wagner*
TI	*Twilight of the Idols*
UM	*Untimely Meditations*
WB	*Richard Wagner at Bayreuth*
WP	*The Will to Power*
Z	*Thus Spake Zarathustra*

ESSAYS

TPhil   "The Philosopher: Reflections on the Struggle between Art and Knowledge"

OTaL   "On Truth and Lies in a Nonmoral Sense"

PHT   "Philosophy in Hard Times"

SE   "Schopenhauer as Educator"

FE   "On the Future of Our Educational Institutions"

Introduction

Traces of Nietzsche: Interpretation, Translation and the Canon

Michael Peters, James Marshall and Paul Smeyers

NIETZSCHE'S LIFE

Friedrich Wilhelm Nietzsche was born in Röcken (Sachen) on October 15, 1844. His father and both of his grandfathers were Protestant ministers. The young Friedrich grew up in a pious environment and was bound to study theology himself. The family was moderately well off, which meant that he would later never have to rely on a personal income. After two years his sister, Elisabeth, was born. She would play an important role during his life and perhaps even more so after his death. When he was five years of age his father died, and his family moved to Naumburg. In attending the famous secondary school in Pforta he met Felix Mendelssohn and became interested in the music of Richard Wagner. In 1864 he enrolled at the University of Bonn. Only a year later he followed his professor of classics to the University of Leipzig.

His talents did not stay unnoticed. Before he graduated, at the age of 25, he was offered a chair of classics at the University of Basel (1869). When Nietzsche's academic career started, everything seemed to point to this young genius who would soon become one of Germany's most important scholars of the late nineteenth century. His friendship with Wagner (31 years his senior), his spiritual mentor, would foster his interest in German music and in Greek tragedy. There was also their mutual interest in Arthur Schopenhauer's *Die Welt als Wille und Vorstellung* (*The World as Will and Representation*), which had changed Nietzsche's outlook on philosophy in his student days but which he gradually disregarded.

Nietzsche's interest in philosophy led him away from the classics, and his first book, *Die Geburt der Tragödie aus dem Geiste der Musik* (*The Birth of*

Tragedy), 1872, chased his students out of his classroom. Because of its dark and mythical style and its metaphysical pretensions—bearing the mark of Wagner—it was also heavily criticized by his colleagues. Among other things this caused isolation and lack of recognition, a situation that was soon enforced by his bad health. His vehement attacks of migraine and the rapid deterioration of his eyesight added to the tragedy of his life. In 1879 he was almost completely blind and had to give up his chair in Basel.

In the 1880s Nietzsche spent most of the summers in the mountainside and every winter at the Rivièra. His illness influenced his style and affected the philosophical content of his works. He alternated between periods of violent suffering and even more violent writing. When he felt better, Nietzsche would spend weeks and weeks of continuous writing (dictating to his friend Peter Gast) in a state of complete exaltation, followed by a total mental collapse and long walks in the mountains and by the sea, where he would contemplate. The most famous example of these outbursts of visionary inspiration can be found in the first three parts of *Also Sprach Zarathustra* (*Thus Spake Zarathustra*), all written in less than a fortnight of sheer euphoria respectively in 1882, 1883 and 1884. Later other published works would follow: *Jenseits von Gut und Böse* (1886) (*Beyond Good and Evil*), *Menschliches Allzumenschliches* (1886) (*Human, All Too Human*), *Die Fröhliche Wissenschaft* (1887) (*The Gay Science*), *Zur Genealogie der Moral* (1887) (*On the Genealogy of Morals*), *Götzen-Dämmering* (1888) (*The Twilight of the Idols*) and *Ecce Homo* (1889).

Little is known about the women in Nietzsche's life, except for his mother, his sister, Elisabeth, and Lou von Salomé (a Finnish high society intellectual) with whom he had a brief relationship in 1882. After his final nervous breakdown on January 3, 1889 (in Turin), Nietzsche led a life of total darkness with his mother until she died in 1897. After that he lived with his sister, Elisabeth, until his death on August 8, 1900.

His sister, who had dubious nationalist and anti-Semitic sympathies, made sure that Nietzsche's work would be misinterpreted to her and others' benefit. Thousands of German soldiers read *Also Sprach Zarathustra*—one of them an Austrian corporal who adopted the ideas about the *Übermensch* and turned them into a bold, materialistic and biologically inspired race theory of Arian supremacy: thus originated Hitler's *Mein Kampf.*

NIETZSCHE'S PLACE IN THE PHILOSOPHY CURRICULUM

Nietzsche's place in the Anglo-American philosophy curriculum—his almost complete absence during the three decades of the 1950s, 1960s and 1970s and his prominence in the 1990s—we take to be part of a first-order problem for philosophy of education. It is not just a problem for philosophy (or for the constitution of the philosophy curriculum, or for the pedagogy of philosophy) but also, necessarily, a problem for philosophy of education. This is because we construe philosophy of education as encompassing what counts as a curriculum for philosophy, and what counts as a pedagogy of philosophy (i.e., curriculum matters and matters of pedagogy) is the province of a philosophy of education. This is certainly a Nietzschean point.

The issues of why and how a philosophy curriculum changes include not only changing intellectual fashions in a discipline that is prone to pride itself on universality, permanence and truth, but also changes in the pedagogy of philosophy, in what counts as philosophy and in who is to be incorporated as part of a national philosophical canon. (In particular, how does a philosopher become enshrined in a curriculum and become part of a national tradition?) Nietzsche seemed to be excluded from the Anglo-American logico-analytic canon on both of these general counts. The situation is similar for the French poststructuralist philosophers and is particularly well illustrated by the attacks on Derrida over the proposal to award him an honorary doctorate at the University of Cambridge. But there have been changes for Nietzsche.

The change in Anglo-American philosophy from an exclusion of Nietzsche to an inclusion of his works in a much more prominent position in the curriculum might initially be considered as merely exemplifying the problem of changing intellectual fashions. But such changes as these in the philosophy curriculum reflect broader questions than those of mere intellectual fashions. They concern the constitution and reconstitution of national cultures, philosophical traditions, sensibilities and styles on the one hand, and the increasing cultural interpenetration and globalization of philosophies or internationalization of philosophical debates (and their intercultural transmission) on the other hand. These, in turn, may effect changes in traditions, fashions, sensibilities and style and, subsequently, the reconstitution of a philosophical curriculum.

These questions are, quintessentially, questions in philosophy of education as much as in sociology of the curriculum and historiography, more generally. They are questions in philosophy of education, and not merely internal questions in the discipline of philosophy, because they concern the nature (constitution, composition, selection) of the philosophy curriculum and therefore impinge upon issues concerning the principles of its construction, the development of courses that prescribe it, the selection of "works" (bibliographies, reading lists) or "problems" and the setting of assignments and examinations. In other words, they are questions that bear upon the question of the *pedagogy of philosophy*. Because Nietzsche's writings touch on these educational *and* philosophical issues, he should be in the philosophy of education curriculum.

One striking example of why Nietzsche may have been excluded from the British philosophy curriculum is given in a remark that Walter Kaufmann

(1990) makes in the preface to the third edition of his *Nietzsche: Philosopher, Psychologist, Antichrist*. He writes:

In 1952, when I visited C. D. Broad at Trinity College, Cambridge, he mentioned a man named Salter. I asked whether he was the Salter who had written a book on Nietzsche, to which Broad replied: "Dear no; he did not deal with crackpot subjects like that; he wrote about psychical research."

Kaufmann reminds us that Broad had been president of the Society for Psychical Research.

Nietzsche's place—his presence or absence, his "traces"—is even more striking in (British or Anglo-American) philosophy of education. David Cooper (1983a), writing now well over a decade ago, begins his study of Nietzsche's educational philosophy by remarking that despite the intense interest in Nietzsche, especially in France and Germany, his ideas on education have been consistently overlooked. Despite being one of the greatest educators of the nineteenth century (according to Cooper), this area of Nietzsche's philosophy has remained hidden and obscured. In the English-speaking world, Cooper (1983a: vii) goes on to remark, the "neglect of Nietzsche's educational philosophy harmonises with a general, if less exaggerated, neglect of his philosophy at large." The reasons for this neglect are for Cooper relatively straightforward: during the 1960s—the period when Cooper was studying philosophy at Oxford (and probably throughout the 1970s as well)—Nietzsche did not figure on philosophy reading lists. British and American philosophy departments did not teach courses on Nietzsche because he was not considered a "real" philosopher. Nietzsche, like Kierkegaard and Sartre (and, indeed, we might add, most contemporary Continental philosophy), was regarded with a certain hostility—a judgment reflecting, in part, "a particular predilection for a certain kind of philosophizing" (p. viii). Sartre's "Existentialism Is a Humanism" figured in undergraduate ethics courses, but Sartre has misunderstood Heidegger to present a facet of humanism, and one that was probably acceptable in Britain. What was not taught was the influence on Sartre of Husserl or indeed Heidegger, and thus the Sartre fragment of existentialism was domesticated.

Since the early 1980s there has been an extraordinary value reversal. In the English-speaking world, as Bernd Magnus and Kathleen Higgins (1996) testify in the new *Cambridge Companion to Nietzsche*, Nietzsche is now all the rage. Paradoxically, perhaps, at precisely the point at which Nietzsche is both overwhelmingly popular and respectable in the English-speaking world, his influence in France is on the wane, or, in the words of Alan Schrift (1995), the French Nietzsche has been eclipsed. Whether the French Nietzsche is, indeed, on the wane in France, or whether the French Nietzsche has simply been "exported" and undergone a series of interpretive "mutations," we would venture the observation that there is a strong relationship between the French Nietzsche and why Nietzsche is currently so popular in the English-speaking world.

Despite being one of the greatest educators of the nineteenth century (perhaps of the modern period) and one of the greatest moral philosophers of all time (as Cooper claimed in the early 1980s), Nietzsche's educational thought and works, with some notable exceptions, have been ignored, or remain hidden and obscured. This was true of his philosophy as a whole and its reception in the English-speaking world until very recently. The question of why it has been treated in this way is a complex one: it involves not only the "style" of Nietzsche (his way of doing philosophy) and the radical nature of his inquiries but also the history of Nietzscheanism, the politicization of the Nietzsche archive and his "association" with Nazism.

NIETZSCHE'S RECEPTION

The history of Nietzsche's reception is complex. A rough provisional picture of Nietzsche following his death in 1900 is provided by Gregory Smith (1996: fn. 4, 68–70): the early dissemination of his work among the Stephan George "circle" of German poets and novelists (including besides George, Thomas Mann and Hermann Hesse—see Kaufmann [1974: 9–16]); the first academic reception of his work beginning in the late 1920s which served to "neutralize or soften" his teachings (Jaspers, 1947), to discredit him by focusing on his mental illness (Podach, 1930) or to characterize him as "betraying" contemporary civilization (Benda, 1927); and from the same period, a "Nazification" of Nietzsche emphasizing themes of the superman ("the blonde beast"), anti-Semitism (mistakenly), the glorification of the state and the importance of suffering (Baumler, 1931; Haertle, 1937).

Smith is less clear in historical terms about Nietzsche's reception following this period. He considers recent interpretations of Nietzsche in terms of the literary qualities of his work in Derrida (1979) and Nehamas (1985); the restoration of the psychological and material referents of Nietzsche's work in Deleuze (1983); and the separation of his political and moral teaching from his philosophy (see, e.g., Warren 1988; MacIntyre, 1981). He does mention, however, Martin Heidegger (1991; orig. 1961) and Kaufmann (1974; orig. 1950), who, he maintains, accomplished Nietzsche's introduction to the Anglo-Saxon world almost single-handedly. Kaufmann's place in the Anglo-American reception of Nietzsche is undisputed. Steven Taubeneck (1991: 160) asserts that there are striking parallels between the reception of Nietzsche in Europe and North America, and he likens the monumental influence of Kaufmann's Nietzsche in Anglo-America to the way Heidegger's interpretation dominated continental Europe in the 1960s and 1970s. Taubeneck (1991: 160) maintains that "Kaufmann's interpretation shaped the reception in English from 1950 to at least 1974, or for nearly [a] quarter of a century."

Heidegger's interpretation of Nietzsche, based on four lecture courses (1936–1940), lectures and essays (1936–1950) and published for the first time in 1961 (see Krell, 1991), was hugely influential in Europe. Clear lines of influence from Nietzsche run through Jacques Derrida (1978), for example, among many other contemporary French "poststructuralist" philosophers. While Smith mentions Heidegger alongside Kaufmann (as one of the two most important Nietzsche interpreters), he significantly fails to mention the French reception of Nietzsche and the importance of readings by Georges Bataille (1992; orig. 1945), Pierre Klossowski (1969), Gilles Deleuze (1983; orig. 1962), Sarah Kofmann (1993), Eric Blondel (1991) and Luce Irigaray (1991) (see further Schrift, 1995, 1996; Peters, 1996, 1997).

Ernest Behler (1991: vii), in his preface to the English edition of his *Confrontations*, suggests that the image of the "new Nietzsche" as it has emerged since the 1960s finds its most characteristic expression in Jacques Derrida's work. In his study Behler (ibid.) suggests that Derrida "highlights Nietzsche's turn toward infinite interpretation, or the affirmation of a view of the world as play, and shows how the style in which such thinking manifests itself must be plural." Such a view of Nietzsche contrasts sharply with Martin Heidegger's interpretation of Nietzsche "as the thinker of the most condensed notion of modern metaphysics, the 'will to power' " (Behler, 1991: vii).

As Behler argues, Heidegger's Nietzsche is the last metaphysician, the one who inverts Platonism and seeks in the "Will to Power" a metaphysics of the subject that discloses the truth of the Being of beings. In *confrontation* with Heidegger:

Derrida views Heidegger's reading of Nietzsche as an extreme type of truth-oriented, unifying, and systematizing hermeneutics that, because of its own attachments to metaphysics, misconstrues the subtleties of Nietzsche's text in a highly reductionistic manner. (ibid.)

Clearly, while not underestimating the importance of Nietzsche to poststructuralism, it is necessary to understand the differences and nuances of the relations of various poststructuralist thinkers to Nietzsche. This is as much a matter of intellectual autobiography—how individual thinkers perceive their relationships to Nietzsche—as it is a matter of intellectual history and philosophical interpretation. It is easy to assume that the relations were one and the same, and consequently to ignore not only the different ways in which poststructralist thinkers such as Foucault, Deleuze, Derrida and Lyotard (to name only an obvious group) formed their own specific relation to Nietzsche, but also how these relations were (are) modulated through other thinkers—Maurice Blanchot, Georges Bataille and Pierre Klossowski, to name the most obvious examples—who are less familiar to the English-speaking community (see Peters, 1997).

Duncan Large, in providing an introduction to a translation of Sarah Kofman's *Nietzsche and Metaphor*, discusses the intensification of interest in Nietzsche in the dozen years following the publication of Heidegger's *Nietzsche* in 1961 in terms of Deleuze's seminal work. He writes:

In tracing the emergence of the new Nietzsche, one would undoubtedly have to consider the contributions of Georges Bataille and Maurice Blanchot, as well as of Jean Wahl, whose Sorbonne lectures series *La pensée philosophique de Nietzsche des annés 1885–1888* was published in 1959, the same year as *Nietzsche devant ses contemporains*, edited by Génèvieve Bianquis, the most outstanding Nietzsche translator and interpreter of the pre-war generation. Deleuze himself credits Pierre Klossowski with having rekindled interest in Nietzsche through two important essays, though it would be difficult to overestimate Deleuze's own definition of the new Nietzsche. (Large, 1993: x)

Georges Bataille constitutes a special case requiring further comment. His *Sur Nietzsche* was published in 1945 (Bataille, 1992), some seventeen years before the publication of Deleuze's *Nietzsche et philosophie*. *Sur Nietzsche* constituted an early moment in the construction of a new philosophical (as opposed to a literary) French Nietzsche. Bataille's work on Nietzsche has had tremendous influence on a wide range of scholars, including Klossowski, Foucault (who came to Nietzsche through Bataille, and Bataille through Blanchot) and Hélène Cixious, among many others. Sylvère Lotringer (1992: vii) claims that it was Nietzsche who "rescued" Bataille from Catholicism in 1920 when he was only 23, turning him against all religion. *Acéphale*, one of a number of journals (including the influential *Critique*) established by Bataille, and the public face of the secret society of the same name, carried a number of articles by Bataille on Nietzsche in 1937. "Nietzsche and the Fascists" (Bataille, 1985a) attempted to reclaim Nietzsche from "the anti-Semitic falsifications" and interpretations of the fascists, including Nietzsche's sister, Elisabeth Förster-Nietzsche, Richard Oehler (Nietzsche's cousin and his sister's collaborator), Mussolini, Alfred Rosenberg and Alfred Bäumler. (Bataille claims that Lévinas also mistakenly identifies Nietzsche with the racist attitude.) Jean-Michel Besnier (1995: 18) claims that:

One cannot understand Bataille well if one does not take his integral Nietzscheanism seriously, if one forgets, for example, that one of his essential political gestures was to want to "wrest Nietzsche from the grip of the Nazis"—that is to say, to preserve the symbol of the irreducibility (of heterogeneity) of thought against the totalitarian enterprise. If Nietzsche could be saved from Nazism then sovereignty is impossible.

"Nietzschean Chronicle" (Bataille, 1985b) argues that the apogee of civilization is a crisis when sacred values lose their force and conventions begin to "decompose." The fascist solution for the recovery of the lost world consists in a restoration rather than a creation: it recomposes society on the basis of existing elements, developing the most closed form of organization (see also Bataille, 1985c).

In *Sur Nietzsche* Bataille says that he thinks of Nietzsche as a philosopher of *evil* rather than as the philosopher of the "will to power" (1992: xxiv), and it is clear that Nietzsche's work is used as a basis for Bataille's energetics and philosophy of transgression, where the practice of freedom is seen to lie within evil. Certainly, it is the posthumous *The Will to Power*, which dominates *Sur Nietzsche*, rather than Nietzsche's *Genealogy of Morals*—a paradox, given Bataille's goal of resolving the problems of morality and its consistency with Nietzsche's own probings of the origin of morality in the *Genealogy* (see Lotringer, 1992: ix).

A more comprehensive analysis of the contemporary reception of Nietzsche (compared to Smith) is provided by Pauline Johnson (1996) who investigates a range of recent interpretations—categories of criticisms—concerned to establish the relevance of Nietzsche's thinking for us today. First, against the totalizing character of Georg Lukacs' influential reading of Nietzsche, Johnson suggests that contemporary receptions declare themselves uninterested in establishing the essential truth of Nietzsche's texts and more concerned to appropriate Nietzsche for their own purposes. (Lukacs in *The Destruction of Reason* thought Nietzsche's claims to the unsystematic nature of his thought disguised its ideological role in the class struggles of its time.) Second, the "redemptive paradigm," by contrast, establishes that "each historically significant reading constructs its own essential Nietzsche" (as in the case of Steven Ascheim's [1992] *The Nietzsche Legacy in Germany 1890–1990*) or that the open-ended and anti-systematic of his texts is Nietzsche's dominant commitment (as in the case of Paul Patton [1993] and Keith Ansell-Pearson [1994]—perhaps, following Derrida) (Johnson, 1996: 25).

Recent "feminist readings," Johnson (1996: 26) suggests, have "looked to Nietzsche to augment and philosophically refine feminism's own struggles against a classical liberal conception of the subject and as a potential ally in its quest to build a new, non-exclusionary, image of social co-operation." Johnson mentions readings by such feminist scholars as Rosalyn Diprose (1989) and Luce Irigaray (1991). Johnson's third category of recent Nietzsche receptions is titled "The critique of liberalism," for which she draws upon Mark Warren's (1988) *Nietzsche and Political Thought*. Warren's "gentle" (as opposed to "bloody") Nietzsche foreshadows the "postmodern" critique of the liberal subject: the "receptive-aesthetic approach" characterized by Alexander Nehamas' (1985) *Nietzsche: Life as Literature*, which insists on an aesthetic worldview on the model of a literary text and an aesthetic, rather than a moral, attitude toward self-fashioning. Johnson comments that Nehamas' reading is a special case of the redemptive view.

Michel Foucault's Nietzsche is categorized as "the historization of life." Foucault also endorses an aesthetic reading of Nietzsche, Johnson maintains, replacing "an old (moral) Enlightenment with a new (aesthetic) Enlightenment rationalization of the world [which] seeks a democratization of Nietzsche's categories of the self." Richard Rorty's (1989) Nietzsche involves modulation of his aestheticism in a different direction—"a poetization of culture" that follows from the collapse of metaphysics. Rorty's appropriation represents a clear third alternative to the "redemptive" and "aesthetic" readings. He tries "to extract a substantive vision from Nietzsche's philosophy adequate to a contemporary interest in evolving new images of social cooperation in a pluralistic democracy" (Johnson, 1996: 31). What is extraordinary about Johnson's otherwise philosophically interesting and fruitful set of categories is the complete omission (with the exception of an "honorary" Foucault) of the French poststructuralist reception of Nietzsche, especially the influential readings by Gilles Deleuze and Jacques Derrida (see above) and more recent interpretations by "analytic" or "post-analytic" philosophers of Nietzsche's ethics.

There has been a flourishing of Nietzsche scholarship in the English-speaking world in the last decade (e.g., Magnus and Higgins, 1996; Krell, 1996), with much of it focusing on ethics (e.g., Schacht, 1994; Leiter, 1997). Leiter (1997) begins his useful synopsis of Nietzsche's Anglo-American "morality critics" in the following way:

Nietzsche has long been one of the most dominant figures in twentieth-century intellectual life. Yet it is only recently that he has come into his own in Anglo-American philosophy, thanks to a renewed interest in his critical work in ethics. This new appreciation of Nietzsche is reflected in the work of many philosophers. For Alastair MacIntyre [1981], for example, Nietzsche is the first to diagnose the failure of the project of post-Enlightenment moral theory—even though, according to MacIntyre, Nietzsche wrongly thinks that such theory is the last hope for moral objectivity. For Annette Baier [1985: 224], he is one of those "great moral philosophers" who show us an alternative to the dominant traditions in modern moral theory, an alternative in which we "reflect on actual phenomenon of morality, see what it is, how it is transmitted, what difference it makes". For Susan Wolf [1982: 433], he represents an "approach to moral philosophy" in which the sphere of the "moral" comes to encompass those personal excellencies that Utilitarian and Kantian moral theories seem to preclude. For other recent writers, he figures as an exemplar of a philosophical approach to morality that these writers either endorse (e.g., Philippa Foot [1973]) or reject (e.g., Thomas Nagel [1986], Michael Slote [1983]). Indeed, in looking at the claim common to critics of morality like Slote, Foot, Wolf, and Bernard Williams—that "moral considerations are not always the most important considerations"—Robert Louden [1988] has recently asked, "Have Nietzsche's 'new philosophers' finally arrived on the scene: 'spirits strong and original enough to provide the stimuli for opposite valuations and to revalue and invert "eternal values"?' [BGE, 203]." (Leiter 1997: 250–251)

By comparison with the new appreciation of Nietzsche's critical work in ethics, there has been little scholarship completed on Nietzsche in philosophy of education (or education more generally) and, certainly, little that marks out Nietzsche as uniquely placed in philosophy as one who devoted considerable attention directly to questions of education as part of his investigations into the genealogy of morals and values. This is curious, if not lamentable, given the new work being completed by Anglo-American philosophers on Nietzsche's critical work in ethics and the centrality of ethics to education. It is further lamentable given the status granted earlier to Nietzsche as educator.

NIETZSCHE AND PHILOSOPHY OF EDUCATION

Little has been published on Nietzsche in relation to the field of education since David Cooper's book in 1983. Only twelve articles have been published on Nietzsche in two major journals in the field of education since 1973—the *Journal of Philosophy of Education* and *Educational Theory*. Moreover, only a handful of articles have been published in *Educational Philosophy and Theory* and *Studies in Philosophy and Education*. These are the four journals devoted exclusively to philosophy of education in the English-speaking world. We will now provide a brief summary of this literature.[1]

According to Eliyahu Rosenow in *Educational Theory* (1973: 370) Nietzsche has "the most consistent working out of the idea of radical free education in the history of educational thought." The same edition of the journal presents a paper by James Hillesheim, who interpreted Nietzsche's educational theory of self-overcoming as the path toward the creation of genius and genuine culture. But there is a silence on Nietzsche in that journal until 1986.

The issue of Nietzsche and education was, however, raised in the British *Journal of Philosophy of Education* in 1980. Between 1980 and 1985, four interconnected papers on Nietzsche and education appeared. They were authored by Haim Gordon (1980), Keith Jenkins (1982), David Cooper (1983b) and Jacob Golomb (1985). Surprisingly, however, no mention was made of the two earlier (1973) papers in *Educational Theory*. One of the contributors, David Cooper, was to explore the topic of Nietzsche and education further in his aforementioned book *Authenticity and Learning* (1983).

In 1986, Nietzsche's educational philosophy again came under scrutiny in *Educational Theory*. Hillesheim and Rosenow, who had been the authors of the 1973 papers, were responsible for three out of a total of five more papers that were published by that journal over the next four years from 1986 to 1990. The other authors were Martin Simons (1988) and Nimrod Aloni (1989). None of the five acknowledged the work done in earlier papers in the British journal. These silences, almost of two ships passing in the night, are somewhat mysterious!

The final effort in the British journal came from Aharon Aviram in 1991. He engaged in a comprehensive summary and analysis of Nietzsche's educational philosophy, based on the entire British debate and Rosenow's argument in the American journal. He acknowledged Hillesheim's earliest work and provided a broad philosophical reconciliation of many apparently contradictory perspectives. By examining the issue from a number of different levels, Aviram was able to give credence to what had earlier seemed like opposing interpretations. Aviram appears to have closed the debate in 1991, proposing that Nietzsche's ideas, though reflecting an animosity toward humanism, liberalism and democracy, could be used to support a liberal democratic view of education. The focus of those articles ranges from an emphasis on the teaching style and message of Nietzsche's *Zarathustra* to a broad interpretation of Nietzsche's other educational writings.

THE COLLECTION

The present volume is unique in that for the first time it brings together a group of educators who, working from Nietzsche's texts both in the original German and in English translation, mark out the significance of Nietzsche's thought for educational theory. It is unique also in that individual chapters firmly link Nietzsche's *oeuvre* to contemporary scholarship and particularly to the work of the French poststructuralists. The collection, therefore, in addition to explicating Nietzsche's relevance and significance for contemporary education, provides an understanding necessary for a proper appreciation of poststructuralism in educational theory.

The contributions, from experienced readers of Nietzsche, were drawn mainly from three groups. The first group worked at the Catholic University of Leuven between November 1997 and February 1998 and included James Marshall. The second, a reading group of Nietzsche scholars at the University of Auckland, met throughout 1998. Finally, there was a reading group at the University of Illinois, at the Champaign-Urbana campus, which met in the fall semester and which included Michael Peters. An "outside" contribution was solicited from Valerie Allen and Ares Axiotis.

In Chapter 1, Juliane Varvaro investigates similarities and differences between the ways of thinking of Nietzsche and Wittgenstein, and how this comparison leads to a shared understanding of ethics, or a way of life. Inherent in this investigation is an attempt to show not only how, through thinking, we inhabit worlds of our own making, but also how these worlds, or the way we see the world, is related to how we are in the world. In simplest terms, it is concerned with how, through thinking, we create worlds of our own making. Consequently, this chapter focuses on both Nietzsche's and Wittgenstein's attempts to leave an earlier culture "in a heap of rubble" by destroying the dualism between "the world of mere appearances" and the "real world." In doing so, this chapter plays off Wittgenstein's "splitting the world" into sense and nonsense, and in turn it describes at length Nietzsche's early attack on the correspondence theory of truth and epistemology more generally. By linking these two thinkers in this way, Varvaro shows the productivity of reading Wittgenstein after Nietzsche, after Nietzsche's attack against this dualism.

In Chapter 2, Valerie Allen and Ares Axiotis start with Nietzsche's early unfinished and unpolished lectures on education, which were contemporaneous with *The Birth of Tragedy*, and argue for a continuity of ideas in these works: specifically, that the Apollonian and Dionysian impulses informing tragedy also underlie the earliest expressions of Greek *paideia*. Nietzsche turns from the hyper-rational Enlightenment ideals of the Humboldt university to different models in his search for a community that nurtures deep thought—the goal of education. Through his allusions to *paideia* and to the nineteenth-century German *Burschenschaft*, key characteristics of Nietzschean thought emerge: thought issues from initiation into community rather than from Cartesian self-seclusion; it exhibits bodily as well as mental grace and fitness; thought is associated less with the quiet consolation of philosophy than with the passion of divine *mania*, suggested by the double meaning of Greek *paideuein* as teaching and torment. *Pathein mathein*, "learning is suffering," encapsulates the underlying connection between education and "passion," and thus between the tragic view of education in these lectures and the origin of tragedy disclosed in *The Birth of Tragedy*. Nietzsche's allusion to the *Burschenschaft* places the present and future of education in relation to the past. The search for guidance for the future is enacted as a revisitation of the past, not to conserve yesterday's traditions but to "think" the university through to its fundamental basis or ground.

Chapter 3, by F. Ruth Irwin, concentrates on genealogy, exploring the works of Nietzsche, Gilles Deleuze and Michel Foucault. In *On the Genealogy of Morals*, Nietzsche espouses a way of evaluating whether cultural mores are "actively" enhancing or "reactively" degenerating the life of society. The reactive aspect of the dichotomy appears to be dominating contemporary Western culture, produced by a palliative approach to suffering, which results in nihilism. The active/reactive dichotomy could be understood in terms of negative differences, but Deleuze argues that Nietzsche is advocating an affirmation of life that incorporates and transforms the negative reactive forces into a necessary but temporary aspect of human society. Foucault investigated Nietzsche's theory of genealogy to create alternatives to the traditional (and nihilistic) belief in ultimate origins, essential truths and teleological endpoints. Genealogy allows the present to derive influences and to open a variety of possible futures, without fixing on an inevitable structure of knowledge. Education could make use of these challenges to redefine the current emphasis on vocationalist skills and reopen creative critique as a legitimate arena of knowledge.

In Chapter 4, Peter Fitzsimons develops a Nietzschean-based critique of the work of the prominent British philosopher of education, Richard Peters. He argues that, from a Nietzschean perspective on the notion of ethics in education, a multidimensional view of the self may be more appropriate than a universal morality in determining a basis for educational direction. Fitzsimons employs Connolly's account of identity formation to provide such a view and a background against which the democratic-liberal position as expounded by Peters can be critiqued. Fitzsimons finds Peters' account wanting both in its own judgments and as a form of totalizing rationality. The author argues for an ethic that respects difference and minimizes the focus on essential transcendent normality.

In Chapter 5, Scott Johnston explores the relations between Nietzsche's work and notions of democracy and education. He reviews much of the work that has been completed recently in philosophy of education. His major question is: "What possibility is there to reconcile the ideal of Nietzsche as educator with current democratic education as it is practiced in America?" To answer this question he proceeds by offering Deweyean definitions of "democracy" and "education." Johnston avoids the notion of *bildung* to focus on an examination of Nietzsche as educator for the schools and the classroom. He develops the notion of Nietzsche as educator through three themes taken from Alexander Nehamas: "The Most Multifarious Art of Style," "Beyond Good and Evil" and "How One Becomes Who One Is." Johnston concludes by arguing: "Ultimately, however, the task is, as Nietzsche would agree, a thoroughly individual one. One must create not only the self that one wishes to become, but also the means, the instruction and the content, if you will, of how one wishes to achieve this stature. Unfortunate as this is to educators, there can be no blueprint for this task."

In Chapter 6, Paul Smeyers deals first with a reading of Nietzsche's philosophical stance as characterized by nihilism, will to power and responsiveness. Smeyers develops the idea that the form of nihilism that has to be overcome, according to Nietzsche, is not so much a matter of replacing old values with new ones as it is coming to value something where previously one valued nothing. Neither is nihilism about taking responsibility for a view of the world and thus opening oneself up to the possibility of different views. Rather, it should be understood in terms of the notion of commitment, an openness to what matters to us. From this position it follows that education involves not the determination of who the student should be but of how she might become. The chapter then discusses Charles Altieri's expressivist ethics—a Nietzschean ethical stance that argues one cannot distribute responsibility (as a consent to bear the consequences of particular actions) without a strong sense of the commitments for which agents make themselves responsible. For the educator, it follows that she is characterized by her willingness to stand for something and simultaneously is willing to care for someone. While her integrative authenticity should rescue her from despair, it should also correct the possible immobilism occasioned by the interpretation of some postmodernist authors. Here, what we take as somehow fulfilling us, to a certain extent also conceived in a naturalistic way, binds us to the ways of structuring our concerns so that others can participate in a common framework. Smeyers concludes that Nietzsche's mission for education is as lively as ever: in the end all education transgresses into (what is perhaps not correctly expressed by the concept of) "self-education."

The possible role of the arts and of education in the formation of Nietzsche's new philosopher is discussed by James Marshall in Chapter 7. Nietzsche's new philosopher is not the traditional philosopher *worker* (academic) but is instead a radical reformer who can provide a way forward, or a solution to what Nietzsche saw as the crisis of Western civilization. He saw the religious and philosophical underpinnings of Western civilization as being incapable of offering any solutions to this (alleged) crisis. Hence he repeatedly attacks or undermines religion and traditional academic philosophy. In *The Birth of Tragedy* Nietzsche distinguishes between two forms of art and two forms of personality—the *Apollonian*, concerned with form and order, and the *Dionysian*, which bursts forth or erupts from nature itself and returns to the frenzy and daring of the world. These two approaches to art are crucial for Nietzsche, for insofar as art is the creative transformation of the world, so, too, the new philosopher in Dionysian fashion can creatively transform the world. This chapter traces what Nietzsche says about these two forms of art and the new philosopher in *Thus Spake Zarathustra*, *Beyond Good and Evil* and *On the Genealogy of Morals*. What Nietzsche offers is not a nihilistic, but a life-affirming, account. Finally, Marshall looks at the educational implications of Nietzsche's position on art.

Peter Roberts, in Chapter 8, continues and enlarges upon Marshall's discussion of the new philosopher, and considers what Nietzsche has to offer contemporary cultural and academic life. In a number of works Nietzsche draws a comparison between "scholars" and the "philosophers of the future." Scholars, Nietzsche tells us, are subservient, unhealthy, brittle, herd animals. They are reliant upon their books, suffer from low self-esteem and are ultimately unable to think for themselves. The new philosophers, by contrast, are independent, creative, courageous free spirits. After summarizing these differences, the chapter sets out Nietzsche's requirements for a good philosphical life and considers his account in the light of the frenetic nature of contemporary cultural and academic life. Bureaucratic and marketized universities, it is argued, provide unfriendly soil for the cultivation of *both* scholars and philosophers. In a world driven by the imperatives of consumerism and competition, few have the time, space and material resources necessary for creative, critical intellectual work.

In Chapter 9, Patrick Fitzsimons points out that in liberal societies education is generally defined in terms of development of the (liberal) self. He sees Nietzsche as presenting us with a critical genealogy of Western philosophy as the philosophy of self and, therefore, with a critique of the liberal self. For an evaluation of liberal education, the liberal values behind the very idea of evaluation must be critiqued to expose their worth. Fitzsimons argues that the liberal self is the social system that, through a critique of the values of liberal education, is the object of revaluation in this chapter.

This Nietzschean critique suggests that liberal education, which purportedly leads to the emergence of a rational, autonomous subject, has actually achieved the opposite of true individualism. What emerges are individuals identical with one another; therefore, contemporary society can no longer be relied on to provide a framework for individual fulfillment. From a Nietzschean perspective, disciplinary education transforms the individual into a docile and obedient subject as it presents a small range of possibilities limited by reason. Nietzsche suggests a way of dealing with such education in order to go beyond it: he wants to destroy the domination of the past by forgetting it, incorporating it, and redeeming it within a horizon of the individual life. Here the task of the educator is to articulate critiques about the merit of the values behind liberal education. The conclusion is that liberal education, inadequate in its underpinning value of reason as its ultimate court of appeal for discovering value, is in need of a radical reevaluation. That, of course, is what is wrong with liberal modes of evaluation.

In Chapter 10, Stefan Ramaekers argues that an understanding of education from a Nietzschean point of view cannot overlook the importance Nietzsche attaches to obedience, which means being embedded in a particular historical and cultural frame. Education is, at least in the early stages, teaching the child to see and to value particular things, or in Nietzsche's way of putting it, teaching the child to "lie." By stressing the importance Nietzsche attaches to obedience, to being embedded, Ramaekers argues against a subjectivist reading of Nietzsche. A subjectivist reading tends to emphasize a radical individualism and takes the individual to be the point of reference of all values and truths. In Ramaekers' view, one of Nietzsche's most important lessons is not to create something radically new but to adopt a serious engagement to what one stands for.

Betsan Martin celebrates Nietzsche and Luce Irigaray in Chapter 11. According to Martin, Nietzsche's penetrating philosophical critique of the values embedded in Western culture, disturbing then as it is pertinent now, could be described as a counter-practice, an historical and cultural exposé that was out of step with his time. Nietzsche's examination directed attention to a genealogy of cultural values and an investigation into the construction of knowledge. The purpose of genealogy was to see how the past overlaps with the present, and the past was "reproduced" through knowledge that remains embedded in a structure of binary opposition. Nietzsche pursued an escape from stifling conformity to social mores, seeking freedom in courageous, artistic individuality—"action at a distance," or an ethics of difference. Although Nietzsche's work was developed to escape the past and present, Luce Irigaray discerned a perpetuation of the paradigm of mastery in Nietzsche. Therefore, she claims that he remains within a binary, or phallocentric, paradigm. Both Nietzsche and Irigaray have sought to go beyond an oppositional paradigm that is premised on negation of difference and to move toward a new horizon for culture that will enable regeneration. Both Nietzsche and Irigaray discerned the liberal investment in equality to be a trap that binds change within a metaphysics of binary opposition. The educational focus of the chapter is on the conditions which these philosophers raised for knowledge constituted on difference—specifically, in the case of Irigaray, on sexual difference. Sexual difference is proposed as a means of breaking both with past history and with the universal assumptions embedded in Western knowledge. For sexual difference, as a new basis for culture, it is necessary to build a symbolization of the feminine as well as to find ways to mediate male-female relations.

In Chapter 12, Michael Peters provides a link with the themes outlined in the Introduction. He sets out to examine Nietzsche's place in the Western philosophy curriculum, and he asks the question why Nietzsche was all but ignored by English-speaking philosophers until the 1980s. Peters sees this question as central to philosophy of education, and he explores it in relation to a brief comparison between Nietzsche and Ludwig Wittgenstein, focusing on how each figure has been "made over" by analytic philosophy. The ultimate source of the question leads historically to the construction of the so-called analytic/Continental divide. Peters maintains that Nietzsche stands at the very heart of this historic separation and that through his concept of nihilism, he is viewed as continuing the Kantian critique of metaphysics out of which Continental philosophy emerged. It is this critique, Peters argues, that is intimately tied up with Nietzsche's critique of Enlightenment humanism, modernity and liberalism. Accordingly, Peters focuses on Nietzsche's critique of modernity not only as the thematic that still decisively separates the problematic of Continental philosophy from that of analytic philosophy, but also as the determinant of the style and content of a post-Nietzschean philosophy of education. Finally, he traces the trajectory of this post-Nietzschean discourse concerning the critique of modernity in the writings of Jürgen Habermas and Michel Foucault.

NOTE

1. The review of the Nietzschean literature in philosophy of education is based on unpublished work carried out by Peter Fitzsimons.

Chapter 1

Learning the Grandeur of This Life

Juliane Varvaro

> For if there is a sin against life, it consists not so much in despairing of
> life as in hoping for another life, and in eluding the implacable grandeur
> of this life.
>
> —Camus, 1991: 87

After Narcissus' deluded lovers ask a goddess that "he may love one day,
so, himself, and not win over the creature who he loves," Narcissus finds
himself trying to quench a thirst that only leads to his destruction. When
bending over the spring, Narcissus falls in love with his own image, upon
which he not only finds self-knowledge, through an understanding of signs,
but also "substance in what was only shadow." Narcissus' excitement upon
discovering that the image was his own, however, brings tears of joy that
disturb the image, making the image he so loved dissipate into nothingness,
thereby leading to his very own death. By taking the object of his love as
an object instead of as a vision, when Narcissus comes to see that it is his
own representation and that it can disappear, he dies of despair. His mistake,
like that of so many others, was in taking an image as permanence, real
"substance," when it was only an illusion, or a representation (Kristeva,
1987: 103–105).

This despairing of life, of representation, of the fleeting substance behind
a mere scaffolding, has found itself illustrated in many ways throughout the
history of philosophical and psychological thought. There is perhaps no discussion, however, that captures the tragedy of poor Narcissus as brilliantly
as that found in Nietzsche's notebooks, under the heading of "On Truth
and Lies in the Nonmoral Sense." In fact, this work exemplifies Nietzsche's

first attempt to bring down the "immense framework and planking of concepts to which the needy man clings" (Nietzsche 1979: 90). More shockingly, however, is the breaking of the world in two that is illustrated by Wittgenstein's *Tractatus*. In his attempt to investigate "what can be said at all can be said clearly," Wittgenstein ends up splitting the world into two different realms: that which we can speak about and that which we must pass over in silence, into sense and nonsense (1963: 3).[1] Years later, however, in 1947, Wittgenstein cries out in *Culture and Values, "Don't for heavens sake*, be afraid of talking in nonsense! But you must pay attention to your nonsense" (1980: 56e). Why might Wittgenstein years later, after drawing the limits of language, of our thought, claim that nonsense, that which we must pass over in silence, be something we *shouldn't* be afraid of talking in? While what we can say about this question will emerge in this investigation, what is really at issue is the hour Nietzsche's and Wittgenstein's similar, but distinct, ways of thinking lead them both to a shared understanding of ethics, or a way of life. In fact, by reading Wittgenstein after Nietzsche, after Nietzsche's attack against "the true world" and "the world of mere appearances," we can see a shared understanding of "this life" and thereby of ethics. Reading in this way may help to show that, through thinking, we not only inhabit worlds of our own making, but also learn how these worlds, or how we see the world, is related to how *we are in the world*. Throughout the process, we may come to see that the nonsense accepted by both Nietzsche and Wittgenstein may in fact be essential to self-knowledge and, more importantly, may be "the implacable grandeur of this life."

The background force shaping this endeavor, however, puts a strange twist on things. As much as this chapter is concerned with thinking, with the way "to think is first of all to create a world (or to limit one's own world, which amounts to the same thing)," this chapter assumes a Nietzschean diagnosis of "the human condition" (Camus, 1991: 99), of the revengeful, ressentiful, man–animal longing to be other than he is. Because of this, this chapter lies within the "conservatism" of both Nietzsche and Wittgenstein, with the ways in which each tries to get us to accept "this life." What happens after this acceptance is of grave import, especially given Nietzsche's questionable political motives.[2] At this point in time, however, thinking our way out of the ascetic, resentful reasoning system seems even more important. This lesson, though seemingly so basic, is a lesson that may have saved poor Narcissus from his despairing death, as well as all others who chose to elude the implacable grandeur of this life.

WITTGENSTEIN: THE DESIRE FOR CERTAINTY

Although the most obvious place to begin this endeavor might be with Nietzsche's and Wittgenstein's similar attack on correspondence theory, we will instead begin with a brief discussion of the *Tractatus*. For it is in this earlier work that Wittgenstein sets out to determine the limits to what is expressible, in the hope of finding the "final solution" to the problems of philosophy derived from misunderstanding the logic of our language (1963: 3–4). However, most interestingly, Wittgenstein tells us at the end of this very preface that "the [second] value of this work consists in how little is achieved when these problems are solved" (1979: 4). The significance of this last comment should not be taken lightly, for Wittgenstein is said to have commented that the value of this work really lies in what was not said. It might be plausible to assume that the real value of this work lies in Wittgenstein carving out a space in which religion, art and aesthetics can be free from the drive for Truth, for certainty. As he later comments in *Culture and Value*, "if you have a room which you do not want certain people to get into, put a lock on it for which they do not have the key," or in this case, place what is of *real value* outside the limits of that which is trying to condense everything into a single, understandable and classifiable unit (1980: 7e, 63e).

In this early work, and similar to the case of Narcissus, Wittgenstein sees language (representations) as being directly related to states of affairs in the world, whereby language is a picture of reality (1963: 2.12). Not only do the propositions in which pictures are displayed have "exactly as many distinguishing parts as . . . the situation that it represents," but the words, the names of objects, making up the proposition relate the objects to each other in a pattern that attempts to show how things stand in the world (4.04, 4.022). Furthermore, by showing us how things stand in relation to each other, the propositions show us the sense of the proposition, whereby to understand a proposition is really to understand the situation that it purports to represent (4.021). We are then able to compare the proposition to reality and thereby determine whether it is true or false.

Even in this earlier work, however, Wittgenstein is aware that expressions do not meet up with the world in this simplistic manner. In the *Tractatus*, however, he claims that either complex propositions can be translated into these simpler propositions or else they are meaningless.[3] There is still another realm, however, that lacks sense completely, and Wittgenstein calls this nonsense, which is everything outside the little room he constructs on the principles of logic. Inside this room, all propositions are of equal value, as "in the world everything is as it is, and everything happens as it does happen: *in* it no value exists" (1974: 6.41). Wittgenstein is led to believe this because of his notion of the world as being outside of human manipulation, as being a realm governed by logic whereby what is mere accident comes to be what is the case (see 6.42). This is probably where Wittgenstein mostly "saw the world split in two"; for propositions, thereby, cannot express what is "higher" (6.42). There can be no propositions that express ethics, because ethics is transcendental and "the will" is only of interest to psychology (6.421, 6.423). Even if human action changes the world, it "can alter only the limits of the world, not the facts—not what can be expressed by means of language" (6.43).

Thus, how things are in the world is "of complete indifference to what is higher" (6.4312). Why things are the way they are is just that they are. We cannot ask, for instance, why God created things the way He did, for when we cannot put an answer into words (as the answer must match up with reality), we similarly cannot put the question into words. This, however, still does not seem to be a good enough answer to the problems of life for Wittgenstein, for the problems of life only vanish in that there can be no questions. That is, the solution is that in fact there are no problems. Why then does Wittgenstein still believe that life has a sense even if we are unable to speak about it? As he questions, "is not this the reason why those who have found after a long period of doubt that the sense of life became clear to them have then been unable to say what constituted that sense?" (6.43).

Since we cannot directly ask what this nonsense is, we shall instead look at the shift that occurs in Wittgenstein's thinking that may allow us to make sense of a claim Wittgenstein makes at the end of the *Tractatus*: "the world of the happy man is a different one from that of the unhappy man" (6.43). What is interesting about this comment and its placement within this work is that it is located in the midst of the discussion on value and nonsense. To some extent, Wittgenstein's closing remark that "what we cannot speak about we must pass over in silence" is directly related to this comment about the happy or unhappy (wo)man. For if (wo)man cannot alter the facts of this world, then (wo)man to some extent is left with being able to alter only the limits of the world, of his/her own world, which is the limits of his/her own language (see 5.62).

Most interesting is how closely related the ideas expressed near the end of the *Tractatus* are to a passage from Nietzsche's *Daybreak*. Take, for instance, a condensed version of these ideas:

for many years now, a certain picture of things has held philosophy captive. At the centre of this picture is the lonely human soul, brooding over its private experiences: experiences which are thought to be unique and incommunicable. This individual is a prisoner of his own body; and he is locked out from the contact with others by the walls of *their* own bodies, which render them mysterious and opaque to him. (Eagleton and Jarman, 1993: 46)

And this sentence from Nietzsche,

my eyes . . . can only see a certain distance, and it is within the space encompassed by this distance that I live and move . . . our ears enclose us within a comparable circle. And so does our sense of touch. Now, it is by these horizons, within which each of us encloses his senses as if behind prison walls, that we measure the world. (D: 117)

What both passages capture is a notion of philosophy, in Wittgenstein's case, and a notion of individuals, in Nietzsche's case, in which (wo)man is limited by his/her own senses or by the language which he or she uses.[4] This view, however, undergoes radical revision for both Nietzsche and Wittgenstein. The revisions that each takes are rather similar. Both argue against a private notion of language and instead contend that language belongs to our commonality, our social nature. Similar to Nietzsche, Wittgenstein's later views of language dismantle correspondence theory, in which words in language (signs) have referents (objects) with which they correspond, or as in the case of the *Tractatus*, propositions correspond with states of affairs in the world. However, Wittgenstein goes further than Nietzsche's ideas concerning language in many ways. Not only does he show the arbitrary link between word and referent by showing the many problems with ostensive definitions, but, more importantly, he shows how integrated language is to everyday practices. He shows how language is an activity that is embedded in social practices.

While Wittgenstein's critique of correspondence theory takes a radically different form from Nietzsche's, this chapter will say very little about this critique. Instead, the critique will be used to show how Wittgenstein is inviting us to see the way in which he philosophizes. Since philosophy is really no more than working on oneself, on one's way of seeing things, he is showing us a radically different way of being in the world, one that might help us to see or catch a glimpse of the happy man (1980: 16e). Although it is readily known that neither Wittgenstein nor Nietzsche was a happy man, this does not diminish the possibility that their views of things might lead us to perceive a new way of being in the world, one that might reflect more appreciation for "this life."

This is not to assume, however, that this new way of seeing things solves anything or leads to happiness. Instead, it is to assume an attitude derived from the end of the *Tractatus* that runs throughout the *Philosophical Investigations* and *Culture and Value*. Let Wittgenstein himself comment:

The way to solve the problem you see in life is to live in a way that will make what is problematic disappear. The fact that life is problematic shows that the shape of your life does not fit into life's mould. So you must change the way you live and, once your life does fit into the mould, what is problematic will disappear. (1980: 27e)

While Wittgenstein ended the *Tractatus* by claiming that problems disappear when we stop trying to ask questions that have no answers, the problematic aspects of life caused by misuse of logic run deeper than us asking the wrong questions. As Nietzsche would say, many problems derive from a "rudimentary psychology" surrounding our use of grammar.

Interestingly, both Nietzsche and Wittgenstein critique various notions, such as free will, purpose and intention, in rather similar ways. This may be due in large part to a similar presumption about the way the world is. As we will recall, Wittgenstein ends the *Tractatus* by claiming that the world is mere accident, with the world being independent of man's will (1974: 6.373). He further claims that "there is no compulsion making one thing happen because another has happened. The only necessity that exists is *logical* necessity" (6.37). Although it can be argued that the later Wittgenstein throws off all metaphysical claims, it is hard to imagine an interpretation free from presumptions about transcendence. And in this case, like Nietzsche, we may be able to say that for Wittgenstein, transcend simply refers to a world that has no necessary order and is thereby mysterious and incomprehensible. Furthermore, when a philosopher says, "look at things like this," this does not translate into "this is how things are." Rather, it is a description attempting to make sense of what we do or what has happened to us in this messy world.

What can we say about the way Nietzsche and Wittgenstein see, or describe, the world? There are really two options here: (1) We can pull all their direct descriptions of how the world appears to them, or (2) we can attempt to catch a glimpse of this through the ways in which each philosophizes. In many ways, however, both ways correspond to each other in that the first preconditions their ways of philosophizing. For when Wittgenstein splits the world in two and creates the realms of what can be said and what cannot be said, he has already described one way in which he sees the world. In the little room, there is a degree of certainty, of accuracy, while on the other side "man exists in this world, where things break, slide about, cause every imaginable mischief. And of course he is one such thing himself" (1980: 71e). As much as we may want the certainty of the logical little room, outside that box, things are radically different. Not only are these aspects of life not easily reduced to logical propositions, but, in attempting to do so, we misrepresent the real messiness of this world. Not only do we have to admit certain givens, as for instance that the world is, but also that life in general is like a conversation: "In a conversation: One person throws a ball; the other does not know whether he is supposed to throw it back, or to throw it to a third party, or leave it on the ground, or pick it up and put it in his pocket, etc." (1980: 74e). And in this conversation, faith and belief play a pivot role.

ATTACK AGAINST THE CORRESPONDENCE THEORY

Nietzsche's attack against the will to truth and against *the* correspondence theory of language is radically different from Wittgenstein's in that Nietzsche directly attacks epistemology.[5] Indeed, part of Nietzsche's problem with history, science and the knowledge drive in general is that these activities typically presuppose that "knowing" is possible and that truth is more valuable than untruth, or appearance. It is supposed that there is another world, one free from our perceptions, which can be known if we can find an objectifying lens through which the real nature of things (i.e., inherent properties, things-in-themselves, essences) can be understood. Nietzsche sees most endeavors concerned with discovering the truth as attempts to separate the knower from the known in such a way that they can separate their perceptions (the way the world seems) from the perceived object (an entity that has an existence free from what we bring to the world). With this separation of the world into "the world of mere appearances" and the "real world," objects are seen as things-in-themselves, with inherent meanings that are non-revisable, objective and universal (TPhil: 133). It is hoped that by finding this truth, this real world, we can free ourselves from the contradictory, deceptive and transitory nature of the apparent world, for this world just causes us grave suffering (WP: 585).

The problem with this, Nietzsche claims, is that there is no such thing as immediate and direct access to objects, and thereby no thing-in-itself, for man is standing in the way, he conceals things (D: 438). What this means is that the Truth, or essence, of a thing cannot be known, for this would require a self-contradictory mediated immediacy, to borrow a phrase from Kaufmann. As Nietzsche says in his notebooks, "we can say nothing about the thing in itself, for we have eliminated the standpoint of knowing, i.e. of measuring. A quality exists for us, i.e. it is measured by us" (TPhil: 101). Or as he warns in *On the Genealogy of Morals* (3:12),

let us guard against such contradictory concepts as "pure reason," "absolute spirituality," "knowing in itself," for these demand that "we should think of an eye that is completely unthinkable, an eye turned in no particular direction . . . these always demand of the eye an absurdity and a nonsense. There is only a perspective seeing, only a perspective 'knowing.' "

This does not mean, however, that an individual's perception can facilitate an understanding of things-in-themselves either; it means that existence is nonsensical without interpretation (D: 125). All we can discover in trying to examine a thing-in-itself is "things upon it," namely, our perceptions, which themselves depend on sensations and such. But, as Nietzsche claims, "The habits of our senses have woven us into lies and deceptions of sensations" (D: 117). In other words, even the senses we rely on to "see" things are inherently faulty: we think that through our senses we can observe things "how they are," but this is not possible: we have no access to "things-in-themselves." Our senses may take in the environment as it appears; our eyes may see a table, but it is nonsense without interpretation and language.

This disavowment with our senses, Nietzsche argues, has led many a philosopher and scientist to posit our reasoning faculties as the means by which to establish the criterion of truth. It was hoped that through scientific rationality the properties of things could be determined and that we could thereby establish the rules for determining the "real" and the "unreal," thereby achieving mind-independent representations of the world (see WP: 584). It is then assumed that knowing is the ability to represent accurately what is outside the mind. Nietzsche asks, however, would not we already have to know what *being* is in order to determine if something is real or not? (see GS: 354; WP: 486). Without already knowing what an accurate representation might be, we are unable to say that it is an accurate representation, and this is not something we can know: we simply lack an organ for knowing, for "truth" (GS: 354).

Nietzsche is willing to admit that we are acquainted with reality, but the reality of our thoughts, language and consciousness, the realm that supposedly makes up the kernel of humankind, makes man most human (TPhil: 94; GS: 11). It is this realm, the realm of thoughts, which we take, in comparison with the realm of actions, willing and experiences, to be the realm of our freedom (D: 125). To this Nietzsche must respond that we are again gravely mistaken: for thinking itself is language, and thereby our consciousness is nothing more than language. While in words we assume we are able to share our experiences with others to thereby break free of our prison caused by sensation, we are mistaken in thinking that words, a social convention, can really give individuals private expressions or allow for self-understanding. How this can be is simple: thought or "consciousness does not belong to an individual's existence but rather to his social nature . . . and that fundamentally, all our actions are altogether incomparably personal, unique, and infinitely individual; but as soon as we translate them into consciousness they *no longer seem to be*" (GS: 354).

What this means is that consciousness, or thought, is not private; there is no such thing as private language. Consciousness developed out of the need for individuals to communicate.[6] As such, consciousness does not really belong to a man's individual existence but rather to his social or herd nature. Those experiences, feelings and thoughts that rise to consciousness are thereby those that have been required by social utility. Similarly, what we call an "inner experience only enters consciousness after it has found a language the individual understands—i.e., a translation of a condition into a condition familiar to him" (WP: 479). As Nietzsche described our situation:

given the best will in the world to understand ourselves as individually as possible "to know ourselves," each of us will always succeed in becoming conscious only of what is not individual but "average." Our thoughts themselves are continually governed by the character of consciousness—by the "genius of species" that commands it—and translated back into the perspective of the herd. (GS: 354)

Therefore, the world we become conscious of is really only a surface and sign world, and is thereby shallow, low, thin, superficial and generalizable. In other words, we can simply know, that is, believe or imagine, that which has been a utility for the human herd and that for which we have already coined terms and concepts (ibid.). This does not mean, however, that Nietzsche is lamenting an inability for language, or signs, to accurately correspond to or capture a deeper level of individuality. All he is claiming is that because of the generalizability and superficiality of language, we are mistaken in believing that words can accurately represent "what's going on."

This leads Nietzsche to start out "On Truth and Lies in a Nonmoral Sense" by saying that men are deeply immersed in illusions and dream images. What man has done is set up in language

a separate world besides the other world, a place it took to be so firmly set that, standing upon it, it could lift the rest of the world off its hinges and make itself master of it. . . . he readily thought that in language he possessed knowledge of the world. The sculptor of language was not so modest as to believe that he was only giving things designations, he conceived rather that with words he was expressing supreme knowledge of things. (OTaL: 11)

Not only is this a nice description of the spirit that pervades the *Tractatus*, but what Nietzsche is hinting at here is that the reputation, name and appearance of a thing, the ways by which we usually measure it, are arbitrarily thrown on it and are thereby foreign to the nature of the thing (GS: 58). What man has done, however, is to take words as representing and capturing the mind-independent meanings of the objects for which they stand. Nietzsche, however, questions this notion. As he sees it,

if truth alone had been a deciding factor in the genesis of language, and if the standpoint of certainty had been decisive for designations, then how could we still dare to say "the stone is hard," as if "hard" were something otherwise familiar to us, and not merely a totally subjective stimulation. (OTaL: 81–82)

What this means is that all language does is "designate the relationship of things to men" (ibid.: 82). When we think we are describing the inherent properties of a thing, all we are really doing is naming the attributes of its appearance, attributes that we ourselves have given it (see GS: 54). And it is only by a very gradual process that we come to believe in a thing, or concept, and thereby come to see our beliefs as being a part of its very existence. As Nietzsche puts it, "what at first was appearance becomes in the end . . . the essence and is effective as such" (GS: 58).

As should be clear, there is no objective reality for Nietzsche. This would not only require an absurdity of the eye, but also the necessity that we "subtract the phantasm and every human *contribution* from the world" (GS:

57, Nietzsche's emphasis). We would have to forget our descent, our past and our training—all of our humanity, for even behind every feeling there stands the judgments and evaluations that have been inherited (D: 35).

Nietzsche is not saying, however, that "things" do not exist, rather he is saying that we have deceived ourselves in such a way that we take our opinions, or language, about things as if they themselves actually represent a separate world of existence, one free from what man himself brings to the world. As Nietzsche sees it,

we have arranged for ourselves a world in which we can live—by positing bodies, lines, planes, cause and effect, motion and rest, form and content, without this article of faith nobody now could endure life. But this does not prove them: life is no argument. The condition of life might include error. (GS: 121)

Earlier it seemed that, by Nietzsche saying that words are arbitrarily thrown onto objects, words just fall from the sky. This is not the case, however, for concept formation is not arbitrary. What is arbitrary is the word's relation to the object; there is no direct or necessary correspondence between the signified and the signifier. However, once we abstract to the level of language itself, it becomes clear that there is a process to concept development and thereby to knowledge. In fact, concepts are created and related to each other; they form an intricate system in which each word is separate from but related to other words (BGE: 20). As Nietzsche sees it, concepts, and thereby knowledge, originate from a complex process of separation, delimination and restriction, as well as from a complex rule system whereby things are classified into certain groups, with each having its own rule-governing system (TPhil: 109).

In the end we categorize things based on their similarities to and differences from already established, and rule-governed, categories, and thereby construct concepts; in the process, we ignore or overlook what is individual and actual in the case at hand (see OTaL: 83). By omitting the uniqueness and individuality of the thing, we are then able to form a concept through categorizing the new into the old, from which we then begin our accumulation of knowledge (see TPhil: 150). Only when we are able to express something new in the language of something old and familiar does it become understandable and knowable (WP: 479; GS: 355).

We forget, however, that a thing, its organization and meaning, is the result of a double process in which we first create a theoretical or narrative description of it and then place it within an already established system of meaning, where it then receives its significance and meaning. By forgetting this, we similarly forget that to have a thought, or know, that something is some object is just to have the right word at hand, or words by which to express it (D: 257). We also forget that things are given their meaning and purpose through a system of classification. This does not mean, however, that we are free to rearrange or create words in whatever fashion we would like; rather, "thought is interpretation according to a scheme that we cannot throw off" (WP 522), and "only that which has no history is definable" (GM: 2:13). Furthermore, "in this conceptual crap game 'truth' means using every die in the designated manner" (OTaL: 85).

The consequence of this, as Nietzsche hints at above, is that reality is "not something there, that must be found or discovered," but rather it is something created and given a place in a discursive system (WP: 552). It is only our belief in this reality, in essences, that gives this process its support (ibid.). This does not mean, however, that this piece of paper is not a piece of paper. All this means is that there are two parts to all things: that which is constant, the actual piece of paper, and that which is fluid, the meaning or utility of the object derived from a complex system of rules governing its place within a system of meaning. For Nietzsche, an object is not comprehensible without this interpretation and classification, with interpretation being the introduction of meaning or sense to something new (GM: 3:12; WP: 604). Thus, concludes Nietzsche, the development of the organ of knowledge was motivated not so much by the desire not to be deceived as by a need to create a world in which we can live. He therefore contends that

one should not understand this compulsion to construct concepts, species, forms, purposes, laws (a "world of identical cases") as if they enabled us to fix the *real world*; but as a compulsion to arrange a world for ourselves in which our existence is made possible:—we thereby create a world which is calculable, simplified, comprehensible, etc., for us. (WP: 521)

As can be seen, Nietzsche is taking issue with something more than language linking to the world. What Nietzsche is directly arguing against is any notion of "essences" or "things-in-themselves," that is, that things have internal or inherent properties. By doing so, Nietzsche is attempting to destroy the distinction between the "real world" and the "world of mere appearances" in an attempt to direct our attention to what is "seeable and thinkable." One might even say that Nietzsche is trying to get us to pass over in silence that which cannot be said and instead is pointing us to that which is shown. However, this is rather complicated for Nietzsche, for a thing "is the sum of its effects, synthetically united by a concept, an image" (WP: 551).

This does not mean, however, that things "effect" other things. What this means is that the properties of a thing are its effects on other "things." If one were to remove other "things," then the object in question would have no properties and thereby not exist at all (see WP: 557–561). In other words, our common understanding that things have a constitution in themselves, whereby the sum of the properties of some object

is the cause of one single property, is an absurdity and very misleading
(WP: 559–561). For the properties of some object are derived from its
relation to other things. As should be apparent from this notion of effects,
Nietzsche sees nature as having no boundaries; only man brings to nature
notions such as shape, size or purpose (TPhil: 123). Yet, as he comments elsewhere, notions such as time, space and causality are not mere
metaphors of knowledge that we use to explain things to ourselves.
"Stimulus and action are connected: how this is we do not know; we understand not a single causality, but we have immediate experiences of
them" (140).

What this means is that Nietzsche is claiming that all we can come to
know about a thing or person is its effects, its appearance. However, because
of the seductiveness of language, we are sometimes misled in the matter of
cause and effect. Take, for instance, the phrase "I think." What does this
tiny sentence assert and lead us to believe?

That is it *I* who thinks, that there must necessarily be something that thinks, that
thinking is an activity and operation on the part of a being who is thought of as a
cause, that there is an "ego," and finally, that it is already determined what is to be
designated by thinking—that I know what thinking is. (BGE: 16)

The irony of this whole process is that before one can even start this
process of questioning, one must already have a knowledge base, or standard, from which one can determine what is happening. As Nietzsche comments, if I did not already assume a standard, then what would prevent me
from not seeing this phenomenon as being related to "willing" or "feeling"
(ibid.). The significance of this is twofold: one cannot attempt to understand
something without already having something by which to measure it, as is
apparent from the concept formation process, and one cannot attempt to
explain the cause-and-effect relation through words.

In relation to the latter notion, our whole description of cause and effect
is an absurdity. In *Daybreak* at 121, Nietzsche comments that we usually
infer from things that occur regularly together in a succession that one is
the cause, the other the effect. However, by doing this, we take the cause
as being something that is its own cause, for if it is the cause, then how
could it also be an effect? To put this another way, take the whole notion
of action. Nietzsche thinks we have completely confused the notions *active
and passive*: we seem to think we know when and how we should act, as if
we ourselves are not acted upon at every moment (D: 120). Or more clearly,
"one must understand that an action is never caused by a purpose; that
purpose and means are interpretations whereby certain points in an event
are emphasized and selected at the expense of other points" (WP: 666). In
simplest terms, we are misled by the terms *cause and effect* and have taken
these conventional fictions as means by which we can explain our behavior.

In fact, all we have done is reify "cause" and "effect" according to an understanding where something presses and pushes until it effects (BGE: 21).

The consequence of these examples is simple: the presupposition of reason leads us into the realm of "crude fetishism." As Nietzsche states in *Twilight of the Idols*,

Everywhere it sees a doer and doing; it believes in will as *the* cause; it believes in the ego, in the ego as being, in the ego as substance, and it projects this faith in the ego-substance upon all things—only thereby does it first *create* the concept of "thing." Everywhere "being" is projected by thought, pushed underneath, as the cause; the concept of being follows, and is the derivative of, the concept of ego. (TI: 5)

What Nietzsche is saying is that our belief in the three little "inner facts"— the will, the spirit and the ego—have led us to posit things as having a "being" or an essence-in-themselves (see TI: Four Great Errors: 3; also WP: 483–492). What we have done is taken the belief in an "I" as the cause of thought and by analogy we have transferred this understanding to other causal relationships. It is this very belief in the self that has led us to imagine "truth" and "reality" (see WP: 483, 485).

Part of the problem, Nietzsche reasons, is that we posit the existence of a subject, of an ego substance, as the cause of everything one does. This, Nietzsche says, is ridiculous. The self, like a thing, does not have "being." Like a thing, we believe the subject is the effect of one cause; we see it as a unity beneath all the different impulses. Nietzsche argues, however, that this belief in a "subject" is a fiction: "it is we who first created the 'similarity' of these states; our adjusting them and making them similar is the fact, not their similarity" (WP: 485). If we have a self, it is just a word for something about the body (WP: 492). We only posit "subjective, invisible life," for example, feeling, willing, thinking, to someone when we see movement in the body (ibid.). In other words, movement is "symbolism for the eye." It is we who then differentiate things into willing, feeling and thinking (see WP: 490, 492).

What Nietzsche is doing here is questioning our common belief in separating things into inner and outer dimensions, into a "soul" and a "body," and thereby into intention and action. He is also directly questioning our separation of the world into a "world in itself" and a "world of mere appearances." For Nietzsche, there is no "material world" and thereby "immaterial world"; there is just the world as it appears to us. And since we can only see effects, it is then we who imagine a cause, purpose or intention after the effect has already taken place. In other words, the subject, doer, essence and so on, is something added and invented behind what is already there (WP: 481). Therefore, a thing, a person, is a synthetic unity created through the double process of interpretation—the reading of signs—and classification—the cosmic game of placement of dice or signs.

NIETZSCHE AND WITTGENSTEIN: LANGUAGE AS AN ACTIVITY

Anyone already familiar with Wittgenstein can probably see many obvious connections of his ideas to Nietzsche. What is interesting, however, is that while Nietzsche seems to be arguing against the views established in the *Tractatus*, the way in which he does it leaves him trapped in a language game, caught between description and explanation. While Nietzsche is attempting to get us to stay on the surface, by describing what he sees us as doing, he at the same time engages in broad generalizing explanations that really tell us "this is how things are" as opposed to just saying "look at it like this." In order to see this difficulty in Nietzsche more clearly, let us now look at the later Wittgenstein in relation to certain Nietzschean themes; in the process, we shall come to see a new way of being in the world.

To begin, let us look at a comment Nietzsche makes in *Daybreak* that comes close to Wittgenstein's own thinking. Here's the aphorism at length: "*Words present in us.*—We always express our thoughts with the words that lie to hand. Or, to express my whole suspicion: we have at any moment only the thoughts for which we have to hand the words" (257). Compare this passage to "When I think in language, there aren't 'meanings' going through my mind in addition to the verbal expressions: the language itself is a vehicle of thought" (Wittgenstein, 1994: 113). For both Nietzsche and Wittgenstein, thought and language are closely related. Not only are words the medium through which we express our thoughts, but one might say that one can only know an object if one has the right words at hand. This is not to say, however, that the word's meaning correlates with the object or that the meaning is in the head. For both Nietzsche and Wittgenstein, the utility or use of the word tells us its meaning. Also, for both, the meaning and significance of the word is derived from the system of signs or language games (for Wittgenstein) or from the already established system of meaning (for Nietzsche).

Wittgenstein begins his *Philosophical Investigations* by examining the correspondence theory of language as expressed in his reading of Augustine. The view he is interested in dismantling is that "Every word has a meaning. This meaning is correlated with the word. It is the object for which the word stands" (1953: #1). Without recounting all the problems with ostensive definition, it should be noted that Wittgenstein quickly introduces two pragmatic ways of understanding language. In the first, he compares words to tools in a toolbox, thereby hinting at the diverse range of words functions (#11). In the second, words are like pieces in a game. With these two analogies, Wittgenstein is able to introduce not only words as instruments (#54) but also language as an activity, in which we speak and respond to speech. Language is a complex system of language games in which word usage is derived from systems of rules that are embedded and are conditioned by forms of life.

By linking word usage to systems of rules and to forms of life, Wittgenstein surpasses Nietzsche in the sense that he does not attempt to explain the system of classification whereby words in Nietzsche's system derive their use and thereby function. However, Wittgenstein does tell us that some word usages are similar enough that they have a family resemblance, in which case they cross over and overlap in the same way as "the various resemblances between members of a family: build, features, colour of eyes, gait, temperament, etc." (1953: #67). For instance, board games form a family, as do such things as reporting an event, giving a command and so on (#23). These similarities are not what tells us the place of a word in our systems of concepts, however; rather, grammar itself establishes the place of a concept in our systems of concepts and thereby its place in the world. In this way, the concept is not derived from the object for which it refers, but rather, by the language games in which it is used. Take, for instance, the question, Is that a dog? Or the question, Is that what we call pain? The problem we usually encounter with this second question is that we are using a grammar that misleads us. This sentence is not part of the language game of naming, and we are thereby led to believe that pain, like a dog, is some object that we can come to know.

What does "to know" mean? For Nietzsche, "to know" or "to understand" means being able to translate, or interpret, something new into the language of something old and familiar. Take, for instance, an example Wittgenstein uses. He asks: "What does it mean to know what a game is? . . . Isn't my knowledge . . . completely expressed in the explanations that I could give? That is, in my describing examples of various levels of games" (1954: 75). In other words, "to know" in this case is "to be able" to describe cases similar to the case at hand. What about being able "to know" oneself or being able "to know" if a student "understands" something. Wittgenstein would tell us to look at the word usage and context. If, for instance, to use an example from Wittgenstein, I were to write the sequence 2, 6, 10, 14, etc. on a blackboard, and ask my students to continue the sequence, how would I know that they knew the sequence? Nietzsche would say, that all we can know is their effects, "the body as symbolism" for the eye—as would Wittgenstein. If the student was "able to go on" and was "able to" go on with regularity, then we could say "they know" or "understand" the sequence.

What about "knowing oneself"? This question is a little more complicated. Let us take an example, however, that may lead us in the right direction. Let's say that someone tells us that they talk to themselves on a regular basis. How would we know that they are giving us an accurate representation of themselves? We would be able to tell by listening to what they say as well as by observing their behaviors. As Wittgenstein puts it, "our criteria for someone's saying something to himself is what he tells us and the rest of his behavior; and we only say that someone speaks to himself if, in the ordinary sense of the word, he *can speak*" (1994: 117).

Do we then watch our own behavior to know if we are in pain? How then do I know if I am in pain? Wittgenstein would tell us that we are misusing grammar, for it makes no sense to say, "I know I am in pain," unless of course there are cases in which another person is questioning what you are saying. Furthermore, there are many different criteria for personal identity, but none determines that "I am in pain" (1994: 198). For "what does it mean to know *who* is in pain? It means, for example, to know which man in the room is in pain." However, individuals usually believe that they know they are in pain by introspection or by way of it being a subjective experience. This, however, Wittgenstein would say, is an illusion. When "I" is used as a subject, it creates an illusion of something that is bodiless, that just has its home in the body. And we thereby end up saying things like "I am having" or "I have got this" as if there was an owner of "the" experience or "the" object. What we fail to see, however, is that words like "I am having" are signs to someone else. Depending on the context and the case at hand, there are different criteria by which we read these signs. Part of the problem is that we take things such as pain or a sensation to be something we can point at, like a chair. In other words, most of the difficulties here arise from the label-object view of language.

To solve these difficulties, Wittgenstein would direct our attention to the way we usually use these words. While this analysis is out of the scope of this chapter, it does hint at the power of grammar, at the ways in which the regularities of grammar tell us the place of a concept in our system of concepts and thereby its place in the world. However, we should not assume, like Wittgenstein's interlocutor, that grammar tells us the possible uses of words, as in the *Tractatus*, that grammar itself groups the diverse cases or uses of words. Rather, the amazing regularities of grammatical use are the product of the ways we live our lives, that is, of our forms of life (Wittgenstein, 1994: 496–520; Pitkin, 1972: 116–120). These forms of life, rules that govern our behavior in different contexts, are what we have to take as givens (1994: 226e), for they are based on the conventional ways in which we do things. It is in fact forms of life that allow us to bridge the apparent gap between "the subjective feeling characteristic of sudden understanding, and the guarantee of future ability to proceed correctly contained in the declaration 'I understand,' between the criteria of understanding and the meaning of understanding" (Pitkin, 1972: 225). In short, what structures our world and makes it stable is really nonsense, for we cannot know, express or say what the rules are that govern the way we do things.

At this point we may want to retreat into the "lucid, ordered crystal palace of mathematics, logic, science, a world secured against all ambiguities"—in other words, into the world, and room, constructed by the *Tractatus* (Pitkin, 1972: 336–337). Like Nietzsche, we might say, Wittgenstein's later work examines our craving for certainty, the ways in which we take the nets we spin to form a solid, stable world that we have just lifted off the ground. One might say that the gap, the mystery and the incomprehensible are problems that philosophers have never taken seriously, at least until Nietzsche. Until his proclamation that "only on this now solid, granite foundation of ignorance could knowledge rise so far—the will to knowledge on the foundation of a far more powerful will: the will to ignorance, to the uncertain, to the untrue! Not as its opposite, but—as its refinement" (BGE: 24).

A NEW WAY OF SEEING

Many have claimed that Wittgenstein's philosophy is conservative, or confining, for it does not allow for effective structural change, as we cannot express the structures, or rules, that are governing our behavior. But this assessment is to miss the beauty of the way Wittgenstein sees the world. Like Nietzsche, Wittgenstein is attempting to get us to see the ways in which we crave answers to questions that often lack an adequate answer. Whenever we ask questions touching on the meaning of concepts that we take as things, his constant retort is to direct us to the ways in which the words are used. Although Nietzsche does not use this approach, his attempt to describe where our belief in "being" came from in the first place is a similar attempt to direct our attention to what is seeable. In doing so, Nietzsche, like Wittgenstein, shows us that our belief in "ego as substance" leads us into crude psychology. Not only does it induce us to assume that there are "causes" of things, but also it shows us that if there are causes, then we can control the effects in such a manner as to change the world.

The problem, however, is that in many cases we cannot control the world, or even for that matter the consequences of our own actions. We live in a world that is outside the crystal palace constructed in the *Tractatus*; we live in a world that is messy, slippery and mysterious and that reflects a gap between existence and being. Refusing to see this reality, or allowing for the basic will of the spirit, a will for ignorance, to dominate our ways of seeing things, leaves us gazing up at the gap, the schism between being and existence, with our mouths hanging open waiting for the answer, waiting "to know." As Wittgenstein describes it,

in this world (mine) there is no tragedy, nor is there that infinite variety of circumstances which gives rise to tragedy (as its result). It is as though everything were soluble in the aether of the world; there are no hard surfaces. What this means is that hardness and conflict do not become something splendid, but a defect. (1980: 9e)

In other words, as Wittgenstein says, in our desire for absoluteness, for transcending "this life," "we have got on slippery ice where there is no friction and so in a certain sense the conditions are ideal, but also, just because of that, we are unable to walk" (Pitkin, 1972: 339).

NOTES

1. This is not to say that these are radically different realms. Sense and nonsense form two different levels of language: that which can take logical propositional form and that which cannot.

2. I am especially thinking of BGE: 61, in which Nietzsche discusses the need of a religion for the masses based on an acceptance of this life.

3. In relation to that which is meaningless, Wittgenstein believes there to be certain propositions that say nothing about the world but instead are the limiting cases that either make propositions possible or not.

4. In both cases, the sentiments expressed by these passages are sentiments that both argue against; it represents a view of philosophy and of individuals that both Wittgenstein and Nietzsche want to dismantle.

5. This discussion on Nietzsche and truth excludes the later developments in his thinking. For an extensive discussion on the changes between the views presented here and his later thoughts, see Clark (1990).

6. Yet the utility of a physiological organ can tell us nothing of its origin. As Nietzsche nicely shows in *On the Genealogy of Morals*, the utility of an object, word and so on, shows nothing other than that a will to power has crystallized an interpretation (see GM: 2, 12).

Chapter 2

Pathein Mathein: Nietzsche on the Birth of Education

Valerie Allen and Ares Axiotis

Of Nietzsche's many abiding insights for which he has come to be known, there is scant one memorable *philosophema* on education attributed to him worthy of the stature of the contributions to this subject by Plato, Rousseau or Dewey, to name the lions of the received tradition of pedagogic theorists. Paradoxically, however, Nietzsche's lectures, "On the Future of Our Educational Institutions" (*Über die Zukunft unserer Bildungsanstalten*),[1] stand as the consummate anti-educational manifesto, against education *qua* education, as defined by Western intellectual practice from Socrates onward. It is not simply a particular *conception* of education that Nietzsche seeks to displace. For Nietzsche the disenchanted university professor, it is the *concept* of education itself that is at stake. He so inveighs against the meaning of the term *education* that by the end he appears no longer to be speaking about the same thing commonly designated by that name. No wonder he has not been allotted his due place among the pride of philosophers of education. As renegade non-theorist of un-education, he is the jackal among the lions, snatching the carcass from their jaws.

Once you relinquish altogether the urge for the "truth" of education to be had, what then is the first virtue of education? the jackal might ask of the lions.

Nietzsche's view remained remarkably unchanged throughout his life. As late as *Twilight of the Idols*, he does no more than restate the same position first articulated in his unpublished early lectures: The first virtue of education is to teach thinking. Not *how* to think or even *what* to think. Simply, to think. "To learn to *think*: our schools no longer have a clue what this means." For thinking, he goes on to say, is no more than a form of dancing. As we learn to dance with our feet, so must we learn to dance with concepts and words. The thinker is but a "dance[r] with the pen" (TI, "What the Germans Lack": §7). The isomorphism implies that thinking and dancing must be learned in a similar way, performatively through initiation.

For champions of excellence, academics, flat-footed plodders, exhibit a remarkable lack of grace. By contrast, the designation of the secondary school in Germany as *Gymnasium* tacitly acknowledges the genealogy of education in the culture of the body—body building and training. In its origin, education always was linked to rhythmic movement, action and flow. Yet for all our talk of the constitution of self-identity through the reiterated rituals of material practice, we rarely consider the sedentary effects of our own daily regimen: "Sit down, write a book, and you will be an academic!"[2]

Were it just a question of footwork, the rest would be easy. But as Althusser wrote on April 6, 1969, no doubt with memories of the previous Parisian summer in mind, ideology never leaves us, and those rituals of daily *habitus*, so thoughtlessly enacted, issue from a powerful symbolic order. The working conditions that have us scrambling from one overdue deadline to another are how we (mis)recognize ourselves as purposeful and productive beings; we grouse heartily about these conditions but nonetheless work freely under them in the privacy of our studies. Our practices of professional self-fashioning are driven by a specular structure of subjectivity; we despise our working conditions, yet by them at least we fashion an identity for ourselves.

So when it comes to thinking, really thinking about the academic economy, there will be no easy points of view to pull out of a hat, no grids or tables, as Nietzsche calls them, to thrust under the nose of a *Tinten*pissing provost. "One should not have points of view, but thoughts!" snaps Nietzsche's philosopher (TI: 150), suggesting that there must perforce be something unsayable about this realm of deep thought, an indirection that will not translate into any decisive point-of-view (*Standpunkt*). Such indecision is at once apparent in Nietzsche's own attitude toward his lectures, which he held in the spring of 1872, while still a young professor at Basel. Delivered even as he was rehearsing a fledgling public voice in his first book, *The Birth of Tragedy*, which appeared in the new year of 1872, these lectures remained unpublished, despite the fact that they were well received at the time. Elisabeth, Nietzsche's sister, remarked that they comprised a fine blend of emotion, enthusiasm and hatred.[3] In "Otobiographies," Jacques Derrida calls into question the "signature" of these lectures, for Nietzsche himself disparaged them in correspondence subsequent to their delivery, admitting that he had lost his way in them and that they ended in pure negativity (Derrida, 1985: 24–25). By the end of 1872, he had decided not even to complete them (two more lectures were intended) and most emphatically not to publish them. Certainly, these lectures have been summarily dispatched, in the only extant English translation of them, published in 1909, as juvenilia.[4] Yet, apart from his preoccupation with the lectures throughout that whole year, there stands a "Preface" (*Vorrede*) to these lectures, "to be *read* [our emphasis] before the lectures, although it has nothing to do with them," in which Nietzsche promises this "book" to readers who are prepared to take time out, to fritter precious hours in deep thought. Readers of publicly performed lectures? An irrelevant preface to a text withdrawn from any audience? The "voice" of these lectures is immediately equivocal, somewhere between those prophecies of Zarathustra that resonate through posterity and echoless words uttered and heard only once.

Something of this Nietzschean *aporia* is evident in some of the metaphors—hardly metaphors any more, so impossible it is to shake off the "literal" issues they denote—by which contemporary writers have attempted to think the university. Such theorizations are marked by a hermeneutic of suspicion, double and indirect, in recognition that the knowledge we produce conceals even as it reveals; and they are remarkable for their debt, acknowledged or not, to Nietzsche's own untimely meditations.

"The University in Ruins"[5] thinks the university's self-reflection by recourse to the analogy with the penchant in Romantic landscape and architecture for fake "primitive" motifs, constructing (at least in part) a terrain of modernity through a past that it no longer is. This search for guidance for the future, enacted as a revisitation of the past, is at the center of Nietzsche's project. Now a university professor at Basel, he inquires after the future of the educational institutions by means of recounting a past encounter he experienced as a student at Bonn. Then, within this recursive narrative, Nietzsche relates how, while a student at Bonn, he revisited the secluded site of a pact made between himself and his friend some years before in order that they might meditate on the course of their own cultural development. This Wordsworthian revisitation of a past scene is wholly Romantic in its anxious awareness of the weight of past and future that hangs within the present. Furthermore, it is by the way in which contemporary culture (mis)reads the past, Nietzsche suggests, that the malaise of the present educational system is made manifest. We might think, perhaps, of what Jean-François Lyotard's meditations upon postmodernism as the "will have been" of the *futur antérieur* owe to Nietzsche (Lyotard, 1983: 341). For Nietzsche's conception of the "future" of education employs not a future simple, but an ironic heterogeneous futurity behind the moment of the present. He writes thus of the behind, the backside of the university's future, less the *Zukunft* than the *After unserer Bildungsanstalten.*[6]

"The University in the Eyes of Its Pupils," the title of Jacques Derrida's 1983 address to Cornell University, gesticulates within the hall of mirrors produced by gazing upon one's self in the reflection cast by another's eye. The punning title of the address mirrors itself in Nietzsche's own lectures. Herr Professor Nietzsche talks about how the university seemed to him when he himself was once a rowdy student furiously practicing his pistols, who in turn experiences the profound encounter with the views of an old philosopher, formerly a university professor himself, who is, by now we re-alize, the disenchanted Nietzsche himself, an angry young man, old before his time. Inside this vertiginous nesting of identities lies the question of who it is who *is* the university. Although it is the old philosopher who has at-tained insight, Nietzsche sees his first duty in these lectures as that of reach-ing the younger generation of scholars.[7] Despite much talk about Nietzschean education in terms of a genius *Führer* (Derrida, 1985: 27–29), such moments of possibility he sets before us issue from below, beyond the official structures of leadership and control wielded within the university. As the pupils of Derrida's Cornell address remind us, students are our wards (Latin, *pupilli*), the eyes by which we see and see our future and our death.

"The Ear of the Other," again Derrida's term for his meditations upon Nietzsche, offers a more direct consideration of his lectures, tracing the other in the autobiographical labyrinth of the self. The ears are those un-closable orifices through which the world passes within; by them, we ex-perience the unstoppable passage of difference. Ears are the organs of education: as students, we're all ears; as teachers we're lent ears; as ignoramuses, we've long ears. Nietzsche is a mute eavesdropper in his own lectures. Noise and quiet shape the whole narrative. Trigger-happy, he and his friend make a racket in the woods with their target practice, angering the elderly philosopher. The clash is not only between youth and old age, but also between the din of a little knowledge and the profounder stillness of wisdom. Silence, the prerequisite of thought, is the one thing the uni-versity disallows, preferring, in the name of productivity, bombination on the page without respite. As Nietzsche points out, this "irresponsible scrib-bling" is part of the academic program of prematurity. The "pantomine" of secondary-level German composition is one of the formative processes by which talent is systematically eradicated (II: 172). Forced into early and over-productivity, all independence carefully doctored, the scholar grows up with nothing of mature import to say. Pulled thus untimely from the womb of pregnant silence, we spend the rest of our thinking lives in incubation, thinking ourselves grandly self-sufficient. The stigma of this splendid pre-cociousness, Nietzsche observes, is the umbilicus connecting our ear to the placenta of our alma mater (V: 231); while our ventriloquizing father, coldest of all cold monsters, coldly whispers into our ears that its interests and ours are one and the same.[8] " 'Ere 'ere," we freely echo. "Hé vous là-bas!" "interpellates" the state, as Althusser observes. "C'est bien moi," we respond without hesitation (Althusser, 1976: 113–18).

"Foreign Body"[9] casts the university as the site of difference. As its ety-mology suggests, the foreign is from outside, yet it cannot logically be from outside until it inhabits that to which it is alien. Doubleness is its given. To think, really think about the university, its being and its future, is at once to subsist in this foreignness of the excluded other, of the un-education that is education; it is to realize the enduring absence of education altogether in these so-called educational institutions, an absence whose very non-existence has to be understood positively as a determining negativity belonging to the self-identity of the university, and without which it simply could not be what it is that it is. Nietzsche himself, a foreigner in Basel, ponders the "German" university and complains of the moribund condition of the university's Germanness. In the second lecture he delineates how the native language, vital and beautiful, is taught as if it were already dead, by "journalists," who, with their fitness-for-purpose writing programs, reduce language to inanimate utility. Germanness, Nietzsche says, is already a spectral presence, a foreign body in the German and German-speaking university, although its ubiquitous caricature persists in the nauseating nationalism of state ideologues such as Hegel. Culture is banished the moment the university constructs itself as that *vomitorium* through whose portals apple-pie students pass in and pass out, only to emerge with their "American" minds now officially declared open. Foreigners, metics, we thus inhabit the schools of our homeland. To be German, we must degermanize (*entdeutschen*) ourselves (HH1: §323).

Nietzsche's prescience and originality in these lectures lie not only in having predicted the twofold threat to the university of state and economy (Nietzsche calls the latter *Lebensnoth* [IV: 209], "the imperative for survival") long before the pathological symptoms had become generally discernible, but more so in his stubborn insistence that these threats are internal to the principle of reasonableness itself, that principle upon which the liberal university is based, rather than accidental circumstances endangering its autonomy from without. In terms of both symptomatic description and diagnostic causality, Nietzsche's lectures throw a long shadow across the writings of later philosphers of education, whose arguments, sympathetic or not, have taken his terms of reference as points of departure.

We can trace two critical traditions in post-Nietzschean philosophy of education: on the one hand, the tradition that emphasizes the dangers of the economic interests vested in the university through the dominance of technical reason—as represented in the writings of Weber, Heidegger, Jaspers, Lyotard, Bourdieu and Derrida; on the other, the tradition that traces the shadowy but sinister presence of the state in academe through the disciplinary regime of administrative reason—here we allude to the writers of the Frankfurt school through to Althusser and Foucault. In each instance, we find an alien logic of abstraction, based on the value-form and the bureaucratic-form of rationality, respectively, coming to dominate education. The debt to Nietzsche's twin critique of the *étatisme* and economism latent in Humboldt's ideal of the liberal university is often ignored, for Nietzsche has, ironically, so often been caricatured as the advocate of precisely the nationalism and individualism he took such pains to criticize. This perceived individualism arises from unnuanced interpretations of Nietzsche's recuperation of ancient Greek heroic culture as an antidote to liberal autonomy, while in the wake of the role played by Germany during the mid-twentieth century, Nietzsche's interest in the integrity of German culture has usually been castigated as reactionary, and the sharp criticisms he makes of the "culture-state" conveniently set aside.

It is important to understand Nietzsche's reasons for his disenchantment with the liberal-humanist university. Inspired ultimately by Rousseau's classic text *Emile*, the Humboldt university gave theoretical and institutional expression to education as the practice of freedom through the ideal of rational autonomy. Implicit in David Hume's "awakening" of German philosophy from its "dogmatic slumber" (the phrases are Kant's) was the realization that science, in offering probabilities rather than certainties, brought the philosophy of mind and the political principle of toleration in line with each other. *Sapere aude*—"Dare to Know!" Certainty, the mark of the narrow mind, belonged to the old regime of intolerance. The liberal-humanist university finally comes into its own, throwing off the shackles of medieval authoritarianism and intellectual circumscription by religion. The Humboldt university model realigns pedagogic structure and practice to promote the freedom of the individual thinking subject as the highest end of culture. Three unifying ideals characterize its rationale: (1) the unity of knowledge; (2) the unity of teaching and research; and (3) the unity of teacher and student. In the lectures, Nietzsche takes issue with each of these points and concludes with a call for education for a post-Enlightenment culture that has overcome the need for the false authority of rationalism.

THE UNITY OF KNOWLEDGE

Classical liberal ideals of education are founded upon an optimistic faith in the universality, generality and self-evident "sensibleness" of the rational subject, to whose judgment all questions of truth, beauty and goodness can ultimately be referred. All theory and practice are ordered to a principle of reason that is systematic and totalizing, rendering all things potentially transparent to the rational point of view. What God was to the Middle Ages, so reason comes to be for the Enlightenment. Nietzsche is quick to spot the ironic echo in the Enlightenment turn that had fought so strenuously to liberate itself from feudal servitude to dogma, tradition and superstition. His objections to the new cultural regime of reason fix upon how the liberal ideal of reason demonstrates reasonableness in all matters save one: the question of the authority of reason to be the final arbiter of culture. Here reason cannot account for itself and its privileged status in demonstrative terms, but must resort to a rational faith in its transcendent power. The Enlightenment is thus characterized by intolerance toward irreducible cultural difference, by its arrogant refusal to regard itself as anything less than the universal end of all cultural development. Insofar as the Enlightenment purports to transcend all historical particularity and contingency in this way, it erases, according to Nietzsche, historical difference, forcing a terminal rupture between itself and the original classical age of reason:

And the reason why it was impossible to bring the public schools in line with the magnificent plan of classical *paideia* lay in the un-German, almost foreign or cosmopolitan character of these educational endeavors: in the assumption that it was possible to pull the native ground from under one's feet and still stay standing upright. (II: 181)

Nietzsche's attack is directed toward Enlightenment hyper-rationality or the (Hegelian) "mad belief in the 'reasonableness of all occurrences' " (IV: 217). When such modern rationality, the voice of *imperium*, appears on the horizon as the universal language of all thought, it muzzles vernacular tongues, standardizing the diversity of dialects into a uniform idiom of abstraction. "Cosmopolitan" rationality cannot acknowledge the localness of its German borders, bounded by the partisanship of particular interests. Unlike classical Greek reason, for whom *logos* meant as much the mastery of native Athenian eloquence as it did the more general powers of valid syllogizing, Enlightenment reason turns imperial precisely at that point when it represses its base genealogy in favor of the noble lie of absolute origins. Because classical culture holds the key to the secret of reason's usurpation, the Enlightenment must above all colonize this terrain as the precondition for the legitimacy of any empire at all. Such is the scandal, according to Nietzsche, of modern classical studies, whose uncritical function it is to claim descent from the very line all trace of which it must obliterate. The culmination of this cultural revolution occurs with Hegel's apotheosis of reason as world-spirit, in the absolute idealism of "thought thinking itself."

A quite recent system basking in scandalous world repute discovered the formula for this self-destruction of philosophy: such a naïve unreflectiveness so pervades now as the historical perspective on things, in taking the greatest unreason for "reason," and in taking the blackest for white that one is occasionally tempted to ask, in parody of Hegel's dictum: "is this unreason actual?" Why, it is precisely this unreason which now alone seems to be "actual" and active. (V: 234)

THE UNITY OF TEACHING AND RESEARCH

Once again, the liberal ideals of the Humboldt model can be understood in terms of what they were reacting against. In the scholastic model of the medieval university, interpretation is not a matter of individual choice but is already hermeneutically implicit, ready to become exegetically explicit from out of the *auctoritas* of scripture. Scholasticism thus does not engage in research but instruction, where the student is initiated into knowledge. In contrast, the "enlightened" university celebrates knowledge as an active process, thereby introducing the idea of research alongside that of teaching. The relation between the object of knowledge and the knowing subject is, in the Hegelian sense, always already dialectical, a matter of continual description and redescription. Consequently, knowledge is inherently procedural and dynamic, instead of being primarily propositional and doctrinal. Learning inevitably participates in the free process of the production of knowledge itself. If knowing is thus always a doing, the "labor of the concept," production rather than representation, being a good student requires exactly the same virtues as does research, namely, observing closely and questioning closely. Conversely, the best teacher is also the best researcher because both must inevitably be interpreters and, hence, critics of the traditional opinions that comprise the stable core of a discipline. The rational and the critical principle become identified with each other, and in this identification, free thinking subjects become accountable to themselves as the final standard of judgment.

Once again Nietzsche impugns the idea of disembodied critical knowing based on the liberal ideal of open and undistorted dialogue within the academic retreat. If knowing is always radically situated, then there can be no such thing as wholly disinterested truth. Rhetoric and politics thus together constitute what must remain unthought and invisible to reason for its effective rational operation. In just the same way as the spurious "reasonableness" of transcendent rationality always enshrines vested local interest, so, Nietzsche maintains, "academic freedom," that categorical imperative of all academics to act under the idea of freedom alone, impelled only by the force of the better argument, is but a euphemism for the profane determination of judgment by the balance of prevailing interest.

THE UNITY OF THE TEACHER/STUDENT RELATION

The Humboldt model of learning is also dialectical in the further, Socratic sense in which the social exchange between student and teacher is formalized in the seminar. The fixed roles in the medieval university between authoritative *magister* and quizzical *discipulus* give way to the anti-authoritarian and democratic encounter, calling everything into question and leaving everything open to interpretation. In the seminar, the roles of teacher and student are not fixed according to status but are freely interchangeable as the discussion progresses. By the same token, the text no longer represents the authority of *scriptura* but is simply a value-free narrative, ever in need of the reinterpretation that safeguards against any servile tendency to enshrine the text as law. In these respects, then, the seminar as envisaged in Humboldtian pedagogy is the secular analogue of the reformed congregation, a community of free-thinkers without priest or creed to impede their service to the greater glory of reason. The aim of this open community of free and equal rational subjects is to progress to a point unattainable by either student or teacher working alone, such that the whole represents more than the sum of its individual parts. But Nietzsche holds the mirror up to the disingenuous ideals of such liberal education, exposing both the absence of any genuine teacher/student dialogue and its vicious circularity. The Humboldtian seminar emerges as the fundamental material ritual whereby the teacher reproduces an ideological imago in the student:

Now the teacher speaks to these students who are listening. Whatever else he thinks and does is cut off from the students' perception by an impassable divide. . . . One mouth speaking, many ears listening, half the number of hands writing: there is the external apparatus of academe, there is the university's education-machine set in motion. (V: 231–232)

Our contemporary universities therefore . . . establish their philological professoriates for the purpose of training new generations of specialist philologists—who in their turn are responsible for the philological tutoring of the schoolboys. This is a vicious circle in which neither philologist nor gymnasium prospers. (V: 235–236)

The avowed purpose of the Humboldtian community of education is ostensibly to produce self-reliant, critical thinkers. Yet behind the theory and practice of education for autonomy, Nietzsche sees an insidious hidden curriculum that breeds rule-conformity and submission to abstract authority. The Humboldtian undergraduate thus acquires a premature self-reliance whose very earliness guarantees that the student will never attain the maturity of any radical critique of value. Under the banner of self-determination, the student's systematic unreadiness ironically ensures the banishment of really "free" and creative thought from the university and maintains the student in unwitting subjection to the authority of abstraction alone: "Happy age, when youth is so wise and cultured that it can spoon-feed itself!" (V: 232).

Autonomy, then, defines the spirit of the Humboldtian educational institution. Where the medieval university was tied to the interests of church and state, the "enlightened" university liberated itself from such allegiance in the name of academic freedom. This "enlightened" university, on the other hand, similarly dissociated itself from the economic imperatives of civil society in its refusal to be merely a vocational institution. From the third lecture onward, Nietzsche challenges this purported autonomy, bringing into relief the latent *étatisme* of the Humboldt university enshrined in Hegelian liberal-humanist apologetics. What is significant in this connection is how institutional self-reliance cannot but depend upon the good-will of the liberal state:

This mutual independence [of teacher and student] is fulsomely extolled as "academic freedom." . . . Only that at a modest distance, behind both parties, the state stands attentively, its eye watchful, reminding them now and then that it is the purpose and principle peculiar to this oral-aural procedure. (V: 232)

Education, for Nietzsche, is in contradiction to the learning process structured as *universitas*. He eschews the term altogether, for its root metaphor ("to turn into one") appeals to a generality, whose regimented space-time is characterized by the transcendentals of unity, totality and identity. Instead, he gives us two significant indications, seemingly unrelated, of what higher education might look like in a future culture innocent of universitization. The first reference is to the classical Greek ideal of *paideia*. To the Greeks, education was a matter of formation (*morphosis*), understood in terms carried over from the plastic and, more generally, the technical arts. To become educated was to be shaped and fashioned to embody the cultural ideals of the community as transmitted by custom and tradition. With the rise of philosophy, Socrates took hold of this intuitive metaphor for education and developed it, reinterpreting the formative process of molding in an exclusive way as the prerogative of reason. Platonic-Aristotelian metaphysics carried this a step further by invoking the category of matter and form (*hyle/morphe*): form being represented as active universal reason and matter as passively subsumable particularity. When Nietzsche refers to *paideia*, however, he alludes to a primordial, pre-metaphysical experience of formation, whose nature has been occluded by the rationalization of education in the *akademia* and the *stoa*.

The second reference comes in the last lecture near the end, almost as an aside. "Look to the *Burschenschaft*" is Nietzsche's catcall to academic good sense. Although the term *Burschenschaft* now commonly refers (and basically has done since 1848) to the frat-boys of German university student societies, elitist and conservative in outlook, it originally referred collectively to the suppressed German student movement dating from the period of the German Wars of Liberation against the French and the years after 1815. *Burschenschaft*, meaning "fellowship," denotes a "club," "society" or "confraternity" and draws from the ancient Germanic "guilds," which affirmed a group's collective identity through a spontaneous solidarity given freely by its initiates and not obligated by any delegated or external authority. The *Burschenschaft*'s *auto-da-fé* at the Wartburg festival (1817) in which a number of books considered un-German were consigned to the flames, along with its association with the murder of the playwright-turned-government-spy August von Kotzebue in the same year, provoked reaction from Metternich, who, with the Karlsbad decrees of 1819, banned the fraternities and held the universities under strict surveillance and censorship. In his preface to the *Philosophy of Right*, Hegel, seeking to justify his acquiescence in state repression of the student movement, accuses the *Burschenschaften* of menacing the progress of modern social rationality in Germany by advancing obscurantist ideals. He admonishes the academics in the movement (specifically, J. F. Fries, a philosophy professor at Heidelberg who had participated in the Wartburg festival) for what he saw as romantic irrationalism. It is in this same preface that Hegel claims that "whatever is rational is actual and whatever is actual is rational." Jürgen Habermas, in the *Philosophical Discourse of Modernity*, simply toes Hegel's line when he characterizes the German student movement of the early nineteenth century as a conservative revolution opposed to the project of modernity. It is thus in this fifth lecture, where Nietzsche invokes the *Burschenschaften*, that he vents his spleen in full against Hegel, quoting this very passage (V: 234).

It is possible to discern an internal connection between Nietzsche's two references—Greek *paideia* and the German *Burschenschaft*—whose implications for higher education are far-reaching. Starting with *paideia*, Nietzsche points out how little we have fathomed the original Greek understanding of the metaphor of formation. The Greeks had achieved a profound insight into the nature of *morphosis*, which was effaced as the metaphor lost its vitality in its transformation into a neutral concept. Formation is not to be understood in instrumental terms of fitness-for-purpose. Fitness implies the teleological orientation of a calculative thinking given over to the logic of means-end reasoning. The confusion thus arises from elevating the technique of the artisan to the status of abstract philosophical truth. Before it ever became leveled to fitness-for-purpose, the morphotic, Nietzsche maintains, was the dynamic expression of two antagonistic formative impulses. On the one hand, it expressed the plastic energies of Apollo, god of dreams, illusion and imagination, of the overpowering appearance of figuration and transfiguration that defies conceptual reduction. On the other hand, it expressed an ineradicable Dionysian drive to intoxication, ecstasy and *mania*, exciting awe and terror in exceeding all division, limits and boundaries. If *paideia* originally conceived itself as morphotic in this twofold primordial sense of rapture, then the formative meaning of education points to the idea of *initiation* rather than that of *fitness*.

The same conclusion follows from consideration of the fact that music and gymnastics were originally the twin pillars of Greek education. For both music and dance are fundamentally ritual elements, media expressive of the ecstatic process of initiation—alteration of consciousness and obliteration of self-identity. Moreover, Greek music and dance were collective expressions, rhythmic sound and movement performed as a *choros*, the group and the activity being designated by the same word. The Greek conception of education as initiatory in origin thus provides the key to understanding Nietzsche's reference to the *Burschenschaft*, since the process of initiation necessarily implies the existence of a Dionysian throng, a *thiasos* ("company" or "troupe") to which the initiate gains admission in order to share the experience of membership. To become educated, then, hints Nietzsche, is to be initiated into the life of a group, and a particular kind of group at that, one that constitutes itself collectively in and through music and dance.

The fundamental unit of education is, therefore, the *thiasos*, the performing collective body. This entails first that constitution of the group and membership within it are not simply a means to an end but, more precisely, the very essence of education. It also entails that education must always be understood performatively as enactment rooted in the concrete context of community life. The repression of the corporate roots of the university in favor of a free-floating cosmopolitanism indicates the rupture introduced by philosophy in the understanding of education: from initiation into a community with local and particular interests to fitness for the universal life of socio-historically transcendent reason.

The term *initiation*, being Latin in origin, naturally gives rise to some confusion: its root metaphor is different from that of the Greek word and consequently does not allow the same inferences easily to be drawn in English. Nietzsche, however, has the Greek word *myesis* exclusively in mind. In Greek, "to initiate" is *myein*, "to shut," "to close" as of ears, eyes and lips. The initiate is the *mystes*, and the manifold process is denoted by a non-unifying plural: *mysteria*.

Following Nietzsche's lead, we are in a position to identify at least some of the more significant aspects of initiation as a guiding metaphor of education. In the first place, by means of the expedient of the image of initiation, Nietzsche returns education to its base origins under the joint signs of Dionysus and Apollo, the two signature gods of the mysteries. In the confluence of these two antagonistic forces, *orgia* ("intoxication") and *katharsis* ("purification"), the tragic Greek spirit had also given rise to *paideia* to confront its crisis of values. In similar vein, Nietzsche regards education-as-initiation as offering modern culture a therapeutic antidote to its surfeit of rationality. The shift from fitness to initiation replaces the idea of mastery with that of mediation. Education is now cast in intrinsically liminal terms, mediating the labyrinthine transitions, both terrifying and exhilarating, of becoming without end. To the Greeks, therefore, *paideuein* had a double meaning—"to teach" and "to torment"—whose echo still resonates in our modern term *discipline*. Realizing that *pathein mathein*, learning is suffering, they understood the profoundly tragic aspect of education, its intrinsic *passion*, and captured it in the image of the initiatory ordeal, which at once loosens to bind, wounds to heal, so that only through death are we reborn.

Second, it follows that the lectures, roughly contemporaneous with *The Birth of Tragedy*, rely on implicit use of the Dionysian/Apollonian distinction to develop the view of the tragic essence of education. The future of our educational institutions is only made manifest by the genealogy ("birth") of education out of the spirit of music. Nietzsche traces the repressed lineage of what presents itself as noble and elevated, its humble beginnings in what rational self-identity is required to exclude as alien to its nature. A therapeutic desublimation of the sublime occurs, a concrete *katabasis* of the transcendent into the chthonic underworld of Dionysian immanence. By the same token, the process culminates in an *anabasis* from the Hades of the unthought into the Apollonian light of refracted appearance. This twofold structure of thought is expressed by none other than the initiatory ordeal of death and rebirth through ecstatic experience. The rootedness of thinking in the *mysteria* is borne out from a different direction by the origin of the word "theory." The *theoros* was no "disinterested" spectator but an active and sympathetic participant in the mystery rites, whose authoritative function was to mediate the contradictory manifoldness of the mysteries by surveying steadily and whole the many ways of becoming. What is spectacular about theory, then, is precisely the perpetual unsteadiness of such *coinicidentia oppositorum* and the continual deferral of totalization in the face of the irreducible Dionysian/Apollonian pull of thought.

Third, as Nietzsche *expresses* it pithily in "On Truth and Lies in a Nonmoral State," the aim of thought is dissimulation, not representation—*Verstellung*, not *Vor-stellung*. The implication for education is evident: If thought is to be the first virtue of education, then dissimulating itself must be the governing principle of educational institutions. This is as it was with Greek *paideia*, which recognized the basis of education in music and gymnastics. Higher education goes astray, then, by its "point of view," which is inimical to deep thought.

Finally, let us now venture a more concrete understanding of the therapeutic nature of *burschenschaftliche Bildung* as antidote to the universitization of higher education. Noteworthy at the outset is that the former is defined by *schole* ("leisure"). *Schole* is neither a straightforward presence, bone idleness, nor mere absence of labor and utility. It is pure *ek-stasis*, whose meaning derives from the combination of the prefix *ex* (out) and the verb *histanai* (to cause to stand) to yield the idea of de-rangement, literally of standing out or apart. *Schole* denotes the negativity of transcendence, that *an-archia* of the unterritorializable. It thus contrasts with its opposite *an-angke* ("necessity"), which, as the word-root indicates, is expressed in terms of the "yoke" of bondage. *Schole* is neither an institution, a "school" in our modern sense, nor a state of being, as the term "at leisure" implies. *Schole* is defined by unrepresentable liminalities, what Nietzsche in *The Birth of Tragedy* (§15) calls *Grenzpunkte* (literally, "border-points") from which alone tragic insight breaks through, where we shut our eyes, ears and mouths to the functional determination of fitness-for-purpose and set everyday life out of joint in order that we may see, hear and speak with *en-th[e]ousiasmos* (literally: "in-divination").

The counter-territorialization of *schole* articulates the space of the *Burschenschaft* as a sanctuary in which the epideictic festival of the mind unfolds its principal powers in dissimulation. A sanctuary is opposed to the ivory tower or the retreat. We withdraw to an ivory tower or retreat; they are at a remove from the center of activity. A sanctuary, by contrast, constitutes a center, an *omphalos*, around which everything else revolves. A retreat stockpiles energy to be expended elsewhere, whereas an economy of excess governs a sanctuary: energy is harnessed from elsewhere precisely in order to be spent *there*. Nietzsche's sanctuary in the lectures is "that distant and elevated spot near Rolandseck" high above the banks of Rhine, far from the corruption of town and university. Only the non-linear space of the sanctuary allows manic experiences of metamorphosis, of becoming-other, of androgynic and theriomorphic transfiguration. Greek *mania*, however, is a difficult word to translate, for its etymology links it with *menos*, which points to a conception of frenzy as intensified and extraordinary power of mind—to think like a god.

As the sanctuary articulates the space, so the festival articulates the time of the *Burschenschaft*. Nietzsche's narrative is set at the close of the half-year of the academic cycle. There is a general holiday from university life, and the student body is in festive celebration beyond the clock of profane time. The irregular rhythm of the festival renders its time heterogeneous and discontinuous, incapable of being parsed into uniform intervals of semester time. Learning oriented to the festival dispenses with the punctuality of the *term*inus by which classes are held, examinations taken, papers graded and meetings scheduled, all with mathematical precision. The festival's economy of time is purposely dithyrambic. Time is measured by reference to the exalted to-and-fro of the procession in the throng of *choros*. In dithyrambic *choros*, the participants awaken to the beat of qualitative, non-quantifiable time, flowing forwards and backwards.

An after-thought may be indulged to dispel rank miscontrual of Nietzsche's view of the tragic character of education. One might object as follows: the invocation of the Dionysian/Apollonian distinction to illumine the origin of education does no more than reground learning within the cultic or, at least, charismatic experience of a concrete community guided by parochial interests. Thus, education as initiation does not ultimately get us beyond mere socialization—internalizing the horizon of a given group. For initiation, it is argued, is a dependent variable, bound to a prior culture and tradition. On this reading, Nietzsche's antidote to the universalizing pretense of cosmopolitanism in education is simply to administer a dose of particularism. According to the tragic spirit of education, however, *schole*, in virtue of its irreducible liminality, can never give itself over entirely either to abstract universality or to concrete particularity. Education, understood in terms of *pathein mathein* of the initiatory ordeal, is thus intrinsically an affair of the limit—superseding determination by state or economy. Far from being in a tributary position to the state or the economy, as with the university, rediscovered *paideia* now takes pride of place, humbling categorical administrative and productive imperatives before the awesome vision of the tragedy of existence. It would therefore be fairer to say that *our* Nietzsche proposes to reground learning on the *pathos* of the *Grenzpunkt*, which is not an experience that can be plotted on the metaphysical dimension of universal and particular. Rather, it arises there at the wound in being where the metaphysical and its tragic other have their common source.

NOTES

1. All translations throughout are our own and made from the German text of Nietzsche's works (Colli and Montinari, 1980: vol. 1). The lectures are cited by lecture number, followed by page number.

2. *Pace* Louis Althusser (1976: 108), who paraphrases Pascal (our translation): "Get on your knees, move your lips in prayer, and you will believe."

3. For *The Birth of Tragedy* as naughty and offensive, see Nietzsche's letter, December 31, 1871, to Gustav Krug; for the popularity of the lectures, see his letter, January 28, 1872, to Erwin Rohde. For Elisabeth Förster-Nietzsche's observations, see Chapter 10 of her edition of the Nietzsche-Wagner correspondence.

4. Stanford University Press is currently in the process of translating the complete Colli/Montinari edition.

5. The title of a special issue of the *Oxford Literary Review* 17 (1995) on the crisis in the concept of the modern university.

6. *After-*, in German, can bear the temporal sense of posteriority, as in *die Aftergeburt*, the afterbirth (although *Nachgeburt* is more common nowadays). As substantive, *das After* means "the anus." The pun was Nietzsche's suggested revenge title in an open letter to Dr. U. Wilamowitz-Moellendorf, who in May 1872 disparaged *The Birth of Tragedy* in a pamphlet entitled *Zukunftsphilologie!* (Letter to Erwin Rohde, July 16, 1872).

7. Letter to Friedrich Ritschl, January 30, 1872.

8. "On the New Idol" in *Z*: I.

9. See the discussion of the seminar called "Foreign Body" at the University of Stirling, Scotland (Royle, 1995: 143–158).

Chapter 3

Nietzsche: Deleuze, Foucault and Genealogy as a Method for Education

F. Ruth Irwin

NIETZSCHE: *ON THE GENEALOGY OF MORALS*

The first section of this chapter describes Nietzsche's *On the Genealogy of Morals* and analyzes his polemic against nihilism. Nietzsche analyzes power in terms of the active/reactive dichotomy of the master and the slave. Deleuze (1983) advocates extricating ourselves from the master/slave dualism through respecting a distribution of difference. In *Zarathustra*, Nietzsche conceptualizes a process of metamorphosis that transmutes reactive forces into life-affirming principles. The second section of the chapter examines genealogy as a method and discusses the implications it has for approaching education. The focus is on the genealogical relationship between power, interpretation and change, and if it is at all possible, a space will be derived where these dynamics may avoid being recouped by nihilism. Foucault analyzes several technical terms related to genealogy: *Herkunft*, or descent, and *Entstehung*, or emergence, as processes of continuity and change. In the absence of a metaphysical faith in the Absolute, these genealogical processes and the historical context increase in significance. Genealogy opens the opportunity for a plurality of perspectives and a means of evaluating knowledge and interpretation in education.

Nietzsche's genealogy is aimed at investigating moral phenomena as the result of historical forces and contingency rather than as metaphysical or teleological universal Truths. This is to say, that for Nietzsche, unlike Kant, morals cannot be understood as universal givens or values that are logically deducible from categorical imperatives. Nietzsche argues that the Platonic division of the natural world of "Appearance" from an Ideal "Real" world outside of time and space is a fallacy. He also argues that there is no inevitable and authoritative essence or law, which is foundational and determines moral codes. Cohesion of interpretation is admirable and necessary but is not to be confused with an ultimate original source, which underlies objects and events.

Having disposed of the "adolescent" assumption that there is a pure origin in the preface of *On the Genealogy of Morals*, Nietzsche discusses the emergence and coherency of ideas, as particular issues reoccur in an individual's life. In contrast to Kant's system of categories, Nietzsche posits increasingly interconnected, interwoven themes that point to a common root, a constellation of senses that constitute the "fundamental will of knowledge." He claims of the will, "I might almost have the right to call it my *a priori.*"

Many commentators take Nietzsche's search for an origin of morality at face value, but for Nietzsche "origins" are quickly subsumed in the constitutive processes of values. *On the Genealogy of Morals* transforms the philosophical task from uncovering the essential Truth to one of situating and contextualizing the emergence of values, in order to understand them more fully and to appraise their ability to enhance or degenerate human interaction.

Genealogy as a method is a blend of psychology, etymology and historical contextualization. Foucault (1977b) argues that it avoids the question of ultimate origins, while looking for the contextual "emergence" of an idea, a power struggle, a dominant class. Relating a similar concept, but from the subjective viewpoint, Solomon (1996) reasons that the *ad hominem* style of argument insists on the psychological and historical contingency of the author of a theory, not simply the logical coherency of a theoretical system.

THE MASTER/SLAVE DICHOTOMY

The first chapter of *On the Genealogy of Morals* on "Good and Bad" and "Good and Evil" explores the dichotomous relationship between the active master and reactive slave. Values derive from either of these poles. Nietzsche finds evidence of the master/slave relationship in such diverse cultures as the Ancient Greeks, the Egyptians, the Christians and the Jews, Buddhism, the Goths, and "modern" man. Various interpretations of Nietzsche's genealogy read it as glorifying the brutality of the master/slave dichotomy, or alternatively as an evolving dualistic equilibrium. These interpretations miss the aim of his "polemic." As Kaufmann (1989: 11) notes, while Nietzsche is attempting "to rise above the slave morality that contrast good and evil, his work also signifies a very broad attack on 'the faith in opposite values.' " The noble master type imposes moral conditions with little regard to their consequences for others. *Ressentiment* is the French term Nietzsche uses (as there is no directly translatable word in German, unlike the close approximation "resentment" in English) for the reactive slave morality of revenge.

Ressentiment morality constitutes civilization, perhaps more even than that of the "noble." While *ressentiment* is prolific, its revengeful motivation ultimately produces a nihilistic approach to life. Describing the dualism itself is therefore not the extent of Nietzsche's investigation. The "master" and "slave" are psychological categories that illuminate existing power plays, in the field of infinite possibilities. Exceeding *ressentiment* is difficult, for it is the established base of existing culture. Nietzsche argues that if we are to exit the cycle of short-sighted exploitation a metamorphosis is necessary.

Nietzsche's discussion of the master/slave bears a striking resemblance to Hegel, bearing in mind that Nietzsche came to Hegel through the rancor of Schopenhauer and has been accused of "not knowing his Hegel." Nietzsche did not attempt to transcend the master/slave with a dialectical synthesis of doubled negative identity. In the master/slave dichotomy the one relies on the other to recognize the self. Rather than this double movement generating a positive recognition, or even as Schopenhauer and later Heidegger might describe it, a "representation," Nietzsche extricates a convoluted dialectical process of polar opposition, an antagonistic and essentially negative identity formation. Using etymology, Nietzsche posits the "master" type as having a self-sufficient identity, thinking of himself benevolently as "good," "noble," "upright" and even "naive."

[I]t acts and grows spontaneously, it seeks its opposite only so as to affirm itself more gratefully and triumphantly—its negative concept "low," "common," "bad," is only a subsequently-invented pale, contrasting image in relation to its positive basic concept. (GM: 37)

In contrast, the slave's impotence causes a defensive self-serving identity, who reacts with a revengeful spirit against the master, eventuating in a peculiar *cleverness*. *Ressentiment* is Nietzsche's term for the reactive spirit of revenge. The etymology of slave *ressentiment* constitutes the other, the "master" as *evil*. Slave identity follows this fact, inventing "as an afterthought and pedant, a 'good one'—himself!" (GM: 39)

The slave revolt in morality begins when *ressentiment* itself becomes creative and gives birth to values: the *ressentiment* of natures that are denied their true reaction, that of deeds, and compensate themselves with an imaginary revenge. While every noble morality develops from a triumphant affirmation of itself, slave morality from the outset says No to what is "outside," what is "different," what is "not itself"; and this No is its creative deed. (GM: 36)

The pressure on the "weak" to create values in a limited field of possibility forces their will back in upon themselves. Among other interpretations grounded in *ressentiment*, they developed the "bad conscience" and the myth of the independent subject. Nietzsche fumes that the numerical dom-

inance of the "weak" is being used to justify the dominance in society of
their reactive morality. The knowledge that is produced annihilates the values of "others." An ethos of quantity finds legitimation in "universal" morals. The slave mentality comprehends humanity as a pathway to an external
Ideal world—a nihilistic reaction to the suffering associated with this one—a
set of conditions Nietzsche describes as "sick" and "degenerative."

THE BECOMING-REACTIVE OF FORCES

As conditions that lay the foundations for subjectivity, the second essay
of *On the Genealogy of Morals* looks at active and reactive forces. The constitution of the human animal into someone who is capable of making promises, and thus producing society, is "the real problem regarding man." As
the subject is exposed to the constant blast of stimuli from the world, its
initial activity is to actively forget or screen the "digestion" of phenomena.
"Forgetting is no mere *vis inertiae* as the superficial imagine; it is rather an
active and in the strictest sense positive faculty of repression" (GM: 57).
Forgetting enables a little *tabula rasa*, which is a necessary precondition for
consciousness to exist. That forgetting of the "incorporation" of manifold
experiences makes superimposing the immediate reactions to the moment
possible. Forgetting allows a quietness in which to regulate and order responses. Having established the ability to forget, the possibility of adjusting
memories, taking account of the present and predicting the future, is opened
up.

The active imposition of memory is the next step toward enduring immediate organic-chemical reactions. Memory is the retaining of a momentary desire, which instigates a long chain of will, overcoming the unforeseen
momentary circumstances that the future presents. The ability to remember
promises is central to constituting personality; otherwise, again, we simply
react organically to whatever the environment throws up at us.

Memory is at the nexus of the body, mind and society. Nietzsche sees the
faculty for making promises as necessary for society to be possible. In turn,
society develops strategies to impose memories on the individual. Fixing
ideas requires a mnemonic device, and Nietzsche holds that society's primitive means of forming individuals was through pain. "Civilized" society has
become more sophisticated in its mnemonic techniques—using education
as a means, as Foucault might argue, to produce "docile bodies" through
the regulation of time, space and knowledge. The power imposed by societies to regulate their members is the point of evaluation. Is this society
actively generating a dynamic that enhances human relations or diminishes
them? Are the moral values that constitute the physical conditions of society
"healthy" or "sick"?

The activity of the self is to "make sense" of the constant exposure to the
manifold impressions of the world. Actively forgetting in order to selectively

recoup these phenomena constitutes a subjectivity that can transcend the moment, and draw commonalities between disparate elements. However, both the activity of forgetting and remembering are ultimately a *response* to the bombardment of phenomena. They are both essentially reactive. Rather than assuming that all action is generically "active," and that reaction is additional to and comes after some initial action, the forces that Nietzsche is characterizing are *all* "becoming-reactive" as Deleuze (1983; orig. 1962) terms it. The initial correspondence between the noble masters with action and slave *ressentiment* with reaction is no longer a viable evaluation of the life-enhancing or life-demeaning effect of active or reactive values. The dualism has collapsed into the negative pole, and (re)valuation per se appears to be inevitably "becoming-nihilistic"—as Heidegger argued at length in his *Nietzsche*.

Nietzsche's dualism of the active and reactive is excruciatingly difficult to escape. Even Nietzsche's criteria for evaluating morals in terms of the metaphor of health or sickness—the "health" or "sickness" of physicality/personality/morality/society—constantly constitute a dichotomy that is in danger of collapsing into its own opposite. Active health is a peak experience. Health only makes sense in its implied opposition to sickness. Similarly, strength implies "not-weakness," or "not-yet-weakness." The peak of the positive pole cannot retain a static position. The dynamism of forces, or "qualities of the will to power" are a translation of one pole into the other.

The becoming-reactive of both active and reactive forces is not a negation of the negative in the Hegelian sense. The negative identity formation that constitutes Nietzsche's master and slave cannot transform into a life-affirming ethic through Hegel's dialectical synthesis. The negation of negation arrives at a temporary appropriation of an affirmative force but never extricates itself from its nihilistic project. It exhibits "a certain *impoverishment of life*. . . . dialectics in place of instinct" (GM: 154). The question is, how does the negative opposition of active and reactive get translated into life-affirming principles, which can discern the value of values? Reactive forces are driven by *ressentiment*, or revenge. This *ressentiment* is not an appropriation but a phenomenological responsiveness. But it means that at the center of humanity is a tendency toward the negative. Deleuze argues that the double negative of the dialectic, the constitution of identity through rejecting what is "other," *cannot* achieve a positive relationship between a person and the world. Only by approaching the world affirmatively can people derive a positive identity that enhances themselves and life:

Nietzsche wants to say that man's species activity or culture only exists as the presumed end result of a becoming-reactive which turns the principle of this activity into a failed product. The dialectic is the movement of activity as such and it too is essentially failed and fails essentially. The movement of reappropriations, dialectical activity is nothing more or less than the becoming-reactive of man and in man. (Deleuze 1983; orig. 1962: 168)

NIHILISM AND METAMORPHOSIS

Nietzsche's task in the third and final essay of the *Genealogy* is not simply to generate a new hypothesis about morality or an alternative method for understanding the derivation of values. His purpose is to rescue humanity from the nihilism he associates with the dominant value structure that permeates society. Genealogy bypasses origins that are "otherworldly" and concentrates instead on valuing the "world of appearance." Beyond blindly accepting, or simply criticizing morality, Nietzsche suggests that "the value of these values themselves must be first called in question." This is not to say that surmising that particular values that reinforce the dominant will to power of one genealogical group is a sufficient enterprise. The simple advantage of one group or another does nothing to analyze the enhancement or degeneration of society. Thus, the Marxist notion that education serves to reproduce labor power for a capitalist society is not limited to a prescription for revolutionizing the relations of domination—as it might be for reversing the master/slave relationship. That would be to restrict Marx's insight into something helpful in the short term but insufficient for evaluating whether the society's values are "life-denying" or "life-affirming." Nietzsche is unmoved by the notion that some groups have more status than others. He wants to critique the blind assumptions of morality. This is not in order to simply regroup them in an apparently more ethical form; rather, it is to assess morals from the perspective of life itself. "What if a symptom of regression were inherent in the 'good,' like-wise a danger, a seduction, a poison, a narcotic, through which the present was possibly living at the expense of the future?" (GM: 20).

The third essay in *On the Genealogy of Morals* is an analysis of a rather oblique and not easily decipherable aphorism from *Thus Spake Zarathustra*. "Unconcerned, mocking, violent—thus wisdom wants *us*: she is a woman and always loves only a warrior" (GM: 97). Here Nietszche is referring to the active, spontaneous and aggressive truths that form society without negating it. Not content with mere description, Nietzsche seeks the *meaning* of ascetic ideals. The book ends depressingly with the analysis of asceticism as the "will to nothingness." The ascetic ideal found a reason for human suffering—it had found a purpose, a meaning:

> Man was *saved* thereby, he possessed a meaning, he was henceforth no longer like a leaf in the wind, a plaything of nonsense—the "sense-less"—he could now *will* something . . . man would rather will *nothingness* than *not* will. (GM: 162; emphasis in original)

Despite the disturbing ending to his book, Nietzsche is not a pessimist. His profound and optimistic recognition was that without the notion of God, humans have to face the fact that life is devoid of *external* meaning.

The function of meaning and truth itself is contestable, a notion that we will examine in the following section on Foucault. Humanity can no longer perceive itself as a bridge to an ever brighter future. Nietzsche sees this as an opportunity to overcome the human-all-too-human engrossment with pitiable purposes and to enjoy the flux of life for its own sake. Each chance is a destiny. There is no option to keep playing the dice until you get a willed result. There is simply one fatal combination. "To laugh is to affirm life, even the suffering in life. To play is to affirm chance and the necessity of chance. To dance is to affirm becoming and the being of becoming" (Deleuze, 1983: 170).

In *Thus Spake Zarathustra*, Nietzsche describes the process of meta-morphosis, each level a necessary component of human existence. The aim is to escape the spirit of revenge as a motor of history. But Deleuze's famous rejection of the double negative of the dialectic in favor of a double affir-mative is not as simple as it might first appear. Deleuze cites Nietzsche's concept of the *Übermensch* (the Overman) as the possible exit from the unavoidably nihilistic "human type." The *Übermensch* is the (idealistic?) overcoming of all-too-human species or culture. The *Übermensch* avoids pit-ying the resentful masses and thus does not deliver its identity to the becoming-reactive of forces. *Übermenschlichkeit* exceeds the negative identity relation through life-affirming laughter. In my reading, it is to re-spect the other rather than annihilate them.

Nietzsche's concept of the "eternal recurrence" is an associated technique for overcoming *ressentiment*. If every moment must be repeated, *ad infin-itum*, rather than our lives being a practice run, an audition or path to another heavenly world, Nietzsche reasons that each moment must become a precious thing, necessary and beyond revenge.

Rebecca Comay (1990) argues that Nietzsche is aiming for a type of redemption, "beyond recuperation, beyond affirmation, beyond the eternal stamp of presence." She maintains that revenge becomes a type of meta-physics for Nietzsche. He accuses it of attempting to transcend time, in a fashion similar to the ideals of Plato or Aristotle. His notion of the eternal recurrence incorporates *wider-wille*—against the will. The play on words co-opts *wieder*—again, and *wider*—against, so that *wider-wille* aims toward a "transvaluation of revenge":

For "revenge" has officially, for Nietzsche . . . the most metaphysical of all structures: the symptom of intolerance of "ill will" toward time and its transiency, the symptom of the slave economy of revenge and exchange, the symptom of reactivity in its most abject form. (Comay, 1990: 24)

Interpretation of the eternal recurrence is hotly debated.[1] Nietzsche's con-ception of events "eternally recurring" is not an indifference to transience but the collating of the past, present and future into something the person can both comprehend (measure) *and* affirm. The eternal recurrence is a technique for finding the positive value of *ressentiment* and retaining the human ability to compose regular and calculable conditions, within which one can make promises.

Deleuze argues that it is not the return of the *identical,* but return of the same, that integrates a distribution of differences, without the reactive element of *ressentiment.* The transvaluation of revenge is the realization that each event, each moment, each chance, is *necessary* It is *amor fati,* the excruciating task of loving your fate. The affirmation of affirmation is not a simple denial of negation; it includes negation as a vital part of operation. Negation, or as Nietzsche terms it, nihilism, must be metamorphosed into something altogether different.

The active/reactive dichotomy is a necessary component of the *Übermenschlich* metamorphosis. In *Thus Spake Zarathustra* the camel simply bears the burden of life, passively shouldering the burden of existing values without evaluating their worth. This is the regular, calculable aspect of the will. Understanding the contemporary morality of mores is necessary before one can reject them. The "No" of the lion clears away the detritus which morality exhibits. This is nihilism in its most obvious and active form. The spirit of *ressentiment* rejects all morals that have emerged hitherto. Thus, the negative establishes a *tabula rasa,* which allows the child to express a "sacred yes" and create new values, and most importantly, with the ability of assessing the value of such values. Thus, affirming life takes over from the earlier passive and then active nihilism. As Deleuze conceives of it, affirmation overarches both active and reactive forces. This should be understood not as a synthesis but as a transmutation, "not a change of values, but a change in the element from which the value of values derives. Appreciation instead of depreciation, affirmation as will to power, will as affirmative will" (Deleuze, 1983; orig. 1962: 171).

Deleuze focused on the Nietzschean concept of force and extricated Nietzsche's rather vague indicators on how to escape the negative oppositional relationship of the master and slave to the possibility of an affirmative *Übermenschlich* overcoming of modern nihilism.

FOUCAULT AND GENEALOGY AS A METHOD

In Nietzsche's *On the Genealogy of Morals* psychology, philosophy and philology are blurred into one tale, whereas Foucault's (1977b) "Nietzsche, Genealogy, History" article extricates the method of genealogy. Foucault concentrates on the flow, disruptions and dynamism of power, as is played out on the surfaces, folds and interstices of human life. He avoids the active/ reactive dichotomy and focuses on the nature of truth, interpretation, historical context and the Will to Knowledge.

Foucault has taken some of Nietzsche's profound ideas on genealogy and derived a genealogical methodology. As an approach to education, genealogy offers a fresh and constructive alternative to the existing paradigm. Genealogy could motivate education to generate an environment capable of opening up new possibilities for knowledge and interpretation. The "distribution of difference" does not pretend to deny power relations, but offers a constructive means of evaluating ideas in terms of affirmative relationships between people and the world.

Foucault owes his transformation of genealogy to the French influence of Jean Cavaillès, Gaston Bachelard, Georges Canguilhem and Louis Althusser, who have themselves followed up Nietzsche's conception, away from static universalism toward the historical development of practices which produce truth. Genealogy retains its Nietzschean focus on language and style. But Canguilhem sharpened the materialist relationship of genealogy to life and the biological sciences with an emphasis on chance and adaptation. Bataille's early work on Nietzsche along the theme of transgression and exceeding moral limits undoubtedly influenced Foucault profoundly. Deleuze's books on Nietzsche, *Nietzsche and Philosophy* and *Difference and Repetition*, also influenced Foucault's approach. Foucault emphasizes the Nietzschean tendency to disrupt logic and challenge the totalizing word with its unequivocal meaning. These aspects are complemented by the concept of interruptions, refusals, reversals of any historical continuity or necessarily linear development.

While providing a good grounding of Foucault's theory of genealogy, the influence of Nietzsche on Foucault entirely eludes Prado, who completely misinterprets Nietzsche as limiting himself to theories of domination: "unlike Nietzsche, Foucault does not think of domination only in terms of the control of one class or individual over another" (Prado, 1995: 37). On the contrary, Nietzsche's task is to go beyond good and evil. Indeed, it is the complexity of Nietzsche's theory of *ressentiment* that prodigiously multiplies the discourses, events and artefacts we call "culture" that takes Foucault beyond the Marxist dialectic that dominated intellectual life in postwar France. Nietzsche renders the relationships of power as productive, receptive and reactive rather than a simple emphasis on coercion or oppression, as does Foucault (e.g., GM; Foucault, 1991). Clare O'Farrell (1997) focuses on Foucault's theory as an analysis of the "other" and the "limit" as the lynchpin of all his theory.

Andrew Thacker (1997: 194) draws out the distance between Foucault and structuralism, by bringing into focus Foucault's emphasis on "relations of power, not relations of meaning." Most commentators on Foucault emphasize the Marxist roots of the French intellectual milieu, placing Nietzsche as the "second component of the Foucaultian context" (Schrift, 1995: 35). In his book on Foucault, Mark Poster (1984) describes the Western Marxist milieu that permeated the postwar French intellectual scene, and argues that Foucault distinguished himself from the dominant traditions of Marxism with a Nietzschean rejection of any possibility of an idealized future. Poster is interested in how Foucault's theory of the overlapping of discourse/practice denies a utopian escape from the power dynamics of the human condition. Although Foucault differs from Western Marxism in its varying forms, he retains the Marxist interest in critically exploring the dominant forms of social organization from a historically materialist position. Poster draws this distinction:

> If by Marxism one means not the specific theory of the mode of production or the critique of political economy, and not even the supposed dialectical method, but instead a critical view of domination which as historical materialism takes all social practices as transitory and all intellectual formations indissociably connected with power and social relations—then Foucault's position opens up critical theory more. (Poster, 1984: 39)

Schrift (1995) notes that Foucault himself attributes the focus of his work to Nietzsche's specification of power relations rather than Marx's concept of the relationships of production. Both Schrift and Marshall explore the significance and confirming role that the 1968 revolution in France had on Foucault's theory. Marshall (1996a) notes that Foucault had long since left the Communist Party by 1968. Despite the strength of the Marxist theories of revolution, the Communists' lack of leadership and involvement in the 1968 revolt reinforced the disillusionment of many intellectuals with Marxism. Coupled to these local objections, disturbing reports of Stalinist atrocities were increasingly difficult to ignore. These political problems affirmed the need for alternative theories of power and the state. Foucault recognized that revolutions might "recodify" power but tend to replace one set of oppressors with another, leaving the existing power relationships intact.

URSPRUNG

In "Nietzsche Genealogy, History," Foucault (1977b) discusses Nietzsche's use of the terms *Ursprung, Herkunft* and *Entstehung*. The meanings are not easily translatable, but literally, *Ursprung* is dividable into *Ur*, or ultimate, and *Sprung* is leap or jump. *Ursprung* implies a "ground" which is sprung away from. Whether the "ground" is an essence of Being, or an Idea, or a Form depends on the emphasis and technical terms of the particular philosopher referred to. They all adhere to the tradition of an enduring Truth, which supersedes time and space. As a whole, *Ursprung* translates to the ultimate original source, a cornerstone of metaphysics, such as Kant's Ideal "Thing-In-Itself." In distinction, *Herkunft* is less definitively about essential origins of Truth. *Herkunft* is a positioning of place and time, a genealogical descent in relation to diverse other constitutive factors. *Entstehung* is translated as "emergence," not necessarily from one origin, but a complex of things that emerge and tie together at a particular time and place. The terms were often used synonymously in Nietzsche's early work, but Foucault notes that by 1886, in *On the Genealogy of Morals*, and in his later writing, Nietzsche makes quite a strong distinction between the terms.

By disparaging a pure origin, Nietzsche abandons metaphysics. The *Ursprung* makes possible a field of knowledge designed to recover its own Truth. The "ground" legitimates "fixed truths," which are a type of "brain sickness" according to Nietzsche. He attributed them to an eschatological and nihilistic way of conceiving the world. A genealogical method insists that there never can be an accurate recognition of an ultimate original source, or its grounding essence, due to the "excesses of its own speech." Truth outside of time and space can only ever be partially recovered, "the site of a fleeting articulation that discourse has obscured and finally lost" (Foucault, 1977b: 143). The "adolescence" of such a search gives way to its impossibility. It is an error, naturalized by long usage, into an "unalterable form." Foucault draws on the image of Zarathustra awakening to illusion at noon, "in the time of the shortest shadow," rejecting "the history of the error we call truth" (Foucault, 1977b: 144). As he outlined in *On the Genealogy of Morals*, when he was 13, Nietzsche wished to discern the origin of evil. He attributed it to the creator of all things—God. However, his mature thinking approaches the question of the constitution of "evil" quite differently. Foucault writes: "He now finds this question amusing and properly characterises it as a search for *Ursprung*" (Foucault, 1977b: 141). In contrast to the search for essential laws at the base of things, Foucault explains,

if the genealogist refuses to extend his faith in metaphysics, if he listens to history, he finds that there is "something altogether different" behind things: not a timeless and essential secret, but the secret that they have no essence or that their essence was fabricated in a piecemeal fashion from alien forms. (Foucault, 1977b: 142)

Having rejected the notion of an essential ground, from which truths originate, Foucault utilized Nietzsche's method of etymology to draw distinctions between origin, atavism and emergence. Genealogy is an alternative method of constructing truth(s) and by extension, morals.

GENEALOGY

Herkunft, which translates to origin, atavism, stock, descent or the affiliation to a group by tradition, social class or blood, intimates race and type. *Herkunft* is genealogy, familiar to those in Aotearoa/New Zealand as *whakapapa*, the knowledge and recital of ancestors. *Whakapapa* positions the subject in terms of status, marriageability, tribal affiliations, politics, access to specialized knowledge and rights to public speaking. *Whakapapa* overtly positions a person's status and rights.

The modern objection to genealogy as method is bound up with democratic ideals of equality. The critique notes that in Maori history, those without *whakapapa* were almost invisible. Slaves had no facial tattoo that inscribed and displayed their position in society. Similarly, the working classes in England did not know the names of their foreparents by more than two or three generations. Genealogy belonged to the nobility. On the other hand, Nietzsche disparages democracy because by regarding everybody as equal, it refuses the legitimacy of genealogical status. Modernity regards the feudal elements as immoral. Foucault makes Nietzsche more palatable to modern readers. Genealogy is both a critique of modernity (its blind presumption that everyone is the same) and difficult to digest because of its feudal despotic roots. Foucault does not detail the feudal or eugenic implications of such lineages of blood, however. This is part of the objectionable Nietzsche, taken up by the Nazis, which Foucault attempts to clean up, without exactly silencing.[2] Distance from racism is attainable by sophisticated language and by framing with dissonance, interruptions, alternatives: "He must be able to recognize the events of history, its jolts, its surprises, its unsteady victories and unpalatable defeats—the basis of all beginnings, atavisms, and heredities" (Foucault, 1977b: 144–145).

The internal contradiction between the ideal of equality and the recognition of a distribution of irreducible difference is transformed when genealogy is taken out of the realm of the individual and used in the context of existing state apparatus (as Gramsci would term it). Genealogy offers education an ethics in which the norm is insufficient because the norm simply masks the existing domination of a particular group in society. Because no truth is fixed, education is a contestable site, and diverse forms of knowledge which are marginalized at present have as much validity to enter the curricula as the present liberal one. This pervasive pluralism, or as Nietzsche calls it, *perspectivism*, offers an equitable politics and a dynamic motor for change. This is a distribution of difference in the mode of Deleuze rather than an oppositional model that sublimates the other in an effort to produce universality. The aim of genealogy is an ethical self-constitution, which is capable of differentiating between things and ideas without being obliged to alienate them.

Robert Solomon (1996) argues that Nietzsche's method is the *ad hominem* argument writ large. Counter to the traditional philosophical prejudice against personalizing a thesis, Solomon cogently argues that logic relies on the *ad hominem*, despite itself. The *ad hominem* argument contextualizes theory. From the Ten Commandments to Kant's categorical imperative, Nietzsche's famous "perspectivism" makes universal moral claims redundant. Each truth claim is historically and socially situated, each theorist psychologically interrogated, in order to associate his logic with his value position—his "will to power." As Solomon describes it, "perspective is *occupied*" (1993: 196). In complementary fashion, Foucault approaches Nietzsche from the dynamics of historical contextualization. The body is "imprinted by history." In Foucault's terms:

[D]escent attaches itself to the body. It inscribes itself in the nervous system, in temperament, in the digestive apparatus; it appears in faulty respiration, in improper diets, in the debilitated and prostrate body of those whose ancestors committed errors. (Foucault, 1977b: 151)

The genealogical critique of Enlightenment epistemology operates in three ways: first it refutes the ahistorical essentialist self (that I, Ruth, would be fundamentally the same person, no matter where or when I was born, and no matter what events I passed through during my lifetime.) Second, genealogy refutes the notion that objective knowledge is possible. Third, it makes apparent the contradiction inherent in the concept of equal and democratic genealogies (in the familial or atavistic sense) which masks existing relations of power.

ENTSTEHUNG

Nietzsche's refusal of an essential origin is related to his statement "God is dead." Rather than look to an eschatological or metaphysical source for moral values, Nietzsche sets our focus on worldly existence. *Herkunft* and *Entstehung*, descending and emerging, are evolutionary principles of life. Chance and necessity are composites of this theme. "Life" replaces "God" in Nietzsche's criteria for evaluating morals.

Entstehung, or emergence, draws attention to the adaptable, changing utility that occurs during history. This is not a Darwinian teleological process in which the utility value today explains the evolution of a particular characteristic. Nietzsche's classic sentence is "The eye was not always intended for contemplation" (Foucault, 1977b: 148). Today the concept of perception implies deep understanding; the Will to Knowledge. Today's utility however, does not explain the evolutionary emergence of the eye. The eye was once for hunting, gathering, escaping. Foucault explains:

These developments may appear as a culmination, but they are merely the current episodes in a series of subjugations . . . Genealogy, seeks to reestablish the various systems of subjection: not the anticipatory power of meaning, but the hazardous play of dominations. (Foucault, 1977b: 148)

Today's circumstances are not the culmination of the wisdom of generations. Domination is integral to every interaction; interpersonal, intergroup, intersocietal. *Entstehung* is as much about the sudden arrival of an "event," with no logical connection to preceding ways of being, as it is about continuance or convergence.[3] It disrupts the rational faith in causality. Historical change is not an inevitable development or a principle of improving adaptation. *Entstehung* incorporates the chance emergence of phenomena—many of which disappear again, without making a significant impression. Some events, however, introduce a lasting shift in the arrangement of things. The emergence of new forces does not simply enhance existing relations. These forces shift the very ground beneath those relations.

It could be argued that genealogy is the tracking of the essential being (of a family, of an idea). Thus aspects "show" themselves over time, and using genealogy as a method we can discern more facets of the essential Idea. However, Nietzsche is far more radical in his conceptualization of evolution. In the second essay of *On the Genealogy of Morals*, Nietzsche explodes the myth of utility and teleological adaptation. Once it is realized that the utility value—the aspect "showing" today—can be disassociated from its utility in the past, this disengages a continuum that revolves around an essential kernel to the object under question. A millstone today is a rough round rock with a hole in it. Once it was the technological masterpiece of peasant civilization, now it is a burden.

In his own writing, Gregory Smith (1996) eloquently puts genealogy to use by tracing the "diversions" that modern theory has taken. He emphasizes that of the theoretical shifts that have evolved none was inevitable, nor are they reversible. In his footnoted explanation of Nietzsche's process of genealogy, he describes quite a different practice from his own. He mistakenly regards Nietzsche's theory as deriving from an Aristotelian search for equilibrium:

For Aristotle, virtue is based on habit which is in turn rooted in the habit background of a distinctive ethos. Hence instead of offering a metaphysics of morals, Aristotle observes that virtue is a mean and offers such moral rules of thumb as advising that individuals aim in the direction of the vice opposite their natural inclinations, thereby maximising the likelihood of hitting the mean. Nietzsche's discussion of morality can be viewed in the same light. (Smith, 1996: 147)

Equilibrium is a conservative assumption that the norm has some basis in a universal "truth" rather than being an incidental (if at the time, important) contingency. Aristotle's discourse of a "balance" to moral traits reinforces the normative dynamics of morals, limiting excess and corresponding disorder. The genealogical concept of *Entstehung* relies on the excessive and unpredictable to avert teleological closure. Foucault puts distance between genealogy and teleological equilibrium:

Humanity does not gradually progress from combat to combat until it arrives at universal reciprocity, where the rule of law finally replaces warfare; humanity installs each of its violences in a system of rules and thus proceeds from domination to domination. (Foucault, 1977b: 151)

The unending, oscillating flow of power is the source of life, the constitution of history. There is no humanist "balance" which we are aiming toward. There can be no "end of history."

Entstehung, or emergence, is the unknowable interplay of force and environmental adaptation. In the Nietzschean-Foucaultian model, power is neither simply repressive nor simply productive. Foucault writes that history is not a long chain of events, objectively or even subjectively described, but that it serves a contemporary purpose. History itself is constituted by the power plays of emergence:

Only by being seized, dominated, and turned against its birth. And it is this movement which properly describes the specific nature of the *Enstehung*: it is not the unavoidable conclusion of a long preparation, but a scene where forces are risked in the chance of confrontations, where they emerge triumphant, where they can also be confiscated. (Foucault, 1977b: 159)

Acknowledging the inevitability of power in the dynamics of historical events incorporates the role of scholarship within the boundaries of strife and existence rather than any privileged external position that views material "objectively." Nietzsche, Foucault and Solomon argue for a type of contextualized interpretation that has given away a pseudo-objective stance and recognizes the implications of the inevitable subjectivity of the epistemological. That is, the atavism of the author produces a perspective, probably not "original" in itself; a perspective shaped by class, ethnicity, time period, place, among countless other transient things, breakfast, esteem, influences.

Following this line of thought, the nature of truth is intricately bound to power relations rather than "essences." Nietzsche describes the "Will to Knowledge" as the creation of new knowledges. Often knowledge is stimulated by reacting against the domination of previously existing material power relations. The self-idealization, the self-stylization of the "active" colonizing class or ethnicity or gender (etc.), is reinterpreted by the "reactive," *ressentiment* of the underprivileged peoples whose creativity is thwarted and therefore directs itself against those who control and dominate society. Unequal power relations generate the will to create new knowledge. This is the play of dominations. In *On the Genealogy of Morals*, Nietzsche writes,

[W]hatever exists, having somehow come into being, is again and again reinterpreted to new ends, taken over, transformed, and redirected by some power superior to it; all events in the organic world are a subduing, *a becoming master*, and all subduing and becoming master involves a fresh interpretation, an adaptation through which any previous "meaning" and "purpose" are necessarily obscured or even obliterated. (77)

Clearly, the genealogical relationship to scholarship exposes one's own epistemological method, while interrogating aspects of history that are relevant in some (possibly obscure) way to the present, creating modes of existing that enhance potential, rather than limiting it to the norms of the present. Nietzsche's standard of evaluation is future oriented. The emergence of disruptions, breaks, parody and humor alleviates the "stagnant odor" of immediate consumption, in favor of the growth and metamorphosis of society toward a life-affirming future. It is this desire for change that Nietzsche terms the Will to Knowledge.

WILL TO KNOWLEDGE

Will to Knowledge is rendered "techniques of interpretation" by Foucault. He explores the concept in detail in his essay "Nietzsche, Freud, Marx" (1990). The Will to Knowledge has a deconstructive relationship with the existing modes of domination. Thus new knowledge is produced, showing up the ways individuals as subjects are interpellated into cultural practices, discourses and institutional structures, which in turn support particular groups and subordinate others. Because the cycles of domination can never be arrested, neither can the Will to Knowledge. The Will to Knowledge is itself a form of destruction because it stops at nothing, interpreting *ad infinitum*. Whereas Nothingness was harnessed by ascetism, the Will to Knowledge knows no limits. Interpretations may never have recourse to a "correct truth" as in the discourse of metaphysics, but that is not replaced with an undiscerning plurality of equally valid interpretations. The master/slave dichotomy was Nietzsche's initial attempt to make judgments concerning the "health" or "sickness" of values. The *value* of values becomes the discerning criteria. Thus interpretation will never be static, but neither will it allow just any meaning legitimacy.

Techniques of interpretation divine the limits of truth, truth in itself. Foucault uses Nietzsche in particular to interrogate the notion of universal absolute Truth. This thesis refutes the last several thousand years of metaphysics. In this ancient story Truth is like God; external, overarching humanity, superseding time and space. Techniques of interpretation displace the idea (still prevalent in liberal democracy) that there is a hidden truth which the philosopher, the psychologist or the sociologist can uncover. That is, if we plumb the depths of the soul, we will discover the hidden and essential self. The ambiguity of language has to be clarified in this schema, to divine a direct correlation with the original meaning. What is sought is a law of resemblance between the sign and the signified, the word and the object. If we strip away social conventions, it is thought, we will expose the state of nature from which we originally contracted to set up civil society. The presumption is, that with stripping away social convention, it is possible to derive an essential origin; we can arrive at a commencement, a ground, an originating foundation of Truth.

Foucault queries the application of this authority of Truth as it applied to Nietzsche, Freud and Marx. He interrogates this interpretation of "consciousness," "false consciousness" and the "unconscious" as an Aristotelian search for essential underlying "laws" or Truths. Instead of plumbing the soul for an internalized essential self, Foucault recalls Nietzsche's description in the second chapter of *On the Genealogy of Morals* of the 'depths' of psychology as surface layers that have folded and creased into an interiority. The mundane experience of daily living has sunk into the forgotten, or has crystallized into memory, and these multifarious incidents constitute our response patterns today. The psychologist excavates, and "the depth is now restored as an absolutely superficial secret." Thus the interpreter is the "truth" teller.

Any interpretation is expounded through language, and here Foucault points to an associated epistemological shift. Words as signs were thought to designate direct meaning. According to the technique of interpretation (and influenced by the structural linguistics of de Saussure) the sign and the signified become reinstated as a hermeneutic device rather than a vector of absolute Truth. Words are no longer presumed to have a direct relationship with an exact concept or thing. There is an unclosable gap between the desired framework and the ability to express it. The sharpness of direct resemblance is thickened as each sign is excavated layer upon layer. Each sign or word is interpellated without beginning or end with other meanings and other signs, no longer solitary or fixed, but reverberating, pulsing, fusing in a complex cohabitation of meaning:

In this sense, it can be said that *Allegoria, Hypnoia*, are *at the foundation of language and before it*, not what are slid under the words afterwards in order to displace them and make them vibrate, but what give birth to words, what cause them to whine with a brilliance that is never fixed. (Foucault, 1990: 83)

The sign's "new function of covering up, recovering, the interpretation" displaces its disciplined correlation with absolute Truth to redundancy. Truth now derives from the perspective of the interpreter. The method of narration, or exploration, is going to define the degree of truth, the terms in which it can be true. No longer can truth claim divine authority, or indeed any absolute authority, for any interpretation can be reinterpreted. Nietzsche notes that a result of active ruling is the ability to define meaning. New knowledge is created by displaying the Will to Power of the godfathers, the existing assigners of systems of interpretation.

The rebuke of unquestionable authority is in itself an indication of our new age's resentful undermining of authority figures. This is one of Nietzsche's themes—that democracy is the disintegration of civilization as we know it. Democratic equality challenges the rights of a noble class to fix meaning, and with it societal structure. The parody of a straightforward resemblance, or attachment, between signifier and signified exposes instead the genealogy of the meaning of the word as a will to power. Each signification is now interrogated—Whose purpose does it serve? How? When? Where? Oscillating, or even countermanding the democratic impulse to reject authorization for its own sake is the Nietzsche/Foucaultian reading of power as producing meaning and culture. Power is not, Foucault insists, always limited to "domination" or "repression." This assessment of power has extensive implications for educational organization, curriculum, assessment, and pedagogy.

Foucault is affected by Nietzsche's warning that the Will to Knowledge is the most perilous of paths. At the center of the interpretation of interpretation (*ad infinitum*) is, Nietzsche contends, chaos and potential madness. As the interpreter passes through the boundaries of interrelational knowledge, she or he is exposed to a vortex of possibility. The danger of probing the inevitable gaps and spaces, the unlimited oscillation of the sign, is to lose one's grip on stasis. Stasis is defined as the underlying stable, even stagnant commonality of the community or system. However, stasis is not a fixed closed cosmology in the manner of Ptolemy but a slow-moving aspect of stability within infinity. The bonds of community can be exposed by the Will to Knowledge as the arbitrary interests of a reproducing structure of hierarchies, such as class. But exposure and disbelief leave a nothingness which, through possibly the last ultimate accurateness, is also the place of disillusioned paralysis. As we lose our universal, absolutist idealism, the danger of narcissism, or worse, nihilism, is apparent.

The counterpoint to the "madness" implicit in the Will to Knowledge is both stasis and the existence of the community of Others. Foucault traces the shift from absolute truth to an interpretation of the already-interpreted. Freud, for instance, through the illumination of the fantasies of his analysands invented the "super-ego." The problematic endlessness of analysis turns into "transference." In other words, the theory is actually co-relational. Foucault, along with Nietzsche, Freud and Marx, individualizes interpretation. They take complete responsibility for knowledge. Freud forgot that he forged his theories on the "confessions" of women. Nietzsche directs us to a philology that is never fixed, an unpositable play with words. At most, signs have a tendency to certain conceptual frameworks. Word and meaning shift according to juxtaposition and the speaker's interpretation of each other's intentions: the intonation, the body language and so forth. But philology should not be understood as the individual expert delving, developing language in isolation. Language preexists us. It is a product of society. The genealogy of a word may uncover historical shifts in power, interpretation, reversals, slides, but these interlocutions are not arbitrary. They are a result of politics, war, thrusts and reversals of power: the life of the community.[4]

Foucault's only direct work on Nietzsche revolved around method: genealogical method, and techniques of interpretation. Both of these concerns displace the humanist assumption that man is at the center of the universe, and Truth (in man's image) is "out there." Nietzsche signaled an epistemological shift that maintained Foucault's interest throughout his career. The implications of this paradigm shift are beginning to show themselves in various fields, including education.

EDUCATION

The reconceptualization of truth, subjectivity, language, creativity and the introduction of the theories of the Will to Power and Knowledge will have far-reaching (and unending) effects on education. Genealogy as a method will enable the revaluing of education, in respect to the relationship of educational institutions with the state, and of internal institutional practice. Opening up and reinvestigating the subject as genealogically produced, rather than essentially fixed, has vast implications for schooling. It challenges the notion of teacher as bearer of a fixed commodity, variously called knowledge or skills. Genealogical subjectivity also challenges the definition of students as blank slates, who absorb and regurgitate the knowledge thrown at them. In the absence of Absolute Truth, the nature of knowledge and its relationship to schooling is open to question. This question is fundamentally a genealogical one: Whose knowledge is being valued, institutionalized and documented as curriculum? Whose authority is assumed to be valid? How and why?

The shift toward a skill-based education started in New Zealand with the introduction of *Tomorrow's Schools* in 1988. This process is justified by the neo-liberal free market as the best means of "equitable exchange" known to humankind. In reaction to the growth of the welfare state, and its increasing emphasis on universal inclusion and equity, neo-liberals swung toward an efficiency model of the school. They wished to maximize "output" while minimizing "input" from the state. This production-line metaphor permeated the organization, structure, curriculum and, to some extent, pedagogy of education in New Zealand. From this discourse arise the marketization of schools and the translating of a broad "knowledge"-based curriculum to a skill-based one, which enhances the individual's opportunities in the marketplace. The curriculum structure of "Unit Standards" is an example of the concept of "value-added" students—a notion that students' learning can be translated into "measurable outputs" which in turn demonstrate school "efficiency." The older liberal concept of self-development in order to make rational democratic decisions has been sidelined. Government mandate itself is no longer important to neo-liberals, as has been demonstrated on numerous occasions since the Labour government swallowed this ideology in 1984 and effectively reneged on the party's manifesto. Neo-liberalism has escaped the Keynesian settlement as the terms for legitimation of the state by devolving responsibility to local bodies, such as the school Board of Trustees. At the same time, the government has retained policy, funding and regulation as a means of control.[5]

The Will to Knowledge does not rely on either universal citizenship or skills in the free market as a justification for education. This is because neither the state nor capitalism is understood as a monolithic institution or global Absolute to which education is subordinate. Education is doubly important when the self is not understood as an essential underlying truth, and must be developed and overcome through the enhancement of a Will to Knowledge. At a time of massive upheaval which is imposing increasingly disciplinary modes of discourse and institutional practices, education stands in a crucial relationship to forming future modes of meaning and values. Education multiplies interpretations of society and the self. In a particular fashion, it is the means to freedom.

Within the Will to Knowledge model, education emphasizes the "who, how, where and when"—contextual questions about knowledge and validity. It puts students in a better position to understand the structure of their society, the way it affects their own lives as individuals and those of any group whose interests they may be affiliated with. Thus, students are able to analyze the given situation in terms of the dominant group's Will to Power and how this may advance or contradict their own position. Furthermore, if their analysis is guided by active principles of affirming life, they can decide whether the status quo effectively responds to their needs of the moment or the future. This has and will entail serious self-reflection among educationalists. It foregrounds the affect of whose knowledge is valued— how it structures organization, pedagogy, the overt and hidden curriculum, and assessment.

The vocational aspect of education reduces every student to an equal sameness, along rational lines, with an added assumption that individuals will "maximize" their "utility." The neo-liberal concept that "choice" is at the root of subjectivity can be disrupted by an interpretation of humans as genealogically produced, social animals. A system of rational choice between *a* and *b* disregards the unconscious constraints of years of socially produced values, the multiple and conflicting layers of meaning attributed to each choice, the short versus long-term economic constraints and the needs of others within the individual's family and social group, let alone the socially constructed system which makes only these two items "available" when infinite options could be presented.[6] Techniques of interpretation and the acknowledgment of the power/knowledge nexus as simultaneously the product and the deconstruction of the dominance of particular groups in society could contribute to the task and position of education as subverting the blind reproduction of norms.

A theorist's context and interests indicate their Will to Power. This markedly affects their stance, regardless of the logical coherency of their argument. The commodification of knowledge curtails valid research and pedagogy to the creditor/debtor economy of exchange. It limits meaning to a reactive nihilism and individuals to a pseudo-objective unit operating in abstract self-interest in the marketplace. The Will to Power operating here is an eschatological faith in the *purpose* of consumerism, as the stimulus of individuals to adhere to a morality of meritocracy and hard work. Its nihilism is "forgotten," despite the accumulation of evidence that an ethos of consumerism creates huge environmental devastation.

Thus, perhaps idealistically, education could be demoted from its universal supervisory role. It is not directly responsible for producing individuals capable of citizenship or vocations. Instead, the Nietzschean-Foucaultian model of education emphasizes "the critic and conscience of society" role. Education could be available to anyone interested in learning and developing their Will to Knowledge. This is a political, subjective and genealogically positioned standpoint, constrained by space and time. It has no recourse to objective idealization of Absolute Truth or to masking the Will to Power of the dominant group in society.

NOTES

1. About the time he wrote *The Gay Science*, during Nietzsche's "scientific" period, he wrote "cosmological proofs" in his notebooks about the eternal recurrence. His subsequent abandonment of science as able to directly apprehend the nature of the world left the eternal recurrence in limbo. Some Nietzsche scholars regard it as central to his metaphysics, most notably Heidegger. For a fuller discussion of Nietzsche's problematic attempts to find "cosmological proofs," see Magnus (1970) and Danto (1980). Regardless of its status for Nietzsche, the eternal recurrence is an important metaphor which he invoked throughout his corpus.

2. Nietzsche sometimes collapsed into atavistic justifications for cultures, but more frequently he exposed the offensive nature of eugenic breeding. See especially *Twilight of the Idols*.

3. See also Foucault, "The Father's 'No' " in *Language, Counter-Memory, Practice*, ed. D. Bouchard (Oxford: Blackwell, 1977), pp. 68–85.

4. See Howie and Peters (1996) for a thoughtful discussion of the entangled intersubjective field of language and social constructions, and its influence on personal psychology.

5. See Dale (1989), Devine (1998), Larner (1998) and Marshall (1997).

6. See Marshall (1996b, 1996c).

Chapter 4

Ethics and Difference: A Critique of R. S. Peters' *Ethics and Education*

Peter Fitzsimons

R. S. PETERS' *ETHICS AND EDUCATION*

For several decades Richard Peters has been the leading figure in the British school of educational philosophy. His text *Ethics and Education* (1966) offers a coherent, well-argued position within the liberal tradition of education and has become essential reading for philosophers of education. In Peters' own words, the book is intended

> to serve as an introductory textbook in the philosophy of education in the field of ethics and social philosophy; secondly it presents a distinctive point of view both about education and about ethical theory. It is hoped, therefore, that it will be of interest both to teachers and to students of philosophy. (Peters, 1966: 7)

This chapter examines Peters' position and critiques his philosophy by incorporating some themes originally articulated by Nietzsche. These themes are more pertinent than ever, given the challenges that traditional institutions are facing from emerging discourses in poststructuralist thought, from transdisciplinary critiques of educational policy and practice, from the challenges of technology in the modern world, and from the recognition of difference as a feature of ethics. It is beyond the scope of this chapter to investigate all of these challenges, but the idea of "difference" will be investigated as a basis for an ethical position, for Peters' ideas are not sufficient to cope with the new demands being made on ethics in education. The aspects of Peters' theory to be examined in terms of their ethics are the metaphysical notion of truth, the universal assumptions behind social justice, the application of democratic principles to political practice and the commitment to reason as the ultimate value.

Although he appeals to "fundamental principles of morality" along with more conservative liberals like Kenneth Strike (1982), Peters also respects "a tradition of reasonableness and tolerance" in advocating a *democratic* approach to education and to ethics. However, democracy is fraught with conceptual and procedural difficulties, and it will be argued that even a democratic approach to liberalism requires a particular identity construction that undermines Peters' own ethical foundations.

Drawing on the work of Stuart Hall, Marshall (1996d) identifies historic tensions between progressive and conservative forces in the development of liberalism—tensions that are played out in differing approaches to individualism and rationality. A conservative strand, emanating from the theories of Locke and Hayek, espouses tradition, voluntary association and freedom from constraint; and opposes the idea of liberating humankind through a system of rational design. A second strand, in its focus on progress, follows the ideas of Rousseau and Hobbes. It favors strong government for social reform, a restrictive notion of freedom as promoting opportunity through social control and an emphasis on welfare rather than property rights. This second strand, in its commitment to the social development of individuals, often develops into large-order rational systems, such as socialism or collectivism, and is sometimes referred to as *revisionist* liberalism.

Gray (1986) supports the distinction between the two strands of liberalism but argues that rather than being separate philosophies, they represent separate branches of a common lineage, with a shared commitment to four elements in the relation between the individual and society:

It is *individualist*, in that it asserts the moral primacy of the person against the claims of any social collectivity; *egalitarian*, inasmuch as it confers on all men the same moral status and denies the relevance to legal or political order of differences in moral worth among human beings; *universalist*, affirming the moral unity of the human species and according a secondary importance to specific historic associations and cultural forms; and *meliorist* in its affirmation of the corrigibility and improvability of all social institutions and political arrangements. It is this conception of man and society which gives liberalism a definite identity which transcends its vast internal variety and complexity. (Gray, 1986: x)

Peters sees the Anglo-American version of the democratic "way of life" as having emerged gradually out of the "practices of our remote ancestors," a way of life involving, "the determination to settle political matters by recourse to reasonable discussion rather than by recourse to force or arbitrary fiat" (Peters 1966: 299). He sees the proper role of government not as an unfettered authority in promoting the common good but as a necessary expedient, subject to moral appraisal and the need to safeguard the rights of individuals and minorities. It could be that his years of teaching in working-class institutions brought about his desire to alleviate the effects of unwarranted privilege and authority through rational argument and democratic process, but he does not make a collectivist appeal to the principles of socialism. Rather, his version of democracy and the ethical position he proposes expresses a firm commitment to individualism, although he is well aware that the individual is grounded in the community of the present and in the social traditions of the past.

Although advocating democracy in principle and practice, Peters' ethical prescription fits easily with Gray's four elements of liberalism—it is individualist, egalitarian, universalist and meliorist. Peters' articulation of liberal ethics promotes the Kantian notion of respect for persons as an important ideal. Nevertheless, his primary emphasis on the rational individual paves the way for the restrictive conception of the "autonomous chooser" (Peters and Marshall, 1996: 85) which is at the heart of the recent neo-liberal reforms in Western economies; and the consequent failure of historical society and community in terms of economic, social, democratic and cultural deficit in what Kelsey (1995) calls "The New Zealand Experiment."

Peters (1966: 45) stipulates three criteria for activities to be considered educational. They are:

1. that "education" implies the transmission of what is worth-while to those who become committed to it;
2. that "education" must involve knowledge and understanding and some kind of cognitive perspective, which are not inert;
3. that "education" at least rules out some procedures of transmission, on the grounds that they lack willingness and voluntariness on the part of the learner.

For Peters, education involves notions of "improvement," "betterment," and the passing on of what is judged "worthwhile." Although it is important to clarify meanings and specify usage of these terms, Peters acknowledges that their respective values have no empirical referent, and so for justification of worth, he turns to the sphere of moral philosophy or ethics, with its non-empirical concepts such as "ought," "right," "desirable," "worth-while," and "good" along with distinctive procedures for inquiry. Ethics is the realm that, for Peters, provides the rational basis for action and consequently the *moral* justification for educational decisions.

In arriving at an ethical position, Peters considers a number of essential elements, including the development of mind, the principle of equality, consideration of interests, freedom and respect for persons. Each of these factors is not enough on its own, and what he advocates is a relation between all these factors where each is tempered by all the others. So, for example, a presumption of freedom does not give an individual the right to act in a way that fails to respect others.

Central to Peters' position is the need to justify one's position, that is, to give reasons for holding that position. If there are no reasons, he argues, it is mere whim whether one action takes precedence over another, and completely arbitrary whether one person's wants are restricted in favor of another's. Peters does not want to privilege feelings as any criteria for ethics, since he believes that feelings derive from a cognitive core and that provided the reasoning is sound, the attitudes that follow will be sustainable. If feelings indicate dissonance, the solution is sought through an examination of the rational basis for those feelings. Significant in this aspect of Peters' theory is the elevation of the rational core above the aesthetic response to life.

From the base of reason, Peters derives other attitudes that he considers essential for an ethical life namely, an overall concern for truth, respect for persons and a feeling of fraternity with others. His philosophical position depends on a presumption of transcendental truth, as he argues:

Any reflective person who asks the question "Why do this rather than that?" . . . must already have a serious concern for truth built into his consciousness. For how can a serious practical question be asked unless a man also wants to acquaint himself as well as he can with the situation out of which the question arises and of the facts of various kinds which provide the framework for possible answers? (Peters, 1966: 164)

The maintenance of the social order is important for Peters as a means of protecting both the security and the liberty necessary for the pursuit of what is good and as a means of preventing abuse and manipulation. Feelings of fraternity and the belief that distinct points of view are important lead him to the principle of "respect for persons."

The principle of fairness or justice is, for Peters, a presupposition of any attempt to justify conduct or to ask seriously the question "What ought I to do?" Justice is represented by the idea that no one is presumed, in advance of particular cases being considered, to have a claim to better treatment than another. For Peters, social justice is best preserved by the establishment of general rules and a large measure of consensus at the level of procedural principles. Important presumptions here are the ideal of democratic consensus and the desirability of democratic institutions based on an "effective tradition of reasonableness and tolerance" (Peters, 1966: 303). He admits to the difficulty of pinning down an exact definition of democracy but suggests it requires some kind of procedure for consulting citizens about state action and policy. Although aware of its frustrations, failings and hypocrisies, he asserts that only a democratic form of life is consistent with the fundamental principles of morality (Peters, 1966: 306).

Peters' "fundamental principles" of morality are fairness, liberty and the consideration of interests, and he argues that their emotional underpinning in respect for persons and a feeling of fraternity for others as persons is accessible only to "rational men." The primacy of the giving of reasons is evident in his earlier work too. Benn and Peters (1959) explore the relationship between social principles and the democratic state, and conclude that, while the ideal of democracy involves such features as free choice, majority vote, impartiality, sensitivity to all interests and the need for expression of alternative opinion, it is the giving of reasons that elevates democracy as a moral system. Respect for persons stems, they argue, from their status as sources of claims and arguments that underlie political ideals like justice, liberty and equality.

Important educational implications of Peters' ideas stem from his notion of democratic government that requires people with relevant experience, an ability to apply abstract principles and a willingness to participate in public life. An ethical basis for education must then, in Peters' view, include such interpretations as *the democratization of education* by insisting that education should be freely available and fairly distributed; *school as a democratic institution* so that the practices of schooling embody the principles of democratic process; and education as *preparation for a democratic way of life* so that students learn the attitudes, values and practices required for participating in a democratic society.

Because the giving of reasons is offered as the basis for differentiating ethics from naturalism, superstition and religious belief, Peters' position constitutes an emphasis on the rational individual in education. In respect of this emphasis, Marshall (1996d) notes the similarities between the Anglo-American traditional strand of liberalism, and the promotion of a neo-liberal philosophy based on the unimpeded freedom of the individual. However, he argues that it would be a mistake to interpret Peters as a neo-liberal, since he emphasizes the Kantian principles of consideration for the interests of others and respect for persons. Peters' emphasis on democracy as a procedural principle thus softens his perspective inside liberal individualism.

Given Peters' incorporation of both traditional and democratic aspects of liberalism, a focus on his philosophy is also a focus on liberalism generally, not only in its basic assumptions but also in how it unfolds in practice. Liberalism requires some form of constraint on individual freedom if anarchy is to be avoided. Those constraints may be *external*, as in police enforcement of the law. They may also be *internal*, as in the Kantian notion of moral duty stemming from the rational nature of the autonomous self. It is worth noting that education policy in the Western world is increasingly underpinned by liberal and neo-liberal assumptions about the rational individual. The prime importance Peters attaches to the giving of reasons is a cornerstone of liberal education and the foundation for his claim that education is an ethical enterprise. However, it will be argued here that the reduction of democracy to the giving of reasons is not the sole foundation for a defensible education. Rather, the interplay of freedom and constraint in the realm of the social world calls for new and inclusive ethical formulations that may emanate from outside the sphere of liberalism.

The preceding pages constitute a necessarily brief summary of Peters' ethical position, formulated in terms of the liberal discourse. His main points have been delineated (without criticism at this stage) in such a way that the reader can assess whether the following critique is based on any misinterpretation of what Peters has to say. What follows now is a different interpretation of the territory described by Peters—a Nietzschean critique of the liberal morality underpinning Peters' philosophy and the practices that arise from it. The particular features that bear further examination are the presumption of objective truth, the universal morality underpinning social justice, the problem of democracy in practice and the essential commitment to reason as the basis of ethics.

Peters describes philosophy as an essentially cooperative enterprise. He suggests that

Advances are made when two or three are gathered together who speak more or less the same language and can meet frequently for the purpose of hitting each other politely on the head. (Peters, 1966: 8)

This chapter offers Peters a "polite smack," which is not so much a dialectical challenge to the internal rationality of his argument as a different description of what it is to be ethical. This move is one that Rorty (1989) would support. He proposes that "speaking more or less the same language" will result in "more or less the same ideas," with intellectual progress as merely the literalization of selected metaphors. What he advocates is a redescription of the territory, since the vocabulary of Enlightenment rationalism is an impediment to new ways of thinking. In line with Rorty's idea of a replacement vocabulary, it is now appropriate to introduce some Nietzschean perspective to the debate in order to prevent hardening of the categories and ossification of the discourse.

A NIETZSCHEAN PERSPECTIVE

As a basis for a critique of the liberal philosophy of education, this chapter draws upon some of Nietzsche's ideas, not as a straightforward explanation of Nietzsche's educational thinking, but as a selective application of three major themes recurrent in much of his writing. This is in keeping with Nietzsche's disdain for rigid discipleship, and his exhortation to go beyond his ideas:

One repays a teacher badly if one always remains nothing but a pupil . . . You revere me; but what if your reverence tumbles one day? Beware lest a statue slay you. (Z, I: 22)

Although it is a creative and unverifiable exercise to imagine how Nietzsche might respond to Peters' arguments, there are enough parallels in Nietzsche's work to ensure that the interpretation offered here is in line with Nietzsche's overall philosophical outlook on life. Although Nietzsche admired Kant as a profound thinker and acknowledged the huge shadow he cast over ensuing philosophers, Nietzsche rejected the world of transcendental ideals as the moral guide for life and saw possibilities for man far beyond the autonomous rational self constituted by Kantian reason. In many respects, the critique offered in this chapter constitutes the rejection of transcendental ideals and a suspicion about the ethics of an exclusive focus on the rational component of the self. Consequently, what follows provides a Nietzschean flavor to an exploration of what would count as ethics in education, without ossifying his ideas, deifying his image and being slain by the tumbling statue of Nietzsche.

At this stage it is sufficient to identify these themes in a general fashion, partly to acknowledge the scope of Nietzsche's thought, but also to see in relief how the interplay of these themes provides new possibilities for philosophers of education not only to engage in democratic *process*, but also to problematize the politics involved in the *definition* of democracy and in the application of democratic principles to liberal practices of education.

As the first of these themes, what has come to be known as *perspectivism* is often used to describe Nietzsche's refusal to accept political rhetoric as metaphysical truth. He refers to truth as "illusion" and "error," or more expansively as:

A movable host of metaphors, metonymies, and anthropomorphisms: in short, a sum of human relations which have been poetically and rhetorically intensified, transferred, and embellished, and which, after long usage, seem to a people to be fixed, canonical, and binding. Truths are illusions which we have forgotten are illusions; they are metaphors that have become worn out and have been drained of sensuous force. (OTaL: 1)

His skepticism is about all truth brought to light by man, as he argues that since man constructs truth through the use of reason, any truth found within the realm of reason is of limited value:

When someone hides something behind a bush and looks for it again in the same place and finds it there as well, there is not much to praise in such seeking and finding. Yet this is how matters stand regarding seeking and finding "truth" within the realm of reason. (OTaL: 1)

Nietzsche does not, however, want to do away with truth altogether. Actually, his early unpublished notebooks offer a radically different account. Written in 1873, his essay "On Truth and Lies in a Nonmoral Sense" offers as the criterion for truth the degree to which a particular description enhances human life and the degree to which it promotes culture by transforming social life. The earlier cultures that Nietzsche admires (e.g., the Greeks) were not constrained by reason, and Nietzsche draws on them to embrace the Dionysian spirit of unconscious desire and its Apollonian transformation through illusion. This accounts for the high cultural value Nietzsche places on art and myth, as opposed to the modern world's emphasis on reason, a world where art and myth are peripheral, and, in terms of rational truth, merely illusion and error. In Nietzsche's life-enhancing model, there is still room for the conventional categories of truth and falsity in that he acknowledges conventional designations as essential for some form of social life. However, there is no recourse to an ideal world to assess accuracy of representation. Rather, that recourse is to the natural world, the world of culture and the world of everyday social practices. In this way, truths (and the attempts to categorize them as "errors" and "illusions") function as life-preserving fictions. The move to a *nonmoral sense* means that there is no appeal to a transcendental world to ascertain truth value.

Turning his back on the idea of truth as a mirror of reality, Nietzsche draws on his background in philology to come up with an alternative epistemology—truth as "metaphor," a word derived from the Greek verb meaning "to carry over," "to carry across" or "to transfer." Since, in a Kantian sense, subject and object are independent of each other, truth cannot be a mirror of reality. Therefore, the idea of transference of meaning between subject and object is better explained by metaphor formation than by the exact replica implied in the mirroring model. Truth as metaphor then suggests the making of meaning from one's existential predicament rather than from an appeal to some metaphysical realm.

This distinction between the metaphysical idea of "truth in itself" and the political utility of various empirical claims to truth is often deconstructed and signaled by Nietzsche with the use of scare quotes to signify dubious claims to truth. A perspectival approach problematizes these claims, interpreting truth as metaphor, as perspective, tentative in its claims, and providing at best a "basis" for debate. Perspectivism then, directly challenges the truth behind a universal morality; it renders inaccessible a meta-perspective on truth; and it questions fundamentalist approaches (e.g., the giving of reasons) as the only basis for ethics.

In spite of Peters' appeal to universal values as the basis of his ethical position, the value of incorporating other points of view is not lost on him. In an appendix added after his *Ethics and Education* was written, he includes a section subtitled *Informal Education*, which acknowledges the importance of being able to see the world from the perspective of another. In contrast to his promotion of education as *initiation*, Peters sees the ability to listen to what another says (regardless of the use that can be made of it or him) as "one of the main hallmarks of an educated man" (1966: 88). He sees educational value in the process of "active participation" in "shared conversation," that is, the construction of "a common world to which all bring their distinctive contributions" (ibid):

By participating in such a shared experience much is learnt, though no one sets out to teach anyone anything . . . and one of the things that is learnt is to see the world from the perspective of another. (Peters, 1966: 88)

There is no suggestion here that Peters is offering a Nietzschean interpretation of life as an infinite diversity of interpretations with no "truth" (in-itself). He is more likely advocating different vantage points on a singular world. Yet, Peters still acknowledges *difference* as implicated in the realm of educational ethics. Although he categorizes these comments as referring to *informal* education, the practical distinction between "formal" and "informal" may have more to do with the politics of schooling than with an estimation of ethical value. Nietzsche's (FE) early lectures on education refer to the label "formal education" as "a crude kind of unphilosophical phraseology" which has more to do with how institutions justify their existence than with a meaningless dichotomy between "formal" and "informal" education. For the purposes of this chapter, the fact that Peters has categorized the acceptance of difference as belonging to an "informal" category of education does not detract from the educational value he ascribes to it. Its value as a shared practice is to some extent in keeping with Nietzsche's notion of truth as implicated in the social world.

The second of Nietzsche's ideas used in this chapter is his concern with life, health and sickness. Contrary to the earlier Newtonian metaphor of life as machine, Nietzsche's inquiry is often conducted at the biological level of humanity, with human life as an organism comparable to plant and animal life. From that perspective, rationality is an overlay and morality is a negation of life energy. For Nietzsche, Christian morality imbues life with evil, guilt and the need for teleological justification, while the rational ethics of Kant replaces obedience to God with the acceptance of duty based on transcendent reason. In contrast, Nietzsche values life as an aesthetic phenomenon above science, morality and truth, with no need for transcendental justification:

Behind your thoughts and feeling, my brother, there stands a mighty ruler, an unknown sage—whose name is self. In your body he dwells; he is your body. (Z, I: 4)

In tracing the development of Kant's ideas from the ideal worlds of Platonism and Christianity, he reveals *How the Real World at Last Became a Myth* (TI: 50). Kant's *Critique of Pure Reason* posits the "real" world as unknowable, and therefore, according to Nietzsche, unavailable as a source of moral duty. But, as he notes, a rejection of the "real" world (world-in-itself) also means a rejection of its derivative—the apparent world. Kantian epistemology then holds little truth value for Nietzsche in that it removes the source of ethical direction to a non-existent realm and prevents the sort of responsibility for one's own life that characterizes Nietzschean ethics. Thus, for Nietzsche, it is a moral system based on a fable.

Nietzsche's "brand" of ethics can be seen as an aesthetics of life, an idea drawn from his picture of the early Greeks, and elaborated a century later by Foucault (1986) as an ethic of care, particularly care of the self. In contrast to a system of rational morality, any ethic that incorporates care for others must, for Nietzsche, flow from an abundance of care for one's self and the joy of living: "When your heart flows broad and full like a river, a blessing and a danger to those living near: there is the origin of your virtue" (Z, I: 22).

Genealogy, another of Nietzsche's tools important in this critique, is linked to the previous two by its methodology. Genealogy problematizes accepted patterns of belief and refuses to take for granted the "tired metaphors" that have come to be known as truth. In that sense, it is perspectival. At the same time, genealogy grounds the critique of knowledge in the lived history of self-constituting human actors and thus affirms life as an aesthetic phenomenon.

Although an understanding of Nietzschean genealogy is of vital importance in coming to terms with the corrosive nature of his philosophy, the concept will not be explained in detail here, since the preceding chapter by Ruth Irwin provides a thorough analysis of its implications for educational thought. Suffice it to say here, however, that the idea of genealogy offers competing explanations for what we take as current reality, defines "truth" as a political contest and provides a vigorous challenge to fundamental rational morality as the only and inevitable basis for ethical theory.

What follows is a genealogical examination of the philosophy of education articulated by R. S. Peters, involving a challenge to universal truth and morality based on transcendental reason, and a claim that codes of morality that disregard "otherness" are not ethical. It thus establishes the rationale that underpins Connolly's (1991) exploration of identity and difference, not as essences of humanity but as "contingency," "contestability" and "intertextuality."

AN ETHICS OF DIFFERENCE

Connolly's (1991) notion of identity is not a descriptive label that can be applied to an already existing self-entity. Identity formation is a political process that rests on social definitions of difference, with the resulting identity not as an inherent truth about one's self, but a self-reinforcing "circle of significations." The contingent and relational nature of the process is emphasized by Connolly as he sees identity constantly exceeded, subverted, obstructed, and confounded both by actors who resist roles for which they have been cast and by audiences imperfectly colonized by the circle of significations within which the prevailing politics of identity moves. (Connolly, 1991: 210)

Social life then is ambiguous, and political "reality" can be challenged as "conventional categories of insistence." Connolly draws on Nietzschean genealogy to interrogate exclusions built into the idea of entrenched identities, to problematize and politicize the forms they have taken and to "salute" uncertainty and ambiguity.

There appears to be some convergence between Peters and Connolly in their formulation of ethical principles, insofar as both could be construed as advocating the idea of ethics as the arbiter of individual behavior within an acceptable social life. However, unlike Peters, whose idea of ethics ultimately hinges on the rational individual, Connolly's ethics is pragmatic and social, as he introduces the notion of "agonistic democracy," a political relationship in which each participant welcomes the "otherness" of difference.

As an ethical strategy, agonism maintains a spirit of competition and adversarial respect, so that instead of overriding different points of view, closing down opposition or enforcing community, contest is welcomed. Thus, rather than needing to eradicate fundamental ethical systems, agonism advances itself as another political contestant in the ongoing discursive game, while at the same time problematizing the nature of that game. In other words, agonism is not only the *form* of a proposed ethics, but it is also the *process* through which such a form might be developed. In some respects, this may be what Peters' has in mind in his advocacy of democratic principles. Yet the imperative of Peters' rational categories precludes the open and ongoing negotiation inherent in the agonistic structure.

Within the ethics laid out above, education can be interpreted as a political relationship in which an agonistic contest may develop and in which contending identities and "otherness" are nurtured. It recognizes the social process in the formation of "self," and in so doing, it aspires to the Nietzschean project of historical culture as a focus for education.

With an appreciation of Nietzsche's perspectivism, the problematic generated by genealogy, the democratic diversity of agonistic contest and an ethic based on an aesthetic care for life, Peters' rational system of ethics now begins to look bounded, and in places rather dubious in its own terms, especially in regard to his emphasis on the importance of respect for persons. Peters' philosophy of education, with its respect for "rational men," establishes rationality as a normative criterion, but in so doing, it excludes much of what is valuable in the social world. Creativity, eccentricity, warmth, empathy and humor are not seen as contributing to a person's worth. Establishing abnormal categories has a compounding effect: the formation of idealized norms not only generates abnormalities such as irrationality, irresponsibility, immorality, delinquency and perversity, but the abnormal are also excluded from contesting the nature of the categories.

Underpinning Peters' ethics is a depoliticized acceptance of the giving of reasons. In other words, reason governs not only those deemed to be living an ethical life, but also those committed to developing an educational philosophy. Rational argument is the only recognized mode of contest in the philosophy of liberal academia, since only the "normal" are admitted to the debating chamber, with the greatest authority accorded to those who are established within traditional disciplines. Political challenge, a querying of an exclusively rational order or a genealogical investigation of the prevailing moral authority, is characterized as postmodern or nihilistic from within the discourse, and the lines of demarcation between "the rational" and "the other" are reinforced. The formation and separation of otherness is divisive in its tactic, not only at the political level of group and social formation, but also within psychoanalytic formulations of the self, with some elements selectively repressed or excluded, on no other ultimate basis than their fit with a Platonic ideal of rational order. This does not fit well with the rhetoric of liberalism, which purports to embrace differing points of view and features a positive attitude toward tolerance and diversity.

While Peters cannot be said to be logically wrong in his argument for a rational approach to ethics (for how could he be wrong when "truth" was hidden behind the "bush" of reason?); it is argued here that "otherness" and "identity" are mutually interwoven, and the idealization of the rational self creates and excludes the "other." Considering the importance Peters attaches to "social justice" as the "rockbottom" foundation of ethics, such exclusion could only be justified by ignoring the selective nature of a politics of normalization and the contingent creation of categories of mental disorders, social misfits and political scapegoats.

If these categories are in themselves not violent enough in their objectification of human beings and their exclusion of vast tracts of humanity, their use in the distribution of social capital contravenes Peters' own idea of social justice, with a person's worth being morally judged according to standards of supposedly "objective" rationality. Ignoring the political forces at work in the production of subjectivity commits social injustice, not only in selectively distributing the benefits of society, but also in excluding all those aspects of the self that are not subject to reason, including the elements of desire and illusion that Nietzsche sees as part of being human and essential to a non-nihilistic culture.

The genealogical critique of the notion of depoliticized individuality (i.e., the Kantian subject) creates new possibilities that undermine the certainty of liberal individualism. This process also creates problems for Peters' theory in terms of his "concern for truth" because, if there are new and unexamined possibilities, or if we entertain Foucault's idea of "numberless beginnings," then the closure of Peters' deductive logic is suspect. His "truth" begins to resemble Nietzsche's "metaphorical illusion," or even worse, as Harris (1979: 129) argues, the intentional promotion of ignorance in the preservation of class interests. While Harris' Marxist analysis is also problematic in its privileged access to the "reality" underneath ideological "distortions," it is valuable in emphasizing the political nature of education in establishing social identity.

Peters' position holds that it is *reason* that distinguishes moral action from private likes and whims. Reason then is a transcendental discourse that can be used to judge private action. In the style of agonistic debate, it is not intended to discount Peters' position completely or to deny the benefits of reason in whole realms of enlightenment activity. However, it is argued here that ethics needs to stem from more than just the rational tradition, for it is hard to imagine a rational approach generating an ethical attitude if there is not already a generous sense of abundance in the self: "When your heart flows broad and full like a river, a blessing and a danger to those living near: there is the origin of your virtues" (Z, I: 22).

ETHICS AND DEMOCRACY

The preface to Richard Peters' earlier work with Stanley Benn (1959) has both authors taking full responsibility for what they see as the theme of the book—the close relationship between what is implied in "being reasonable" and the principles and institutions of the democratic state. So it is assumed that these ideas can be taken as a strong influence on his later text *Ethics and Education*. Their justification for democracy as a system draws on the theory of natural rights, stemming from the individualism of the seventeenth century (and in particular John Locke), which, they say,

recognized the moral principle that every person must be respected as a source of claims, and must not be treated as a mere instrument; and further, that all interests must be weighed impartially. (Benn and Peters, 1959: 350)

They vigorously defend their position with a number of prescriptions for democratic processes. For example, democratic leaders are bound to give reasons for their decisions if they want to maintain voter confidence; politicians must listen to their constituents and attend to a great variety of sectional claims; electors need full information about possible alternatives; channels of publicity must not be monopolized by any particular interest or party; the dangers of persuasion by organized propaganda must be minimized.

In spite of their optimistic theory, their analysis acknowledges some of the difficulties inherent in the practices of democratic government. They acknowledge that the concept of a "unified will" is utopian in that conflicts will always exist, but they see democracy as the best way to deal with the inevitably conflicting claims. They see the majority principle as important in a democracy as a means of ensuring sensitivity to the widest possible range of interests. It is this sensitivity, they say, which distinguishes democracies from "plebiscitary dictatorships."

Peters (1966) suggests that democracy attends to the "fundamental principles of morality," that is, fairness, liberty and the consideration of interests. The age-old problem of liberty is not resolved by such a suggestion however, for it is still problematic how much freedom the individual can have in a system that is aiming for consensus decisions. In practice, democracy allows some voices to be heard as long as they fit within accepted parameters. Even though no *one* person is fully represented by a majority, majority democracy is still posited as the best *system*. Peters concedes, however, that democracy is impracticable because of its extraordinary demands on ordinary citizens (Peters, 1966: 304).

In modern parliamentary democracy, the party that wins the largest share of the vote assumes power, and sometimes that party represents the *majority* of voters. However, in democracies that feature proportional representation, it is becoming increasingly common that the party in government does not represent a majority. In the case of coalition governments, the balance of power is often held by a very small minority. Democratic systems of government, therefore, not only exhibit the injustice of excluding a large number of voters who must abide by the decision of the majority (or in some cases, the decision of the minority), but they also negate those who refuse to vote on an issue, those with insufficient information to take part, those who object to the authority under which the vote is held and in Peters' admission, the 80 percent who don't know what to make of it all.

Many of Benn and Peters' prescriptions for democratic government are missing in the age of televised politicianship. Politicians, under the guidance of public relations consultants, spend more time making an impact than listening to constituents, press conferences are timed for maximum publicity, journalists and reporters are governed by commercial presentation and information is likely to be delivered as commercial sound bites compatible with advertising schedules. Rather than Peters' "well-informed constituent expressing a rational opinion," today's voter is more likely to be a well-massaged consumer of television images.

Politicians often use the aggregate term *the public* to prescribe how individuals should think about an issue. The public is certainly not a self-constituting group, but represents the category of "otherness" in political decision making, those about whom the decisions are made in the interests of "communal harmony." The agonistic position allows for and even promotes the existence of active minorities who can ensure that competing points of view are recognized and that any harmony that arises does so from a space where separate voices are protected.

Democracy in practice ensures gradual incremental change, preserving the prevailing order and removing the need for messy revolutions or authoritarian decree. Liberal democracy then, like its attendant rationality, is attractive as an ideal, but to believe that the ideal is achievable ignores Peters' own admission about the "frustrations," "failings" and "hypocrisies" of such an ideal in practice. News media constantly present violent images of "peace-making" and "truce-monitoring" troops destroying whole countries and killing people in the interests of liberation, world peace, security and democratic freedom while their governments benefit economically from providing postwar aid to those same nations. National identities are formed by constructing and denigrating otherness through such terminology as "insurgent dissidents," "communist infiltration" and "fascist regimes." The language of our liberal society has not yet adopted such phrases as "creeping democracy," "capitalist rebels" or "liberal guerrillas," or learned to examine the ideals of liberalism or democracy from alternative perspectives. Everyday "common sense" assumes the status of truth, especially our metaphysical notions of the self, the transcendental nature of truth and the capacity of language to give accurate descriptions of reality. A genealogical approach, by adopting a different political and historical perspective, problematizes the ethics of many practices in our systems of democracy and thereby undermines the certainty of Peters' prescription for democracy as the ethical basis for education.

In highlighting the importance of discussion, Benn and Peters acknowledge that discussion presupposes a consensus on fundamentals, for where this is lacking, they say, men will treat one another as scoundrels and differences of opinion will be undiscussable:

Where men start from different assumptions, there are no adjustments and no compromises generally felt to be fair and reasonable. In such conditions politics is a cynical grasping for whatever advantages temporary power combinations can secure. . . . without appropriate attitudes, and the will to conduct politics in a rational and tolerant spirit, democratic institutions work undemocratically. (Benn and Peters, 1959: 353)

If it has done nothing else, this chapter has surely suggested that different assumptions are not only inevitable, but are to be welcomed as part of an ethical difference. The presumption of consensus suggests at base a fundamentalism that prescribes the limits of what can be said, denigrating the possibility of agonism and precluding anything but cosmetic differences. In Rorty's terms, the result is the literalization of prevailing metaphors and an impediment to new ways of thinking—anathema to education.

An ethics based on agonism favors a non-closure on identity, an acceptance of differing conceptual schemes and a softening of the criteria for what would count as a point of view. Peters' ethical basis for education is welcomed as one such point of view but is resisted in its entirety because it searches for an idealized version of the truth. If Peters were to achieve the closure inherent in the universal ethic that he seeks, his work would fall prey to its own moral judgments, based on its exclusivity, its rigid prescription for a particular identity and its insistence on a transcendental rationality as the true order for human life.

Any recommendation for an ethical formulation needs to be procedural rather than substantive, inclusive rather than exclusive and ongoing rather than finite. Nietzschean perspectivism does not lay out a totalizing plan for action, or even a coherent philosophical framework for universal agreement. What is advocated instead is an ongoing problematization of the rational overlay on social life and a continuous interrogation of the discursive practices that subjugate "otherness." In calling for multiple points of view:

The Nietzschean critique of dogmatism, grounded as it is on a perspectivist position that calls for multiplying points of view and avoiding fixed and rigid posturings, may be an important voice to heed in constructing a politics that can challenge the panoply of emerging fundamentalisms. (Schrift, 1995: 125)

Chapter 5

Nietzsche, Education and Democracy

Scott Johnston

INTRODUCTION

Nietzsche's cultural critique, as well as his penetrating deconstruction of traditional metaphysics, extends well beyond his time. Indeed, Nietzsche's relevance for today seems well established by the attention Anglo-American philosophers have paid to him since Kaufmann's exhaustive, if somewhat simplistic, reconstruction of his *oeuvre*. Disciplines outside of traditional philosophy have also utilized Nietzsche to their advantage. Education is in no way excluded from this fact.

There have been many educational Nietzsches, particularly in the past 25 years. All of these claim in one way or another to unlock the hidden educator in the philosopher. There is, for example, the educator-Nietzsche that is reconstructed entirely from *Thus Spake Zarathustra* (Gordon, 1980). The author of this particular exegesis wishes us to believe that Nietzsche's educational "theory" can stand alone and complete from this one text. The author, by omission, discounts the possibility that either earlier or later works can have validity for an educator-Nietzsche, even though much of Nietzsche's early writings, and indeed some of his later, concerned themselves with the state of education in his time (see Cooper, 1983a). Then there are the "one-theme" Nietzsches. We also have the Nietzsche who utilizes sublimation in an educational manner (Sharp, 1984). And a Nietzsche who advocates "free" education (Rosenow, 1973). There is also the Dionysian "agonistic" Nietzsche (Hillesheim, 1973), as well as a metaphysical Nietzsche, the "pedagogical anthropologist" who ultimately views all cultural criticism as broadly educative (Aloni, 1989). We have the aristocratic, anti-university, anti-system Nietzsche, who purportedly argues the dismantling of the-then German educational system (Bloom, 1987), as well as the Nietzsche who remains sympathetic to education, advocating as he does an aristocracy of the self (Simons, 1988). Not surprisingly, only one recent commentator attempts to tackle in any forthright fashion what ultimately figures as the larger question looming on the horizon: the question that follows from all these attempts to hermeneuticize Nietzsche for their particular educational goals (Sassone, 1996). This question is: What possibility is there to reconcile the ideal of Nietzsche as educator with current democratic education as it is practiced in America?

Before this question can be adequately posed, definitions of "educator," "democracy" and "education" must be provided. For our purposes, educator will not be maintained in the broad sense that previous authors of Nietzsche's educational teachings have used. The educator of these authors often manifests as a cultural (*Bildung*) educator, an educator of humanity who is as removed from the classroom as any other philosopher attempting to address what are considered sociocultural issues. An examination of Nietzsche as educator for the schools and the classroom will therefore be stressed.

Second, democracy must be defined. The working definition of democracy for the purposes of this chapter comes from Dewey:

A democracy is more than a form of government; it is primarily a mode of associated living, of conjoint communicate experience. The extension in space of the number of individuals who participate in an interest so that each has to refer his own action to that of others, and to consider the action of others to give point and direction to his own, is equivalent to the breaking down of those barriers of class, race, and national territory which kept men from perceiving the full import of their activity. (Dewey, 1944)

This is so because Dewey was the first, and arguably the most influential, individual to provide a sense of how a democratic education could appear (Kaminsky, 1992). To this day he remains the most noteworthy of all philosophers of education, even though his great treatise was written over 70 years ago.

Third, education must be defined. Again let us return to Dewey for this enterprise:

Schooling is part of the work of education, but education in its full meaning includes all the influences that go to form the attitudes and dispositions (of desire as well as of belief), which constitute dominant habits of mind and character. (Dewey, 1935)

Again, the stress here is on the formal aspect of education noted by Dewey, that is, schooling. Furthermore, the arguments herein are restricted to a view of Nietzsche as educator for free spirits, free thinkers. This involves an examination of Nietzsche's utility as an educator for the "higher man [*sic*]."[1] Previous Nietzschean exegeses have already elucidated an aristocratic child pedagogy. I do not wish to repeat this enterprise. I agree in the main with those authors who visualize Nietzsche condoning an aristocratic and authoritarian view of pedagogy for the populace. However, throughout Nietzsche's cultural critique, a distinction is present between those values typical of the masses and of the higher man. This distinction is notably manifest in terms of how Nietzsche wishes education to be undertaken for the higher man as opposed to education for the masses. This issue will be taken up further in this chapter. Furthermore, the higher man cannot be culled from children; a sense of self-identity is a prerequisite. Therefore, the scope of this undertaking must be restricted further to higher education.

What would "Nietzsche as educator" look like? Those who envision such a Nietzsche must walk a tightrope; balance is important. Although Nietzsche was not a systematist, certain ongoing themes are prevalent in his oeuvre. To ignore these would be to overlook a very large and important avenue of Nietzsche's thought. At the same time there is a tendency, well explicated by French poststructuralism and its antecedent German roots, to resist all attempts at any systematic approach to his work. There is, for example, the Nietzsche of *Ecce Homo* who claims:

To communicate a state, an inner tension of pathos through signs, including the tempo of these signs—that is the meaning of every style; and considering that the multiplicity of inner states is in my case extraordinary, there exists in my case the possibility of many styles—altogether the most manifold art of style any man has ever seen at his disposal. (EH: 74)

This is the anti-metaphysical Nietzsche at work. To bring Nietzsche together on any theme or issue is an extremely difficult task and can rapidly result in a faulty exegesis if one is not sensitive to the aforementioned balance. Alexander Nehamas' *Nietzsche: Life as Literature* (1985) strikes just such a balance. There is a literary interpretation of Nietzsche here—one that pays particular attention to Nietzsche's themes while remaining cognizant of his playful anti-metaphysical tendencies. Nietzsche's "truths" are cast as metaphors, which is in keeping with his early pronouncements regarding the nature of knowledge and truth. The themes that Nietzsche utilizes, and Nehamas identifies, will be given much weight here, for it is through the use of these themes that Nietzsche provides us with insight into the inner workings of his text. To avoid these metaphors is to ignore the few, but vital and ultimately necessary, overarching themes that resonate throughout his work.

The question of what a Nietzschean pedagogical model will look like must be addressed further. Since Nietzsche designed no such explicit model, it must needs be constructed from his text. The metaphors will be utilized as the cornerstone for any such interpretation. As to which themes to choose, three will be selected that seem the most appropriate to deal with the issue of Nietzsche as educator. These themes are "The Most Multifarious Art of Style," "Beyond Good and Evil" and "How One Becomes Who One Is." These titles are chosen directly from Nehamas' *Nietzsche*, although the interpretation of the content constituting these metaphors will no doubt be somewhat different, owing to this chapter's emphasis on the ideal of Nietzsche as educator.

These metaphors span the entire corpus of Nietzsche's work, both early and late. Therefore, a single text cannot possibly be the basis for such an endeavor; neither will one theme, to the detriment of others, suffice. The locus of Nietzsche as educator is Nietzsche's philosophical anthropology. Nietzsche as educator concerns who man is, how he behaves, and why he must overcome himself. There can be no separation, no artificial dualism, to use Dewey's term, between Nietzsche's conception of educator and Nietzsche's conception of what is "fully" human.

Implicit in this analysis of Nietzsche is a view that considers the author's most valued task to create, through his works, a series of themes or metaphors that demonstrate a means for the person to fashion him or herself into a particular type of individual: a self-overcoming individual (see Nehamas, 1985: 183).

The cultural criticisms that were heavily emphasized in Nietzsche's early works (*Birth of Tragedy* through *Human, All Too Human*) give way to this tendency in his later works. *The Gay Science*, wherein the Overman, Eternal Recurrence of the Same, Amor Fati and Self-Overcoming are introduced, heralds the shift in focus. Of course, those cultural criticisms remain; only the end to which they are applied has changed.

To say that Nietzsche is thematic merely points to the fact that Nietzsche has as his purpose a general concern. In this case, it is the self-overcoming individual who, utilizing a variety of metaphors, of perspectives, is able to reach toward his or her goal. Themes are ideas, motifs; they are not the rigid, inflexible attributes of a system. Rather, they have the ability to mutate, to transform. Themes are closer in approximation to perspectives, to metaphors, than mere marks in the system. This view of Nietzsche's themes, of his metaphors, owes much to a continental reading of Nietzsche, beginning with Heidegger and Jaspers, and continuing with Deleuze and the French poststructuralists. The perspective of Nietzsche's themes as metaphors was not a widely held view in Anglo-American settings, dominated by Kaufmann's liberal humanist reading of Nietzsche as a systematic thinker. The publication of Jaspers' *Nietzsche* (1947) and Heidegger's *Nietzsche* (1991), as well as a selection of Deleuze's, Foucault's, and Derrida's works, has helped to restore a balance to the Nietzsche scholarship. Scholars such as Nehamas have been able to profit from these readings and thereby adopt a more equitable view of the thinker.

This brings us back to the question of the utility of Nietzsche as an educator for our democratic society. The argument is that, ultimately, there are too many hurdles, too many difficulties, be they philosophical, social or political, for a systematic adoption of a Nietzschean education or a Nietzsche as educator at the local, state or national level. The question that is begged in the writings of those previous Nietzsche scholars, as may be expected from the lack of a response, may finally be answered. And it is no. The impetus for such an undertaking, if indeed there can be such a possibility, begins and ends not with the school, not with the instructor, but with that multiplicity of individual characterizations known collectively as the self.

THE MOST MULTIFARIOUS ART OF STYLE

Nietzsche struggles to free himself from the confines of metaphysics. Although we must agree with Heidegger (1991, vol. 3) that Nietzsche ultimately fails in his project, nevertheless, a powerful critique against this foundation of philosophy is launched. Future thinkers such as Heidegger and Derrida carry on the assault, ostensibly bringing metaphysics to its destruction.

Central to Nietzsche's critique of metaphysics is an emphasis on the fragmentation of the states of unity, integration, absolutism and wholeness. Nowhere is this emphasis more notable than in those statements that become recognized thematically as perspectivism (see Lingis, 1977: 43).

Perspectivism arises as a result of Nietzsche's contention that there are no fixed, immutable truths. Rather, truths exist as a matter of individual perspective and are in turn played upon by social and cultural forces:

What then is truth? A moveable host of metaphors, metonymies, and anthropomorphisms: in short, a sum of human relations which have been poetically and rhetorically intensified, transferred, and embellished, and which, after long usage, seem to a people to be fixed, canonical, and binding. Truths are illusions which we have forgotten are illusions. (OtaL: 84)

Nietzsche's multiplicity of styles allows truth to be embedded in a diverse range of assorted opinions and maxims. Precisely what is true about these is neither their mutually agreed upon fixity or absoluteness, nor their social importance. Rather, it is the determinateness with which the individual who posits, who invents and develops, these truths, is able to self-identify with them and have them exist to provide meaningful and authentic value to his or her life. For "Truth is . . . not something there, that might be found or discovered—but something that must be created" (WP: 552).

Nietzsche's debt to Hegel is evident, for he recognizes that truths held by the masses exist because of social and cultural forces; that is, they are born of historical conditions. Although Nietzsche agrees that social forces play heavily on the acceptance of truths, he readily argues that truths are reducible in the last to the individual. Social and cultural forces do not create the truths that are in turn accepted by the individual, as Dewey (1950) would argue. Rather, the self-affirming individual creates his or her own truths and then tests them against the predominant truths of the masses for goodness of fit. It is in this way that Nietzsche argues that one can reject outward truth—valuations—and that one can "overcome" other truths in favor of one's own.

But can one infer from the preceding that, since truth is not an immutable fixity and truths rely on individual perspectives in turn influenced by social and cultural forces, all views and opinions are equally as correct as good as each other? The answer, perhaps unexpectedly so, is no (Kaufmann, 1990). Nietzsche does not value each and every truth as equal. In point of fact, he took upon himself the task of being a cultural critic of the age. Indeed, Nietzsche had many "styles," and he utilized them to frequently contradict each other. The use of a perspectival method allows Nietzsche to juxtapose accepted truths with deviant ones in order to expose these truths for their contextual nature and thereby to argue that one truth is as epistemologically operable as another. In this way, individual truths long held in check by hegemonic, sociocultural truths could at least emerge on what might be called a level playing field. Leveling the field allows individual truths to compete with socially constructed ones. This strengthens the worthiness of the individual, who remains in perpetual conflict with social, cultural and historical forces.

A manifold art of style supports, in the main, a view of diversity. But perspectivism also argues for diverse opportunities beyond the paradigm of truth. In terms of education, this can mean diverse bodies of diverse students studying diverse topics in diverse schools.

Nietzsche is adamant regarding the primary place of the individual in all social and cultural matters. We therefore, agree with Rosenow (1973) that, at the very least, a total break from education as it is currently practiced is what would be needed if one were to adopt a thoroughly Nietzschean stand on education. It is precisely the lengths, however, to which Rosenow attempts to produce a systematic Nietzsche, while ignoring completely the anti-hegemonic, multifaceted, perspectival Nietzsche, that is disconcerting (see Rosenow, 1973: 370).

Although Rosenow is correct in assuming that one must be skeptical of a Nietzschean education because it is inherently anti-social, Rosenow nonetheless argues for the existence of education on the basis of the possibility of a "free education," one that "eliminates the possibility of interpersonal communication and which isolates man" (Rosenow, 1973: 370).

Education for Rosenow must therefore exist beyond or apart from the social, a concept that would certainly make Dewey uneasy. However, since Rosenow discounts the possibility of interpersonal communication, he must therefore discount by the same argument the possibility of mutual dialogue between teacher and student. Self-education seems the only appropriate option when the social is removed. And since education has historically involved itself in the dissemination of knowledge from teacher or mentor to student, the term *education* seems no longer an appropriate title for what occurs in Rosenow's conception of the activity.

Systematizing Nietzsche in this way ignores the thematic evidence embedded in his perspectivism—the notion that things must succumb to a multiplicity of styles. To systematize Nietzsche in such a way is to contain him. And this is precisely what Nietzsche wants to avoid (see EH: 33).

To be fair to Rosenow, however, one must agree with his diagnosis, prodded on as it is by Hillesheim's (1986) critique that contemporary education provides a jumbled and confused message with respect to the desirability of the dual metaphors of self-mastery (self-control) and self-overcoming.

With Rosenow (1973) we see the first glimpse of a view that deconstructs education's utility for the self-overcoming individual. He goes on to argue: "Therefore, whoever wishes to adopt Nietzsche as an educational philosopher must stop midway and accept him partially" (Rosenow, 1973: 316). Turning this around, one could argue that, to accept the ideal of a self-overcoming individual in toto, one must stop midway and extirpate the "ideal" of education not partially but completely.

A similar misappropriation of Nietzsche has been undertaken by those (e.g., Bloom, 1987; Sharp, 1984) who, utilizing a faulty hermeneutic, wish to attempt a reconstruction that fits their particular ideological belief. Bloom champions a view that has become one of the most pervasive of the contemporary trends in education: the so-called Back to Basics movement. Its argument is that schools have become too fragmented, standards too lax, curricula too broad (see Pulliam and Van Patten, 1995). Bloom sees as necessary a toughening of standards: higher entrance scores, more rigorous evaluation, teacher and student competency testing and a return to a "basic" curriculum, emphasizing the humanities and hard sciences. In particular, he argues for a return to an aristocratic education along the lines described by Plato in *The Republic* and championed by Socrates. Bloom calls upon Nietzsche the "aristocrat" to help him further these goals:

Nietzsche sought with his value philosophy to restore the harsh conflicts for which men were willing to die, to restore the tragic sense of life, at a moment when nature had been domesticated and men become tame. That value philosophy was used in America for exactly the opposite purpose—to promote conflict—resolution, bargaining, harmony. (Bloom, 1987: 228)

Bloom makes a number of useful points in regard to Nietzsche, particularly in reference to Nietzsche's misappropriation by ideologues bent on utilizing the philosopher for their particular political activities. However,

Bloom, too, falls into a similar trap. Although he concedes that Nietzsche's task is to overturn hitherto accepted social and cultural values, no mention is made of the thinker's myriad cache of perspectives. For Bloom, the current educational values are synonymous with a rejection of instrumental reason and unity in curricula, a playful acceptance of other's cultures and values, and a questioning of tradition. In contrast, Bloom would cast aside these values for an aristocratic education, a Great Books emphasis similar to Adler's (1982), a firm foundation in the liberal arts and sciences, and a return to philosophy as a structured and educable discipline. In order to appropriate Nietzsche for these goals, Bloom has to emphasize the overturning of values. But these are not the values that Nietzsche himself is set on overturning; rather, they are the values that Nietzsche champions: heteronomy, fragmentation and diversity.

Does Nietzsche thus emphasize an anarchistic education for children? He does not. In fact, he values obedience, rigorous study and stern discipline (see e.g., WP: 482). But there is a disparity here between elementary education and "higher" education, on which Nietzsche heaps scorn: " 'Higher' education: essentially the means of directing taste against the exceptions for the good of the mediocre" (WP: 492). For Nietzsche, the then-current organization of higher education in no way prepares the individual for the task of self-overcoming. That institution is simply a hegemonic presence designed to reinforce the insipid cultural decay that was prevalent at the time. To argue a return to an educational philosophy or a system that espouses an aristocratic higher education in a "Back to Basics" style is not Nietzsche's ultimate intention. Instead, his aim is to remove the individual completely from education as it existed at that time. It is Nietzsche's goal to have those capable of doing so, in effect, reject the hegemony of the educational-cultural institution (*Bildung*) in favor of their individual self-overcoming. Nietzsche's "hard school" exists as the nexus for the means to the creation of a thinking individual who could then potentially cast off his or her education in favor of what would ultimately emerge as a self-overcoming (TI).

The aristocratic Back to Basics movement has resulted in a general call for improvements in education that move away from a stress on diversity and multiplicity and back to one of uniformity. The net effect of this particular narrative of education is to argue that diversity has had a negative effect on education. Therefore it is proposed that the discipline once again shorten its boundaries and thereby contain the plurality, the diversity, that has of late begun to characterize higher education in this country. What lies just beneath the surface of much of this particular educational ideology is a justification of education as a predominantly social medium intended to produce a capable and enlightened citizenry. This view of course goes back to Plato, by way of Dewey. It is implicit in much contemporary thinking. In contrast, it must be reemphasized that Nietzsche champions an education that develops the individual so that he or she may be able to attain the lauded status of self-overcoming. Education is merely a means for Nietzsche, and not a self-contained telos, as Bloom (1987) seems to suggest. Any education that does not champion the individual in his struggle to self-overcome, to overcome, in effect, the social and the cultural influences that impinge on him or her, must be in league with those social and cultural forces that alienate the individual from him or herself. Such leads Nietzsche to conclude that education, as it is coterminous with the dominant social and cultural forces at play, contradicts a person's nature (see "Philosophy in Hard Times").

The aporia of a Nietzschean/democratic education must by rights be taken up. Sharp, for example, concludes that Nietzsche views the educator or teacher as that individual who has the stated purpose of assisting the student to reach his or her liberation from the teacher. In the main, this is correct. For example, we find in *Thus Spake Zarathustra*: "Now I bid you lose me and find yourselves; and only when you have all denied me will I return to you" (Z: I #3). Nonetheless, Sharp misunderstands Nietzsche's radical individualism when she writes:

The good educator for Nietzsche is one who can seduce the students into a love of knowledge and truth and who can show them the usefulness of sublimation as a means to an end, and nothing more. He also must have the ability to manipulate the environment at all times so that the student is endlessly challenged with experiences which involve growth and expansion of his horizons. (Sharp, 1984: 102)

What is disconcerting about this particular statement is the appropriation of Nietzsche to what is ultimately a Deweyan task. Nietzsche does not create a telos out of growth, as Dewey, in *Democracy and Education*, is capable of producing. Indeed, Nietzsche rejects the whole doctrine of ends (see WP: 500).

Nietzsche recognizes the futility of struggling with the cultural and social environment, an environment that education is supposed to help overcome. To self-overcome requires the very overcoming of education, as far as education is itself a product and a minion of the dominant society and culture. In "Schopenhauer as Educator," Nietzsche argues:

The difficulty, however, lies for mankind in relearning and envisaging a new goal; and it will consist in an unspeakable amount of effort to exchange the fundamental ideal behind our present system of education, which has its roots in the Middle Ages and the ideal of which is actually the production of the medieval scholar, for a new fundamental idea. (UM: 175)

As such, education, insofar as it is firmly rooted in the social and the cultural, cannot be entertained in a properly Nietzschean manner. Nietzsche can be no more appropriated to Dewey than any other thinker. Although there are certainly elements of Nietzsche's thought that come close to Dewey's, one must nonetheless remain cognizant of Nietzsche's anti-hegemonic and anti-democratic stance. That a multiplicity of styles, of seeming contradictions, should be more highly valued than an overarching view or paradigm is basic to Nietzsche. One can appropriate Nietzsche for a particular view, cause or ideology only if one is willing to have him appropriated equally and for all others. Attempting to categorize Nietzsche in a singular fashion perverts the very argument the thinker utilizes to overcome metaphysics, the dominant culture and the self.

BEYOND GOOD AND EVIL

Nietzsche's critique of the prevailing European culture is primarily an issue of morals. Of particular concern to Nietzsche is the state of nihilism, of cultural decadence traceable to Christian influences and to the hegemony exerted by ratio, a hegemony traceable to Socrates, that pervaded Europe at the fin-de-siècle. Characteristically, it is these tendencies that Nietzsche wishes for the individual, through the Will to Power, to overcome (see EH: 79–80). This self-same opposition to the search for absolutes, this same embracing of all fullness, leads Nietzsche to the Transvaluation of Values. In the same sense that no a priori truths can be admitted, no canonical valuations or fixed principles of justice can likewise be said to exist. "To be moral, correct, ethical, means to obey an age-old law or tradition. Whether one submits to it gladly or with difficulty makes no difference; enough that one submits" (HH: 66).

Nietzsche follows Hegel's *Rechtsphilosophie* in his insistence that moral laws rest within and upon the sociocultural sphere that culminates in the state. But whereas Hegel champions the dominant sociocultural values that coalesce to form Objective Mind, Nietzsche pauses to critique those social values and their manifest Hegelian notions:

Man cannot be made responsible for anything, neither for his nature, nor his motives, nor his actions, nor the effects of his actions. And thus we come to understand that the history of moral feelings is the history of an error; an error called "responsibility", which in turn rests on an error called "freedom of the will." (HH: 43)

Nietzsche's resolute disbelief in a fixed and canonical ethic, together with his scorn of the contemporary Christian-Platonic-European culture, leads him to challenge the prevailing valuations in a hitherto novel manner. For Nietzsche argues an overcoming or transvaluation of the then-dominant values through a reversal of what is to be considered good by that which is clearly evil. In this manner, Nietzsche posits the possibility of a realm defined by extra-morality, a realm in which the hitherto dominant valuations become meaningless.

The overturning of the hitherto accepted valuations in favor of opposites would, for Nietzsche, result in a cultural catastrophe. Indeed, this is prophesized in numerous places throughout his *oeuvre*. Nonetheless, Nietzsche sees this as a necessary precursor to what will ultimately emerge in phoenix-fire fashion from the ashes of the ruined cultural landscape: the self-overcoming individual, able to posit his or her own valuations as over and above the decadent values of the mass culture.

To be certain, this would not be a simple task. For not only must valuations as they exist be deconstructed, but that individual who posits his own valuations as self-worthy must be content to endure the suffering consistent with the self-imposed alienation that breaking away from the dominant sociocultural traditions necessitates. That individual must, according to Nietzsche, not only accept his or her fate, the fate of alienation, of disparagement, of loneliness, but embrace it as well:

My formula for greatness in a human being is amor fati: that one wants nothing to be different, not forward, not backward, in all eternity. Not merely bear what is necessary, still less conceal it—all idealism is mendaciousness in the face of what is necessary—but love it. (EH: 258)

One of Nietzsche's resolute goals is to champion the self-overcoming individual. This means in the first instance to point the way to an overturning of prevalent sociocultural valuations that are considered hegemonic, decadent and lamentable. For Nietzsche, education, as a process, does not assist a self-overcoming individual to overcome hitherto accepted valuations; rather, education serves paradoxically as a medium for their transmission.

Education cannot supply the task of overturning valuations that education itself contains within. Education is a social function. It exists to produce citizenry who are able to interact intelligently with each other, thereby maintaining the ideal of democracy. No discipline and no science, education included, is value free.

To adopt a Nietzschean view of education would, in the main, necessitate a movement away from the social ideal to an individual one. What characterizes education, however, is precisely its social function: to educate means, in a historical sense ranging from Plato to Rousseau and onward to Dewey, the dissemination of knowledge from the one to the other. Nietzsche, however, castigates the values of this interpersonal function, of the shared intersubjective relationship that education favors and within which it participates, in favor of an intrapersonal, intrasubjective and individual one. Education cannot supply the task of an individual transvaluation because, simply put, it *contains* (Ornery et al., 1996). The ideal and the practice of education contain discreet yet pervasive narratives that are passed from teacher, policy and curriculum to the student. While these may exist on a subconscious level, they nonetheless influence. Valuations that reflect the dominant social ideals are contained within these narratives, and these narratives work, in turn, to contain those individuals who encounter them.

We see this tendency in the works of our most prominent educator-philosophers. Dewey (1944), of course, is no exception to this. Dewey attempts an overturning of the then accepted educational values. Education prior to the turn of the twentieth century was purposefully designed to augment an individual's mind: through a fixed and canonical reading of selected texts, combined with an aristocratic, "top-down" instructional style. It was believed that education could somehow improve a person's intellectual situation, regardless of the lifeworld surrounding him or her. Dewey attempts a unification of the self and the world; the fragmentation brought about by an artificial and pedantic curriculum and an isolated didactic instructional technique is to be replaced by a methodology emphasizing the individual's thoroughgoing interconnectedness with the world. For Dewey, education is designed to foster intelligence: the ability of the person to utilize the connections between experience, society and culture and to emerge as a fully functioning individual capable of self-sustainment in the modern world. For Dewey, education is always to be considered a social and cultural function.

Now Nietzsche would not disagree with Dewey that morals and morality traditionally exist within the social sphere. Nor would he probably disagree with the passage of social norms from person to person via that medium of communication known as speech. What Nietzsche does disagree with, however, is the ideal of social morality. In the main, Nietzsche argues that to self-overcome, to "transvalue all values," requires a renunciation of social valuations. This thought is inimical to Dewey, who would argue that just such an activity splits an individual off from society, resulting in an individual existing outside and beyond the boundaries of the social as self-governance, of the particular self-control that Dewey characteristically equates with the Hegelian concept of freedom embodied within society in the *Rechtsphilosophie*. Any and all such thinkers who wish to create a parallel between Dewey and Nietzsche must confront this issue.

Educators who wish to appropriate Nietzsche for their particular agenda seem also to forget that, for Nietzsche, the task for man is to overcome the hegemonic valuations that characterize the decadence and insipidity of the then-contemporary European culture. In short, the task is for man to overcome himself. Any talk of education that does not serve to fulfill this task is antithetical in the main to Nietzsche's concern. It is to commit the error of projecting one's valuations onto Nietzsche.

Gordon (1980) utilizes Nietzsche's *Zarathustra* to point out aspects of an educator that seem, in his view, worth emulating. Gordon correctly argues that the starting point for any discussion of "teaching" is the pupil.

He argues that, to teach as Zarathustra, one's approach must be "anti-dogmatic and anticatechistic" (Gordon, 1980: 191). Certainly, to a Nietzsche who stresses always the individual, together with the overcoming of the dominant valuations, as well as oneself, this is correct. Finally, Gordon (1980: 191) contends that to have Zarathustra as educator is to celebrate the joys of life, "to express . . . love in a joyous dance." There is certainly in existence this quality about Nietzsche. Nonetheless, Gordon errs in assuming that, because Zarathustra attempted to teach his disciples utilizing the aforementioned techniques, the realm of education, of a formal instructional methodology, can thereby be validated. In point of fact, Zarathustra's educational techniques fail: he is not able to reach the higher men that he strives so hard to obtain (see Higgins, 1988). His techniques, as challenging and unorthodox as they are, ultimately prove unsuccessful, leaving Zarathustra with the realization that only the self-overcoming, self-affirming individual, utilizing his or her own valuations, can reach the so-called higher state.

In contrast, Hillesheim (1973–349) projects onto Nietzsche an aristocratic "agonistic" educator, one whose "primary concern is with the education of these few rare individuals." Hillesheim argues that, because Nietzsche makes allusions in his literature to the production of the genius, of higher men, Nietzsche necessarily commands a strong education for these higher men. But Hillesheim, too misreads Nietzsche's higher purpose. And this is that those self-overcoming individuals, if they are to truly become "higher" men, must cast off the shackles of society, cast off the shackles of an education in favor of what ultimately must be termed self-instruction. For, as Nietzsche argues, "Not 'mankind' but overman is the goal!" (WP: 519). Now Hillesheim is correct in advancing the view that the masses, the herd, are unable to forecast social welfare. But it would be a mistake to agree that the Overman, those higher men whom Nietzsche, particularly in his early works and up until the fourth book of *Zarathustra*, designated as the true cultural leaders, necessitates an education crafted for "the intellectual and artistic elite" (Hillesheim, 1973: 353).

To effect a self-overcoming individual, an Overman, requires something that education ultimately cannot provide. It requires a moment-to-moment, hour-to-hour, day-to-day self-realization of one's strengths and weaknesses, together with a profound ability to suffer well. It cannot be imitated, as Hillesheim (1990) seems to believe.

HOW ONE BECOMES WHO ONE IS

Nietzsche's self-styled metaphor "Become Who You Are" is an amalgam of all his other metaphors. From Amor Fati through the Will to Power and the Eternal Recurrence of the Same, to the Overman and the Most Multifarious Art of Style, there exists an underlying assumption that what will ultimately come to the fore is a self-overcoming individual. The self-overcoming individual is one whose locus of existence is within.

The task of becoming who one is requires a tendency toward a heightened self-preservation: a selfishness that concedes to itself that even the appearance of the most "selfless" acts is of ultimate gain for the individual. This selfish, self-overcoming individual is celebratory. He or she is one who both understands and responds joyously to the vagaries of life. In this respect, the self-overcoming individual is one who is able to suffer and suffer well. Several examples of this are provided.

The self-overcoming individual replaces will with the Will to Power, a will to create and live within one's own truths: static being gives way to a dynamic becoming. Every moment of every day of every year is spent in self-overcoming, an eternal cycle of return:

Have you ever said Yes to a single joy? O my friends, then you said yes too to all woe. All things are entangled, ensnared, enamored; if ever you wanted one thing twice, if ever you said, "You please me, happiness! Abide, moment! then you wanted all back. All anew, all eternally, all entangled, ensnared, enamored—oh, then you loved the world. Eternal ones, love it eternally and evermore; and to woe too, you say: go, but return! For all joy wants—eternity. (Z: 323)

The new system of valuations provided by and for this individual takes its point of reference from the individual, and not from the outward society, church, state, nation or culture. Education, bound as it is to the dissemination of social customs and habits, is ill equipped to assist the self-overcoming individual in his or her chosen task. Although education can certainly provide instruction and content that the individual can use to gain knowledge, the valuations that are passed along with this knowledge are antithetical to the selfish, transvaluing, self-overcoming individual that Nietzsche maintains. At best, education can provide a solid base from which the individual is able to gain a myriad of diverse perspectives—something like the diversity that is currently in vogue in many educational circles today. And Nietzsche would certainly argue that, if education is to remain a function of society (and this he certainly does), it must improve the opportunities it has to foster a critical mind.

All else is of secondary importance. Indeed, some of Nietzsche's admonitions of the then-German educational scene would make Bloom, Adler and various other "Back to Basics" organizations extremely satisfied:

Educators are needed who have themselves been educated, superior, noble spirits, proved at every moment, proved by words and silence, representing culture which has grown sweet—not the learned louts whom secondary schools and universities today offer our youth as "higher wet nurses." (TI: 510)

Viewing Nietzsche's polemic as presented could easily bring one to the conclusion that Nietzsche valued a harsh, aristocratic education in keeping with his dictum to produce "higher" men: sound, self-overcoming individuals able to return the German spirit and culture to a long-forgotten state of excellence. In point of fact, this is not the case. Although Nietzsche laments the state of *Bildung*, he does not supply the needed material for its improvement. The reason is that *Bildung* has degenerated to a point where anything less than a total destruction would not suffice. Nietzsche may have indeed prophesized this coming destruction with a glimmer of hope. Nonetheless, his answer to the crisis of culture was not to rebuild; rather, it was to break away, to demolish.

To reconstruct culture, whether through education or through some other means, is not Nietzsche's task. Instead, it is to point the way to the possibility of a new individual, a self-overcoming individual, one able to create and live within his or her own valuations. Education merely exists as a means of creating social beings. Education is a necessity of society that, as with other necessities, must be overcome to accomplish the aforementioned task. Nietzsche would concede that as so long as education provides the pedagogical function of shaping people, it best performs the task with what could be termed aristocratic and noble standards. Even this is suspect, however, because he would also favor a view that considers differing approaches in instruction and curriculum. Can an aristocratic and noble education be conjoined with a diverse, multifaceted, pluralistic one? There certainly is no clear answer to this question.

Education, beyond the most basic attempts to instill in the individual a firm grasp of essential skills—those of, for example, language, logic, critical examination, in short, "learning to think"—is antithetical in the main to the task of encouraging potential self-overcoming individuals toward their anticipated end. Education can be but the beginning: the real work rests firmly with the individual. This is why Aloni's task of creating a pedagogical dimension out of Nietzsche's critique of anemic educational institutions is misguided. Now Aloni's attempt to rescue Nietzsche from other-imposed cries of nihilism, utilizing the theme of Nietzsche as educator, is admirable.

Aloni ignores the overriding evidence suggesting that, for Nietzsche, education is neither liberating nor empowering. If individuals wish, as Aloni maintains, authentic, autonomous and creative lives, they must achieve this goal outside of education, for this is entirely a personal goal. Education is simply the means to the task of thinking. Education cannot, as Aloni (1989: 305) suggests, provide "conceptual means (such as the Will to Power, the Overman, and the Dionysian) for promoting the rise of noble cultures and great human beings." If these are indeed to arise, they will do so precisely because they form outside of education, outside of that hegemonic environment that, paradoxically, creates mediocrity, not nobility.

Simons (1988) fashions an Overman closer to the spirit of the free-thinking inner individual than perhaps do any of the other commentators. Simons' pronouncement of the self-sustaining, self-overcoming individual proves premature. He argues that Nietzsche is indeed able to tolerate a schooling for the majority, for the herd. But it is precisely in his inability to see that the Overman must overcome the vestiges of democracy, society, school and schooling that Simons is exposed. Simons suggests that schooling itself my serve to suppress individuals, but he dismisses the possibility that the whole philosophy of education might be complicit in this; rather, he entertains only the possibility that certain schools may be corrupt. He refuses to affirm the notion that education itself, not simply schools of a certain kind, is the point of contention for a self-overcoming individual.

Sassone (1996) is the first commentator to tackle the difficult issue of the appropriation of Nietzsche for a democratic education. Her attempt is a bold and ambitious enterprise. She argues for a democratized Nietzschean pedagogy, that is, teaching practices that are at once allied with both Nietzsche and democracy. Nietzschean teaching practices and democracy are seen as compatible. This is so in part because of an assumption that the democratic Nietzsche is one who champions "being in-and-for-self" (Sassone, 1996: 515). Hegelianizing Nietzsche in this way allows Sassone to fix the democratic Nietzsche as firmly supporting a self-referential view.[2] The Deweyan ideal of democracy as conjoint communication among peoples is seemingly cast aside in favor of a more radical and ultimately individual ideal.

The self-referential, self-observational individual is certainly a goal to which Nietzsche aspires. An erroneous assumption, however, creeps into Sassone's argument. This is the equation of pedagogy, or the general dissemination of Nietzsche's themes to a captive audience, with education, the formal dissemination of (shared) knowledge. The two are not coterminous. It may indeed be appropriate to argue that Nietzsche's themes, Nietzsche's statements, constitute a pedagogy, inasmuch as Nietzsche himself alludes to this in *Zarathustra*. Nonetheless, Nietzsche has no illusions about the role of formal education in the dissemination of his themes. For this is an impossibility, inasmuch as the effort that leads to self-overcoming is an entirely self-involved task.

In Sassone's (1996) estimation, democracy exists coterminously with a self-referential, self-observing individual. Indeed, in this relationship, individuality is argued to be predicated upon democracy, and vice versa. The social import is briefly mentioned but only toward the end of the essay, and the exact relationship of the individual to the social in terms of a Nietzschean pedagogy is left unclear.

The strains begin to show at the point where Sassone tries to merge the individual and the social. Democracy is principally a social activity. Sassone probably recognizes this and therefore attempts to evade the aporia of exactly how to reconcile a social institution such as education with a view of individual self-reflection, fulfillment and observation. While summarily emphasizing the importance of the social in democratic Nietzsche, she avoids the difficult question of how to be at once both social and radically individual, as Nietzsche—if we are to agree with Sassone—seems to desire. For Nietzsche, though, there is no question of a reconciliation between the realms of the individual and social. One simply has to overcome the social if one desires in turn to self-overcome. To propose a democratic Nietzsche requires one to fashion a compatible solution that does not give too much control, too much weight, to either the social or the individual. A democratic Nietzsche cannot exist in this respect and at the same time recommend to the individual a radical turning away from society and the social in favor of oneself. Nietzsche chooses where Sassone cannot. And the choice he makes is the individual.

EDUCATION AND THE FUTURE OF NIETZSCHEAN RESEARCH

Ultimately, I agree with Cooper's critique of Gordon's "Zarathustra as Educator" wherein he states:

The "legislation" of this new aristocracy is self-legislation. . . . The "power" of philosophical men, as we know from Nietzsche's discussions of philosophy and the will to power, is the creative power to revalue, construct perspectives, confer meanings, and escape the constricting mediocrity of the values and ideas which dominate in the "herd". . . . The riches of the masters are those of spirit and character. (Cooper, 1983b: 125)

Inasmuch as education is a social institution, with social valuations, it contains. It is hegemonic. It self-creates and maintains its specific narratives, and it in turn passes these along to its pupils. It aims to produce critical thinkers: individuals who are able to utilize their training and skills in a purposeful fashion (see Bloom, 1987). It aims to enlighten, to emancipate (Rousseau, 1979; Kohli, 1995). But Dewey is perhaps most correct when he argues that education's chief function, above all else, is to provide intelligence of a kind that will allow the production of a democratic citizenry. This is clearly not what Nietzsche's overriding task with respect to the individual seems to be. The production of an enlightened, emancipatory, democratized citizen is antithetical to the self-overcoming individual that Nietzsche champions: one who would cast off the vestiges of sociocultural valuations in order to become who he or she is.

The question, therefore, is precisely what kind of instruction, what kind of curriculum, would Nietzsche accept? To answer this question requires one to specify precisely what task it is that he or she wishes to accomplish. If the task is self-overcoming, Nietzsche's primary goal for the individual, then the answer is simple: a self-created and self-instructed teaching and curriculum. There is no room for education in this achievement. But if the goal is to educate the masses, then the answer can be found in what Cooper considers Nietzsche's educational corpus.

The noble and aristocratic education for the masses has been well documented, particularly by Bloom, Rosenow and Hillesheim. In contrast to this, the emphasis that Nietzsche places on the self-instruction necessary for self-overcoming has received scant attention. Sassone (1996) and Simons (1988) are perhaps the first to consider this facet of pedagogy. There are many examples, many maxims, in Nietzsche that one can point to for assistance in this endeavor. Ultimately, however, the task is, as Nietzsche would agree, a thoroughly individual one. One must create not only the self that one wishes to become, but also the means, the instruction and the content, if you will, of how one wishes to achieve this stature. Unfortunate as this is to educators, there can be no blueprint for this task. At the most elemental level, there is a requirement to integrate Nietzsche's themes into a schema; a schema that will function solely for that individual. Again, this is perhaps why educators who utilize Nietzsche for their respective "philosophies" hesitate to challenge that most basic labor of the Nietzschean corpus. It is because, ultimately, there is no place for a reasoned discussion of the techniques, of the content of self-overcoming beyond those general opinions that Nietzsche himself proffers in respect to this goal. There are no "shared" methods of instruction, no curricula that can be perused, no contents to be discovered. There is only the Nietzschean individual.

NOTES

1. Unless otherwise noted, gender-specific nouns and pronouns such as "man" and "he" are considered to include both masculine and feminine.

2. Of course, Hegelianizing the individual in this way ignores the fact that for Hegel, being in and for itself was inchoate; it was empty without the referential "being for other" that completed it, and propelled it toward actuality. See "The Science of Logic" in Hegel (1990).

Chapter 6

Nietzsche and Education: Learning to Make Sense for Oneself, or Standing for One's Ideas

Paul Smeyers

NIETZSCHE AND EDUCATIONAL THEORY

Whether it is because of his provocative style or simply because what he writes always rings the bell of emancipation is not clear, but without doubt Nietzsche does not leave many educational theorists indifferent. Praised by few, reviled by many, he seems more than ever to be omnipresent in the general philosophical scene. The revival of interest in Nietzsche has much to do with poststructuralism, taking its inspiration in a particular (Deleuzean) reading of his work. Given that so many within the philosophy of education are presently occupied with poststructuralism, it is not surprising to find more and more papers focusing on Nietzsche. Quite a few analysts consider *Thus Spake Zarathustra* as *the* text par excellence to unlock the hidden educator in the philosophy. Others focus on a number of his early writings, on some of his later ones or on those in which he concerned himself explicitly with the state of education in his time. Taking their inspiration more generally from his philosophical works, there are authors who, depending on the particular aspect they are interested in, offer different kinds of "Nietzschean educational theory." Aloni (1989), for instance, indicates three pedagogical dimensions: a radical redefinition of the aim of education (conceived as the recovery of health and worth); a pedagogical anthropology, that is, Nietzsche's search for the favorable conditions under which great human beings and noble cultures can come into being; and finally, his works themselves.

In a recent paper in *Educational Theory*, Johnston (1998) enlists a Nietzschean interpretation that uses sublimation in an educational manner, another that advocates "free" education, a further Dionysian "agonistic"

Nietzsche, a metaphysical Nietzsche, a "pedagogical anthropologist" who ultimately views all cultural criticism as broadly educative, an aristocratic anti-university anti-system Nietzsche who purportedly argues for a complete dismantling of the German educational system, and one who advocates an aristocracy of the self. I will return to Johnston's paper later in this chapter, for the impression that is given there is, to say the least, confused. But so many interpretations demand an answer to the question of why Nietzsche's oeuvre fascinates so many who reflect on educational contexts. This is even more so, as the numerous papers dealing with Nietzschean issues relevant for education contain a lot of criticism too.

Clearly, it is easy to show that Nietzsche has been misinterpreted in ways that are both sinister and potentially dangerous—for instance, when he was posthumously adopted as the approved philosopher of the Nazi Party. The fashionable criticism concerning his subjectivism is another matter, however. In his reflections on liberal education, Arcilla, for example, describes the Nietzschean subject as one who could simply not care about justifying her beliefs and actions to others and who could exclusively concern herself with self-centered desires or values:

Although Nietzsche calls on us to create and organize our own worlds, he appears to demand that we live only by the rule of whim. Are there to be no guides for the will? Is everything permitted? Is all external constraint to be considered simply an enemy will, fit only to be resisted and overpowered? Under such conditions, is it possible to create a culture that can be commonly affirmed? With these questions, which threaten any conception of social order, we begin to appreciate the cost of his renunciation of the problem of reason, a renunciation that makes him, in the eyes of many, the prophet of nihilism, or at least of the quintessentially postmodern question: Whose values? (cf. Arcilla, 1995, p. 78)

As already indicated, this criticism is not uncommon. It is therefore a serious question to ask whether Nietzsche's thoughts, so often formulated in a typical rhetorical style, are still worth studying (and if so why), or whether we are happily now, as some would claim, far beyond Nietzsche.

Johnston characterizes, quite correctly, the impetus for any Nietzschean education:

[it] begins and ends not with society, not with democracy, not with the school, not with the teacher, but with the multiplicity of individual characterizations known collectively as the self. (Johnston, 1998: 68)

Nietzsche agrees, so Johnston claims, that social forces play heavily on the acceptance of truths, but he readily argues that truths are reducible in the last to the individual. The self-affirming individual creates his or her own truths, tests them against the predominant truths of the masses for goodness of fit and thus rejects outward truth-valuations and overcomes other truths in favor of one's own. Of course, Nietzsche does not value each and every truth as equal; rather, he took upon himself the task of being a cultural critic of the age, thus juxtaposing accepted truths with deviant ones in order to expose truths for their contextual nature. Johnston continues:

Leveling the field allows individual truths to compete with socially constructed ones. And this strengthens the worthiness of the individual, who remains in perpetual conflict with social, cultural, and historical forces. (Johnston, 1998: 69)

Three questions need to be answered here. First, does this make sense within Nietzsche's overall philosophical position? Second, what in general follows for psychology and education from Nietzsche's philosophy? Third, is there still a need to focus on this issue, or have other philosophical positions already dealt perhaps even more adequately with it?

Nietzsche's concept of "self-overcoming" is a revision and revaluation of the traditional concept of self-mastery or self-control, as Rosenow (1989) accurately states. This concept is based on the idea that a human being possesses two or more dimensions and that it is her task to subjugate the rival and contesting powers to one of them (her true essence). The task is to struggle with oneself and to suppress instincts and evil inclinations and to subjugate them to the sublime element. As the ability to master one's impulses and inclinations is not inborn, external authority is necessary. Although educational theories differ in the way they design the constraints, they all aim at the internalization of external authority to become an integral part of personality; the termination of it becomes the point of departure for self-education. It is this concept of self-mastery that Nietzsche challenges. A human being is an individual, whose essence is uniqueness and singularity. The human being has to overcome all that represses her nature and denies her freedom. This includes not only conventional moral values, but also the reverence for scholars and philosophers with which her education has imbued her and finally, as Rosenow argues, "for the sake of surpassing and transcending the self" (1989: 313). The authentic self-overcoming of the false idea of self-mastery imposed by the political and religious establishment requires constant exertion and a readiness for renunciation and sacrifice. As Simons argues: "Less safety, less mutual protection, less kindness and love, less ease and more contests must be welcomed because of what they would produce. . . . The superman will say YES to life whatever life brings and must exist in the constant pain of battle" (Simons, 1988: 345–346). Why does Nietzsche so urgently take up the task of edifying and enhancing of the human being: the diagnosis of nihilism?

A READING OF NIETZSCHE'S PHILOSOPHICAL
STANCE: NIHILISM, WILL TO POWER AND
RESPONSIVENESS

That we must take a certain sort of responsibility for what we say about the world is roughly what is implied by Nietzsche's saying that "God is dead." Good sense can no longer be made of the idea that the ways in which we view the world are justified by something standing above, beyond or behind the world itself. Instead, it answers to nothing more than historically and psychologically conditioned human needs. Nietzsche teaches us the importance of perspectives: the need to see all concepts and values in context. The idea that the sense one makes of the world is either inherent in the world or imposed on it from the outside is unintelligible. Neither nature, nor reason, nor revelation can provide the moral standards for the governance of life: "The total character of the world . . . is in all eternity chaos" (GS: #109). The human condition generates specific and severe moral or practical imperatives, that is, a radical emancipation of the creative will. At the basis of this position is a tension between the idea that morality is, on the one hand, an artifact of the human will and, on the other hand, an incessant belief that there is a binding ranking order of human desires and ways of life. The form of nihilism that has to be overcome is therefore not so much a matter of replacing old values with new ones as it is coming to value something where previously one valued nothing. Neither is it about taking responsibility for a view of the world and thus opening oneself up to the possibility of different views. The Nietzschean notion of responsibility should be understood differently, in terms of the notion of commitment, an openness to what matters to us.

Although a commitment to truthfulness is in some way definitive of modern life, we nevertheless seek to avoid taking responsibility for that commitment. It is this failure that leads to the specific form of nihilism of indifference with respect to what we have become in the present age.[1] Where Nietzsche claims that we lack a culture, he is therefore not referring to the sense of being untutored in the finer things of life but to a form of life in which sense is made (which for Nietzsche is fundamentally a practical matter). He has set himself the task of making clear both the fact of and the reasons for our failure to speak responsibly. The most fundamental ways in which we grasp the world cannot be understood as forms of interpretations that we project onto that world. Indeed, culture calls for a form of obedience. Nietzsche means to show thus how we resist the meaning that we find in the world. Obedience does not equal slavishness. Mere slavishness does not tend to produce something for whose sake it is worth to live on earth. *Beyond Good and Evil* is clear on this point:

What is essential "in heaven and on earth" seems to be . . . that there should be *obedience* over a long period of time and in a *single* direction: given that, something always develops, and has developed, for whose sake it is worth while to live on earth. (BGE: #188)

Nietzsche holds that we do not choose or otherwise decide what constrains us. The obedience he speaks of is therefore not a kind of interpretation. Tragedy expresses the culture's authority for its members. What is most important for us cannot be grounded either by metaphysics or by science. That what we care most about surpasses our possibilities is the lesson tragedy teaches us. Through it the members of the tragic (Greek) audience were identified with their culture; they were obedient to its authority and let themselves be constrained by it. Only as an aesthetic phenomenon can life thus be "justified," according to Nietzsche (cf. BT: #8). Tragedy and the demand for reasons represent two different kinds of responses to the same basic problem, something Nietzsche calls "suffering." If, following Schopenhauer, we understand this kind of suffering to be nothing more than ordinary human misery, then, we will conclude that Nietzsche means primarily to reject any attempt to do away with that kind of suffering. But this is rather a side effect. It might appear that the problem confronting Nietzsche's Greeks was that they suffered from a lack of reasons. The tragic Greeks suffered from life in the sense that they were open, "responsive," to the authority of their culture. From the (Nietzschean) tragic point of view, I no longer see my culture as standing over against nature, but I am simply obedient to its authority. (I let this or that count as courageous to me). Thus, for Nietzsche the possibility of being mistaken by itself provides no reason to worry about whether one has somehow gone astray from the very beginning; this does not give a reason to distrust one's instincts. That we have no real choice but to apply the concepts in the ways we do is in his view merely a fact about this particular community of speakers and reflects nothing about the way the world is. To make sense cannot be conceived as something that is imposed upon or projected into the world. We simply have no idea what the object of such an imposition could be. The struggle to make sense is the struggle to overcome the resistance to make sense— and tragedy may be seen to function as a tool of such overcoming.

Tragic obedience to the authority of culture is achieved by overcoming, *not* to let things count as they are—that is, how they are described in human practices. Obedience to this kind of constraint is what is meant by "making sense." Being is not something to be explained by the notion of imposition. The character of being, for example, of a table, is just that: being a table. Such an expression refers to the place where interpretations come to an end, that is, the world itself. When we make sense, we let our interpretations come to an end in understanding. We "make sense," we are intelligible, but we do not in a philosophical sense create it. Thus, in our talk about the world, there is no gap between us and the world that is bridged in doing so. Something has the character of being if it exercises constraint or power over us. "Power" is Nietzsche's name for the constraints that making sense exercises on us. These are, according to Nietzsche, psychological in nature. "Will" is his name for a commitment to make sense, and "Will to Power" is a way of talking about the fact that we make sense. Making sense as something that we do (of meaning as something that we impose) can, however, only be spoken of in a psychological, and not in a philosophical, sense. "Will to Knowledge" refers to the commitment to truthfulness. The man of knowledge's commitment to truthfulness is pious, and to the extent that it is, Nietzsche condemns that commitment as nihilistic (i.e., an unwillingness to acknowledge the historical character of that commitment). Overcoming resistance to the historical character of our commitment does not consign the man of knowledge to the view that the modern Will to Knowledge is a historical contingency; rather, it acknowledges that this commitment is a necessity for us.

The intuitive picture behind so-called aestheticist readings of Nietzsche is roughly that we are to transform our lives (make something of ourselves) by realizing that our natures are not discovered but remain to be invented. This idea of self-creation has to be interpreted differently. When Nietzsche talks of giving one's life style, he means that one would overcome resistance to recognizing the particular life one has, properly understanding what we have become. He conceives of human life as a struggle to make sense, that is, a struggle against our unwillingness to let ourselves be intelligible.

Nietzsche's distinction between the individual and the herd is the distinction between a life in which what we have become matters to us and a life in which it does not. The true individual will not speak a different language from that of the herd, but the herd fails to speak. The distinction Nietzsche makes is about the difference between speech and what we might call "mere talk." The individual should, however, not be construed as someone who stands outside her community and speaks a different language. To speak is to be intelligible, to make sense, and intelligibility expresses one's membership in community. We are not to achieve a standpoint outside the present age, but rather to overcome resistance to the perspective that is ours, that is, that of the Will to Knowledge.

Therefore, pity and responsibility are in Nietzsche's eyes incompatible. An ethics whose only permitted motivation for action is a desire to avoid suffering would not have much to recommend it. The morality of pity is hostile to that particular form of the perfection of human life. The person inclined to pity is unable to let someone suffer (i.e., Nietzsche's metaphor for a certain form of reading—a kind of passivity, a capacity for letting someone speak, a capacity for listening). Nietzsche also believes that the pitier's desire to help demeans the sufferer; this implies that it is the independence or separateness of the sufferer to which the morality of pity objects.

By offering a psychological account of notions such as guilt, sin and redemption, Nietzsche tries to undermine the traditional vision of a sharp distinction between human beings and the other animals. He argues that the fact that we feel both responsible for what we do and yet ultimately powerless to do other than we do, that we feel, as it were, victims of ourselves, is a feature of our lives that has a complicated psychological and sociological history. Minimally, Nietzsche's claim is that nothing counts as a promise where nothing counts as anything at all. If speaking is seen as a form of promising, then the point of saying that man must be made calculable, if promising is to be possible, is that no one speaks where there are no similarities between judgments we make. It is in this deeper sense that promising may be said to be a social activity. Thus responsibility, as well as custom, is required for true humanity. In obeying the laws of the community, the individual member is keeping what Nietzsche considers to be a promise, a "pledge," in order to enjoy the advantages of society. To say of someone that she has the right to make promises then means that she speaks intelligibly, that she takes responsibility for what she says. Where on the other hand the community itself fails to make sense, where talking the way the herd does is in fact a failure to speak, the notion of an individual can be understood differently. To give one's word (as the sovereign individual has the right to do) is to incur an obligation to let oneself be understood—that is, an obligation to overcome one's unwillingness to do so, to renounce one's desire to remain opaque.

Nietzsche intimates the possibility of a new relation to the phenomena, a relation in which we have learned to let them be. On the one hand, we accept them in their pristine and unsayable integrity; on the other, we transform them through continually renewed mythic and artistic renderings. Tragedy is for Nietzsche a way to overthrow nihilism by the discovery of the special value of what is near to us, the value of what seemed to be unimportant.

The things around us are wonderful because they are fragile. One can love them, they can become precious and things we care for, because they are not immune from the uncertainties of life. Realizing this, the little things of life can achieve a new significance for us, which may lead furthermore to a better attunement to the world. The latter, however, is not to be taken as similar to "resting in peace," which cannot be reconciled with Nietzsche's idea concerning self-realization and the emancipation of the creative will. It is meant rather to temper the ambitions of reason itself by focusing on its limitations and its presuppositions.

The nihilist despairs because she longs to value something but in good faith cannot, for she believes that only values believed to be objective can in good faith be professed, and the nihilist no longer believes in objective values. To acknowledge certain values as one's own creation indicates a willingness to protect them, to fight for the legitimacy of these values, to sustain their influence in the world, to accept responsibility for the consequences of their influence. The weak lack the will for these difficult tasks and responsibilities. It is Nietzsche's hope that the nihilist will be captivated by the portrayals of human types strong enough to create values without deceiving themselves about the origin of these values and thereby be converted to the Nietzschean perspective. What has ultimate significance is the *creation* of value as different from the *value* of what someone creates.

PSYCHOLOGY AND EDUCATION FROM A NIETZSCHEAN PERSPECTIVE

The positive task of Nietzsche's educational psychological and unmasking method is to assist us in overcoming the repressive culture and to entice us into discovering in, and for ourselves, the genuine roots of our creative powers. Nietzsche does not admit a radical (Freudian) psychological determinism. Instead, he contends that we have the liberty to shape our selfhood and ideals by freely choosing our education and exemplary figures. By subjecting our intuitive admiration for great individuals to psychologistic self-analysis, we come to realize what we value authentically and what we really are. The road of a human being toward authentic freedom and spontaneous creativity (essential to self-overcoming and re-creation) requires two stages: liberating ourselves from the external layers imposed on us by institutional conditionings, and freely adopting and assimilating moral norms. In a blind, automated, Darwinian world, where all our transcendental goals have disappeared, we must create new immanent aims. But this needs to be done according to the basic Nietzschean intuition of complete immanency, as Golomb argues:

There is only one world, one nature and its forces, and there are no transcendental or supra-natural powers: there is no "pure reason," there is no other world, different and better than ours. Hence, everything that belongs to man and his culture—and is related to Nietzsche's moral ideal of the qualitative progress of mankind—must originate from and be explicated exclusively within the human context. (Golomb, 1985: 107)

With this in mind, Nietzsche will expose prevailing pseudo-ideals and false values that are deflecting human effort from its utmost goal.

Along similar lines Williams (1993) claims more in general that there is some measure of agreement that we need a "naturalistic" moral psychology. This means in effect that our view of moral capacities should be consistent with, even perhaps in the spirit of, our understanding of human beings as part of nature. Williams argues that in this matter Nietzsche is helpful as he leads us toward a realistic, rather than a naturalistic, moral psychology: not the application of an already defined scientific program, but rather an informed interpretation of some human experiences and activities in relation to others. He interprets Nietzsche's doubts about action as doubts not about the very idea of anyone doing anything, but rather about a morally significant interpretation of action in terms of the will (understood as something "simple" and as a peculiar, imperative kind of cause). "Willing" has to be conceived as a complex of sensations, thinking and an effect of command. For Nietzsche, morality does not consist of principles but of practices. As Solomon (1986: 80) argues: "It is *doing* not willing that is of moral significance, an expression of character rather than a display of practical reason." Talk of "creating new values" may confuse us because Nietzsche does not reject morals but only one version of morality, which has as its instrument the universalizable principles formalized by Kant.

Nietzsche holds that the child alone can "create new values," and this creation, unlike the creation often attributed to traditional values, is not given to us fixed and finished all at once in a revelation from heaven. The child is "innocence and forgetting." She gives a sacred yes to all existence, for she is beyond resentment of her body and the world which characterized traditional values:

The child is innocence and forgetting, a new beginning, a game, a self-propelled wheel, a first movement, a sacred "Yes". For the game of creation, my brothers, a sacred "Yes" is needed: the spirit now wills his own will and he who had been lost to the world now conquers his own world. (Z: 1, Zarathustra's Speeches)

The values Nietzsche envisages arise out of the creative process itself, involving an ever renewed engagement with the flux of phenomena, with the perpetual birth and death, and new birth of existence. Thus we look for the ways to overcome nihilism which enable us to affirm this world. Not the discovery of a metaphysical truth is aimed at but the restoration of the integrity of the phenomena.

In dealing with Nietzsche's early educational thought, Golomb claims that, although "authenticity" as such does not appear as yet in Nietzsche's writings, the application of this notion does not entail any anachronistic fallacy. This concept does not refer to an external correspondence between sentences and their objects. Neither is it an internal coherence between various statements. It indicates integrity and harmony between the innermost self and its external manifestations. The emphasis is thus shifted to the existential correspondence between the life of a human being and her personality. This existentialist tendency initiated by Nietzsche marks the transformation from truth to truthfulness and from an abstract theoretical concept to existential authenticity. As Golomb argues:

A man is true in the sense of life if he accepts it in all its harshness. If genuine selfhood is repressed and prevented from expressing itself, a deepening alienation develops between the person and his acts; between the person's innermost core and all the social and ideological influences that seek to suppress it. (Golomb, 1985: 100)

To rear great men is, for Nietzsche, the highest task of humankind. Because only education can provide for the growth of genius, it is the highest duty. He himself assumed the task of educating the educators, which is a self-education, that is, a recognition and removal of the streaks of decadence. He holds that all philosophy originated and was carried out in the service of education. True education always entails the active influencing of the soul. The individualistic nature of education is a consequence of the educator's need to express herself selectively, thus structuring the needs of her students. Education is aimed through devotion to bring out the very best in someone. However, it has everything to do with control, eventually with controlling oneself, being the coordinator of one's own instincts as Nietzsche calls this. Thus individualism in education is just the opposite of unrestrained development: "All education begins with the opposite of that which one now praises as academic freedom, with obedience, with subordination, with discipline, with servitude" (GM: #4).

What defines education is not the acquisition of facts or skills or technique, but the transmission of passion and will from teacher to student. What the teacher has to teach simply is not transmissible to a crowd. The educator is to serve as a model for her students, and authority and discipline are considered to be indispensable. Education is not the determination of who the student should be but of how she might become who she and only she is. The true educator celebrates success when her students become worthy of demanding their independence. The disciplined training that allows the student to end her servitude to custom and morality ultimately results in the end of her servitude to higher men. The true educator is she who successfully demonstrates a solitude to her students. She serves as the model of how one may escape herd life and bear one's individuality heroically. Only she who has mastered her solitude is worthy of being an educator, a catalyst in the formation of other solitaries.

A matter of considerable debate has been the so-called anti-social and subjective nature of Nietzschean authenticity. For instance, Rosenow (1973) is skeptical of a Nietzschean education because it is inherently anti-social, but he argues nonetheless for the existence of education on the basis of a "free education" that eliminates the possibility of interpersonal communication and that isolates man. According to Johnston (1998), however, this implies that Rosenow must therefore discount by the same argument the possibility of mutual dialogue between teacher and student, thus leaving self-education as the only appropriate option. That is, if it is given what is historically involved in education, it is at least still appropriate to use "education" for the kind of activity Rosenow has in mind.

Another misappropriation of Nietzsche has been undertaken by authors who, like Bloom, emphasize the Great Books approach, thus, as Johnston argues, offering an aristocratic kind of education. Though Nietzsche would surely agree with a rejection of instrumental reason, he also champions heteronomy, fragmentation and diversity through his perspectival outlook. Again, this does not mean that he is a proponent of an anarchistic education for children. He does value obedience, rigorous study and stern discipline as far as elementary education goes but ultimately rejects the hegemony of the educational-cultural institutions (of higher education) in favor of one's individual self-overcoming for which education is a means. For Nietzsche, however, education as a process does not help a self-overcoming individual to overcome hitherto accepted valuations. It can quite evidently not supply the task of overturning valuations that education itself comprises. A Nietzschean view of education would in the end necessitate a movement away from the social ideal to an individual one, in favor of intrapersonal, intrasubjective and individual values. Such a self-overcoming individual requires something that education ultimately cannot provide: "a moment-to-moment, hour-to-hour, day-to-day self-realization of one's strengths and weaknesses, together with a profound ability to suffer well" (Johnston, 1998: 77). This kind of individual cannot be disseminated but must be self-taught. This is why it is not correct to project onto Nietzsche an aristocratic education for a few rare individuals. Although education performs an important function in terms of the masses (passing on the acceptable values from one generation to the next), for the self-overcoming individual this education, too, has to be overcome. Johnston therefore concludes that there can be no question of a reconciliation between the realms of the individual and the social. One simply has to overcome the social in one's desires in turn to self-overcome. Is Nietzsche (only) making a logical point, and is the latter conclusion not correct then?

A RECENT REFORMULATION: ALTIERI'S EXPRESSIVIST ETHICS

Elements of the Nietzschean stance have recently been taken up by Charles Altieri (1994). The question he focuses on concerns the embeddedness of the subject on the intersubjective level, which at the same time leaves enough room so that one may distance oneself from it and from the self as well. Expressing oneself to earn (see further) an identity depends, as Altieri claims, on the capacity to make the identification (to align one's connative sense with the activity being performed) and the possibility of taking reflective responsibility for that investment or identification. Identification is not simply a matter of attentive investment. It does not lie simply in how one acts but in how one wants to be understood as one cares about the action. The play of investments must be interpreted first in relation to what seems to have shaped the agent's investments in the past and then in terms of how that past can be mediated into a future. Although such mediations involve concepts, they need not subordinate the agency to the categories so implicated. Instead, we have to rely on the expressionist sense of a dialectic between subject and substance so that the claims for identity must be understood as continuous with the actions. Although responsibility is, Altieri argues, necessarily an individual matter, accepting it also deeply implicates the person in a social grammar and in specific dialogical relationships.

The ethical theory Altieri is arguing for will pay particular attention to how concerns for ethical identities provide interest in pursuing moral values. It will produce a thicker "psychological" account of those interests than is common in analytic ethics. And finally, it will argue that we can define self-reflexive moral judgments in terms of how the first person engages others from whom identities are sought, and through that dialogical model it will show why the agent might want to submit itself to impartial third-person criteria for assessing its actions and even its projects. Thus Altieri constructs a path from expressivist psychology to related notions of ethical value that afford agents a coherent and substantial structure for representing their own interests in caring about those values and in following the dictates that this care will produce. He does admit that ultimately ethical reasoning is a circular process, as our interests and our arguments, even our arguments about the need to take impartial attitudes toward specific interests, are deeply implicated in one another. But he continues to indicate that

what obligates us derives from what we take as somehow fulfilling us, and what allows us to seek understanding from others also binds us to the ways of structuring our concerns so that they participate in a common framework. (Altieri, 1994: 156)

Developing his theory, Altieri relies on two metaethical principles. We need to cast our reflections in terms of whether agents' actions can win judgments that they are worthy to be happy, and we need to specify how agents can be said to become candidates for such judgments. Worthiness involves fear, but it also invites relating to idealized figures. He does accept the notion that worthiness does not equate with rightness, but he claims that the possibilities introduced by ideals of worthiness provide a model of motivation that can bring back into ethics the forces shaping the kinds of narcissistic structure, reuniting the ethical with a complex of positive impulses and interests basic to fully civilized lives.

Subjective agency is characterized in such a way that we can understand agents as responding to concerns about worthiness without thereby being seduced into subjection and subordination. Altieri follows Wittgenstein when he writes that what people accept as justification is shown by how they think and live. They are expecting this and surprised at that, but the chain of reasons has an end. We are advised to be satisfied by recognizing that we are on a track allowing us either to rest or to go on without a nagging sense of confusion and contradiction. On the basis of the asymmetry between first- and third-person stances, Altieri treats actions as if their intelligibility depended on the reasons agents might give for them. Because explanations in terms of causes do not seem as feasible, the reasons define the force of agency, and thus Altieri gives a kind of substance to subjectivity. But he also wants to avoid existential relativism, which he does by accepting that ethical decisions stand out against a background of dispositions, habits, practices and social expectations and require a more complex model of self-constitution than we find in existentialism or even in post-structural idealizations of singularity (cf. Altieri, 1994: 161). Taking responsibility for meanings is different from choosing meanings. Instead one chooses among meanings or tries to reconfigure their relation to actions and contexts. In effect, what one does is define oneself by placing oneself anew within a world suffused with meanings. Here the intelligibility of the reasons for an action comes to an end within the parameters of a community's grammars. Consequently, Altieri is ready to accept that insofar as the good depends on how agents are understood rather than being based on universal principles, there will be social groups for whom a person's reasons do not count and whose moral priorities may even be incomprehensible.

Ethical theory should try to characterize what might be a common thread in individual situations and to provide some sense of how agents might make the best use of their powers to develop and exchange ethical concerns. Altieri will try to show that his version of expressivist desires can represent connative drives so that they do not require specific acts of self-ownership at every moment but instead find satisfaction in working toward long-term projects and stability within the practices they engage. The following lengthy quotation makes clear where he stands:

What makes an act expressively "mine" then is not quite consent (nor any reference to some attribute of "me" that one finds objectively in it) but a more general willingness to, or need to, have myself represented by it. And what makes it moral is my willingness to, or need to, have that identity judged not merely as a state to be responded to but as one to be assessed in terms of whether in pursuing it as I do I become worthy to be happy. The scope and depth of any particular appeal to moral identity depends on how much of one's life one wants or needs any particular gesture to carry. Or, to put the same point another way, the scope projected for any one act of identification depends on how many other identifications one wants or needs to subsume within it or give purposive roles through it. To complete the identification, then one must adapt oneself to complex social expectations which derive in part from promises or commitments we make to specific others, and in part from the many cultural grammars for assessment that we learn in adapting ourselves to the multiple practices folded into contemporary life. (Altieri, 1994: 204)

Altieri sees the person in the process of negotiating for an identity with an audience imagined as a tribunal whose understanding, if not whose approval, is necessary for the agent's being confirmed in the substance that the expressive activity seeks. Although the audience can be almost entirely imaginary, to grasp the various roles it plays it is better to envision it as representative of an actual community. He concentrates on how the second-person function contributes to the identification process and thus treats the conferring of identity as a dialogical process responsible to cultural grammars but capable of modifying that grammar to accommodate specific expressive traits. Thus one invokes modes of judgment that not only bring to bear the necessary knowledge and sympathy to assess actions, but also the flexibility to take into account the transformations that the agent might work on the vocabulary shared with the audience. That flexibility also gives, Altieri argues, a useful way to imagine how agents internalize social norms, not as rigid rules or conventions to be manipulated, but as aspects of dialogues by which we both try to invoke approval and work toward personalized identifications with the cultural structures framing our investments. The "you" serves both as constraint that holds one to obligations and as a source of idealization that pulls the agent toward certain versions of its and its audience's "best selves."

In intimate relations, how we perform the action and, even more important, how the doing reveals and extends certain qualities in relationships becomes the central concern. It is not so much that we owe particular considerations to others (as if they had rights to make claims upon us) than that we want certain pleasures for them and certain identities as lovers, friends or parents for ourselves. In this sphere of agent–relative relations, we treat the terms of justification less as an accord with principle than as an attunement to the distinctness one wants to feel and think characterizes one's close relationships. Here obligation proves almost entirely a sense of duty to oneself, a sense of how one can represent oneself to oneself as if one were worthy of certain predicates in the eyes of those with whom one is engaged. Here we monitor ourselves to ask whether or not we are living in accord with what we project as not simply a good life but the best possible ways of maintaining those relationships. This ethics of attunement is content with analogs of the beautiful in which the way one experiences oneself in a range of specific harmonies with others becomes an end in itself.

Parallel to Kant's position on aesthetic judgment, Altieri argues that in moral theory the agent pursues a sociality fundamental to its own self-enjoyment. The agent does not want universal agreement for its own sake but seeks a mode of assessment that will allow it to maintain in the eyes of others, and hence in its own self-representations, the identity of one who bases judgments on internalizing sharable models of assessment. Such an agent must follow third-person procedures, but by positing a second-person basis (for accepting such conditions) one secures that our relation to the procedures takes on considerable flexibility. Moreover, one secures that the procedures need not be grounded in terms of some independent principle. One thus remains responsible to specific determinations of ends, but one also places those determinations within complex discursive frameworks and clear expectations about the actions that must follow to secure the desired identity.

Personal identity is thus connected to accepting certain social procedures, not as imposed but as necessary for certain realizations of ourselves. Indeed, what makes a judgment binding is not the coercive power of the judge but the commitment of the agent. The sense of responsibility that Altieri is proposing redistributes the relation between passive and active basic to re-sponsiveness. Expressivist theory argues that one cannot distribute respon-sibility (as a consent to bear the consequences of particular actions) without a strong sense of the commitments agents assume. Thus responsibility is defined by the consent to the practical consequences deriving from acting in accord with the identities we invest in:

What counts as consequences cannot be fixed abstractly. Instead the relevant con-sequences one accepts are determined by correlating a construction of a particular situation, an agent's specific version of some identity, the culture's grammatical ex-pectations about that identity, and the pressures that exemplars of that and related identities bring to bear on how we both define the situation and develop paths of action. (Altieri, 1994: 220)

Altieri's position can be seen as making use of a particular reading of Nietzsche which does make sense. It could be fruitful in educational contexts as well.

NIETZSCHE'S LEGACY FOR EDUCATION

If education can be conceived as an answer from one individual person to another, particularity, care, integrity and trust are of the utmost impor-tance, and so is what "being authentic" means. Of course, an agent cannot articulate a project concerning who she wants to be without a context of intersubjectivity. Such a project must constitute a particularly illuminating example of what can be done in a certain social predicament. Furthermore, authentic identity presupposes a moment of recognition on the part of an-other. Authentic identity can thus mean pursuing a project in which a willed uniqueness is expressed and the wish is for others to recognize this unique person whom we want to become. The agent is willing to take the risk that her intended identity will not be recognized. Recalling the intersubjective origin of identity, the need for recognition and the intersubjective nature of reflective judgment should dispel the impression that authenticity is yet another restatement of the philosophy of the subject. If the educator is characterized by her willingness to stand for something and simultaneously willing to care for someone, then the philosophy of authenticity, thus conceived, should also help the educator out of the problems that the Enlightenment projects and that some of its critics have pressed on her. While her integrative authenticity should rescue her from despair, it should also correct the possible immobilism occasioned by the interpretation of some postmodernist authors. Here, what we take as somehow fulfilling us, to a certain extent also conceived in a naturalistic way, binds us to the ways of structuring our concerns so that others can participate in a common framework.

Aviram (1991), too, argues that Nietzsche's ideal of man, the Overman, can and should be conceived as an educational ideal in postmodern democratic societies. Nietzsche's hostility toward education can be understood as expressing his battle against all justificatory tendencies based on firm foundations. His warning can be seen as a kind of way to help us overcome our insecurity and the rationalizations this generates. Nietzsche makes it clear that in the things we do, we do not operate in a vacuum of power relations but that these are masked by quasi-arguments. Both making sense and overcoming refer, though not necessarily, to not letting things count as they are. Struggling against our unwillingness to let ourselves be intelligible is a perpetual task. For Nietzsche, that all knowledge presupposes experience and that all experience is individual lies at the basis. But far from being a champion of subjectivism and arbitrariness, it will be clear now that Nietzsche was doing more than simply making a logical point (the subject as the locus of meaning giving). Nietzsche's language is persuasive and necessarily visionary. For education it has a mission that is as lively as ever: In the end, all education transgresses into what is perhaps not correctly expressed by the concept of "self-education."

NOTE

1. This understanding of nihilism is different from Sartre's existentialist version. There the meaninglessness of life in general is recognized, and a distinction is proposed between those who can face up to this fact and those who cannot. For Nietzsche, however, the meaninglessness of our lives refers to *as we now live them*, but he also insists on the possibility of rectifying the situation.

Chapter 7

Nietzsche's New Philosopher:
The Arts and the Self

James Marshall

INTRODUCTION

In *Thus Spake Zarathustra, Beyond Good and Evil* and *On the Genealogy of Morals*, Nietzsche talks of a philosopher who is not the traditional philosopher *worker*, but is instead a radical reformer who puts philosophy to the service of life. This new philosopher is seen as providing a way forward, or a "solution" to what Nietzsche, in his essentially pessimistic assessment of the then existent forms of Western life, saw as the crises of Western civilization. He saw the religious and philosophical underpinnings of Western civilization as being part of the problem, as being Tartuffery, and thus being incapable of offering any solutions. Hence he repeatedly attacks or undermines religion and traditional academic philosophy.

This chapter traces what Nietzsche says about two forms of art and the new philosopher through the above three sources. While there is a pessimistic tone to Nietzsche, the interpretation given to Nietzsche here is not a nihilistic pessimistic account but a life-affirming one.

According to Richard Schacht, Nietzsche eventually

emerged as one of the most controversial, unconventional and important figures in the history of modern philosophy. His influence upon European philosophy in the twentieth century has been profound; and he has belatedly come to receive considerable attention in the English speaking world as well. (Schacht, 1995b: 619)

In his own lifetime, his work was generally ignored, and its later appropriation by Fascists and Nazis no doubt helped in his work being further ignored. An early French revival of Nietzsche's work was Georges Bataille's

1945 book on Nietzsche. This work was immensely influential among French thinkers, and Foucault's introduction to Nietzsche was through Bataille, via Blanchot (Foucault, 1983: 24). But it was probably Deleuze's 1962 book on Nietzsche (translated as Deleuze, 1983) that was the main influence on poststructuralist thought in France. Recent English-speaking texts on Nietzsche tend to be interpretations. This chapter will be an interpretation of Nietzsche, and it will put Nietzschean ideas to service, but it will not claim that these ideas represent fundamental or profound truths. Instead, it will be argued that certain Nietzschean ideas may be helpful, if not important, for understanding the self, the arts and arts education.

Nietzsche was deeply concerned about the underpinnings of Western civilization and culture and the crises that he saw Western civilization as facing. These crises, he believed, were the outcome of the fundamentally flawed underpinnings of Western civilization. Thus he sought continuously to undermine these religious and "philosophical" underpinnings, but he also attempted to provide a way forward for humanity by proposing a radical philosophical alternative to more traditional and academic philosophy. But the interpretations of Nietzsche here are both different in kind and varied within kinds, and the extent to which his "way forward" overcomes a basic and fundamental pessimism is arguable (Young, 1992: 3).

According to Magnus and Higgins (1996a: 3), there are two faces of Nietzsche, recognized by virtually all commentators and critics. Briefly, one face is turned to the past and emanates in an autopsy of the Western cultural heritage; this is a negative *deconstructive* face and one that has been emphasized by his critics. The second face, which is more positive and *constructive*, is turned toward the future, providing suggestions for new forms of Western life. But when this second face is examined further, there seem to be not one but two faces. The first is a reconstructive face that is seen as replacing traditional philosophical answers to the perennial philosophical questions. The second and more interesting face, which has influenced among others both Heidegger and Foucault, was that of a cultural physician (cf. Wittgenstein). Here there is an attempt to liberate us in a therapeutic manner from the need to ask, pursue and theorize about the traditional and perennial philosophical questions. This is a notion of philosophy as therapy that has not only influenced both Heidegger and Foucault through Nietzsche, but is also to be found in the later Wittgenstein. The interpretation given here will be in the second vein but qualified as to the extent to which his new philosophy is liberating.

In reading Nietzsche as a positive reconstructionist then, there are differences of opinion between scholars. In the first reconstructive face, Nietzsche is seen as contributing to the ongoing tradition of "the metaphysics of presence" (a metaphysics privileging substance or what is, a mind/body dualism, and a logocentric emphasis on the epistemic priority of a meaning-endowing subject). This tradition has become part of modern philosophy from, at the

least, Descartes and Kant. Others, in the second face version, see the negative and destructive side of Nietzsche as already being constructive, as in,
for example, Wittgenstein, who said (1953: #123): "A philosophical problem has the form: 'I don't know my way about.' " On this interpretation of
philosophy as therapy which can be traced at least to the ancient Greeks
and, more recently, to Hume, philosophy is therapeutic and calms, diverts
or rejects a great majority of the perennial philosophical questions and answers. For Wittgenstein traditional (academic) philosophy asks the wrong
questions and provides misleading theoretical answers to them because, mis-
taking the apparent form of a proposition for its proper logical form by
reference to its grammar, we end in a series of perennial puzzles. These
puzzles are caused because language has gone on holiday. The therapy then
is for the self not to be misled by such questions; it is not to attempt to
solve them by pursuing academic philosophy, for that may only lead to great
anxiety for the self. (See the instability and anguish which arose for Bertrand
Russell in his early work on logic and mathematics, recorded in his autobiography [Russell, 1967: 152] and discussed by Monk [1996, e.g., 158–
159]).

THE INFLUENCE OF SCHOPENHAUER

Nietzsche was strongly influenced by and heavily indebted to Schopenhauer's (1816) *The World as Will and Representation* (W1). Thus Chris-
topher Janaway (1989: 342) says that Nietzsche's most radical views can be
traced to Schopenhauer's conception of the subject as both willing and
knowing. Yet Gilles Deleuze (1983: ix) claims that Nietzsche has "hardly
any predecessors" and recognized only one—Spinoza. Julian Young claims
that "Nietzsche *breathed* Schopenhauer and cannot be understood without
him" (Young, 1992: 4). Russell (1946: 788) says that, while Nietzsche is
the successor of Schopenhauer, he was superior to Schopenhauer, especially
in the consistency and coherence of his thought. This handful of differing
assessments of the relationships between the philosophies of Schopenhauer
and Nietzsche illustrates the problems associated with reading Nietzsche
(and of course Schopenhauer).

It was early in his professional life that Nietzsche published the essay
"Schopenhauer as Educator" in which he extols Schopenhauer at the expense of various university professors of philosophy and praises Schopenhauer for his individuality—"a philosophical loner" (Magnus and Higgins,
1996: 27). Schopenhauer might therefore be used as a model for developing
one's own individuality (see, e.g., Wittgenstein, 1961, 1963). But what Nietzsche adopted from Schopenhauer was not adopted uncritically, and in his
later writings he appeared to have moved on and away from Schopenhauer,
proclaiming his metaphysics to be false and his writing to be not only pessimistic but decadent. In spite of this "rejection," Nietzsche remains deeply

indebted to Schopenhauer, and Schopenhauer is central to understanding his work.

A common view of Nietzsche is that he comes to abandon the Schopenhauerean pessimism that permeates *The Birth of Tragedy* and to adopt a much more positive approach to life and culture. That is to interpret him as a positivist reconstructivist. However, the extent to which Nietzsche abandons his earlier pessimism is not clear. Is his positive way forward merely a way of ameliorating the fundamentally impossible situation in which humans find themselves (according to Schopenhauer), or is it a way of liberating the self from those conditions?

Schopenhauer's account of the self is important for understanding his account of art, for that account depends on his notion of the self. But Nietzsche is highly critical of this account of self (which also influenced Wittgenstein's account of the self in the *Notebooks* [1961] and the *Tractatus* [1963]) Thus a central criticism by Nietzsche of Schopenhauer's metaphysics is that the self remains a riddle, an "it," to which Schopenhauer can only offer a guess—the will. The "I" as a thing in itself is indefensible, according to Nietzsche, and cannot be predicated with the attributes that Schopenhauer wishes to attach to the will because

A totally obscure, inconceivable x is draped with predicates, as with bright coloured clothes which are taken from a world alien to it, the world of appearance. Then the demand is that we should regard the surrounding clothes, that is the predicates, as the thing itself. (Quoted in Janaway, 1989: 343)

In *The Birth of Tragedy* Nietzsche introduces Schopenhauer's distinction between the knowing subject as the eye, or pure representing subject, and the self as will (BT: #1). (This is done through the distinction between the Apollonian and the Dionysian.) This distinction is to be found in *The World as Will and Representation*, Vol. 1 (W1—Schopenhauer, 1969) Briefly, the world as experienced and as given in sense perception is the world as we know it, and not the *real* world. (To this extent Schopenhauer is Kantian, maintaining the idealistic distinction between the world of appearance and the real world.) It is a creation of the mind, a representation to the *eye*, an appearance, and it is not the underlying Kantian world of "things in themselves." In similar fashion to Berkeley, individual things would not exist without an experiencing subject (Janaway, 1994: 24). But what is this experiencing or knowing subject, this "eye" or subject of representation? Is it the self?

The answer for Schopenhauer is "no" because, as the subject of representation, it is not itself experienced in the world of representation. It is certainly not a Cartesian substance; nor is it an individuated self, for it is at best an eye. There is then a problem about the self (cf. Wittgenstein's *Note-*

books and *Tractatus*). Schopenhauer's answer to this problem is his account of the *will*:

the answer to the riddle is given to the subject of knowledge appearing as an individual, and this answer is given in the word *will*. This and this alone gives him the key to his own phenomenon . . . shows him the inner mechanism of his being. (W1, 100)

The subject of knowing appears as an individual self only through a relationship with a body, but, Schopenhauer argues, this body is known in two ways: as an object among objects given in perception and as "what is known immediately to everyone" (ibid.). What is known when my body moves is not only what I know when I see another body move—an event that merely *happens* and that I *observe*—because I am aware that movements of my body are expressions of my will. This is an anti-dualist account of will, for "the act of will and the action of the body are not two different states objectively known . . . but are one and the same thing, though given in two entirely different ways" (ibid.). "My body and my will are one" (W1: 100). For individuals, then, the self as "thing-in-itself" or ultimate reality is the will.

But Schopenhauer talks also of the World as Will, characterizing the ultimate reality of the world as being "the" Will. This *extension* of the concept or notion of will from sentient human beings to a world force, and the ultimate reality of nature, is at first sight strange, if not peculiar, and certainly questionable philosophically. Schopenhauer is well aware of the problems associated with his extension of the use of the term (W1: 111), but he supports this move by two main arguments (Young, 1992: 6; cf. Janaway, 1994: 29). The first argument stems from a perceived atomistic account of science to the effect that it is unable to account in general terms for the hidden essence of the phenomena, which it "explains." Therefore, there is need, Schopenhauer argues, not only for some underlying general "explanations" but, also for an underlying general theory that makes all "forces" in nature *homogeneous*. Again, this argument is questionable. The second argument is an analogical (or conceptual argument) in which he accepts that "will" has application to sentient beings. However, he extends its use by analogy from humans' desiring, hoping, suffering, and so on, to such examples as magnets turning toward the pole(s) and striving "for ever closer union with the earth" (Young, ibid.).

The will, however, uses its organs to control the world for itself and in order to live. It perceives objects, evaluates them and uses them for its purposes. Objects are thus perceived not only in space and time but also in relations of cause and effect and their uses. Because we are continuously striving, directed by the will to life, we relentlessly appropriate objects, which carries with it the possibility of everlasting suffering. According to Schopenhauer, there is a form of penal servitude associated with willing, which is dispersed only "where everything which moves our will and shakes it so mightily is no more" (W1: 196). Thus while we are the subject of willing, we cannot attain happiness or peace. Only if we cease to will can objects be stripped of these relations and possibly be known as they really are, as "things in themselves," and peace and happiness attained. Schopenhauer believed that this was possible in the case of aesthetic objects.

His view is that artists and others can gain experience of things as they really are, if only fleetingly. This requires for Schopenhauer a questionable merging of Platonic ideas and the Kantian notion of a thing in itself. Things in themselves are *unknowable* and cannot be objects of representation. But Platonic ideas exist in objects and to this extent are knowable.

But the knowledge which is attained by artists may be of two kinds, according to how Schopenhauer is to be interpreted. First, it may be directly of the Platonic universal idea—say, of the species *horse* in a particular horse in a painting. Or it may be indirectly, as the notion of a horse as depicted by the artist in a painting may be a representation by the artist of the universal *idea* of horse. So it is not the idea of horse that is perceived, but the particular horse is perceived and represented as the idea of horse (Young, 1992: 15). Either way, as Janaway comments, this running together of Plato and Kant, and the subsequent collapsing of the exclusivity of the Kantian categories of thing-in-itself and object, causes some strain (1994: 61).

By no longer considering the relations of place, time, causality and the uses to which an object can be put, we can consider the *what* of an object (W1: 178–179). This involves collapsing the distance between perceiver and perception so that what is known is no longer the individual thing but the Idea. At the same time, the self "has lost himself, he is *pure* will-less, painless, timeless *subject of knowledge*" (ibid.). To gain knowledge of the universal idea is then to lose the self of this world and thereby gain access to peace and happiness. This can be attained, Schopenhauer claims, in aesthetic experiences, for whenever we have an aesthetic experience we cease our endless willing. Divested of the metaphysics and in more prosaic terms, the arts can be seen as involving both knowledge and a "time out" from the relentless pressures and stress of modern life.

This account of the self and its accompanying metaphysics is criticized by Nietzsche, as we have seen above. According to Young (1992: 25), however, Schopenhauer is "the figure of greatest importance" for *The Birth of Tragedy*, in spite of his acknowledgment that there is considerable controversy over Schopenhauer's influence on that work. But, according to Young, the controversy is essentially over the extent to which Nietzsche endorses Schopenhauer's pessimism, and not over Nietzsche's incorporation of substantial elements of Schopenhauer's theory of art.

Nietzsche uses Schopenhauer's metaphysics in *The Birth of Tragedy* in his introduction of the two great gods of Greek tragedy, Apollo and Dionysus. The distinction between the Apollonian and the Dionysian plays an important role in Nietzsche's writing. According to Nietzsche, the Greeks were well aware that life could be inexplicable, dangerous and at times terrible, but this awareness did not result in an overpowering form of pessimism and a turning of their backs upon life, as in the case of Schopenhauer. Rather, they attempted to transcend this terrible world by transmuting it (and the life of human beings) through art (Coppleston, 1965: 171). On this interpretation of *The Birth of Tragedy*, Young says:

the Greeks were nevertheless able to survive and even thrive, psychologically speaking, through the effect of their art—through more specifically, the effects of their two types of art, Apollonian and Dionysian art. (Young, 1992: 30)

THE BIRTH OF TRAGEDY

It is an overcoming of the pessimism thesis that I shall adopt as my reading of *The Birth of Tragedy* and Nietzsche. Nietzsche (and Foucault following him) is concerned about the present. Nietzsche's early attacks on historical scholarship included the rejection of the present by historians for a pursuit of knowledge for its own sake, thus treating the present as but an episode in an unfolding chain of events, and thereby stifling joy and creativity (Magnus and Higgins, 1996b: 26). Hence for him, in the overcoming of pessimism, art is to be used to ameliorate or overcome the present. Thus the ways in which the Greeks grappled with pessimism, and their "solution," are important for us now.

Nietzsche opens by contrasting Apollonian and Dionysian art with (plastic) sculpture/(non-plastic) music, and dreams and drunkenness. Apollo, as the metaphysical counterpart of the Schopenhauerean eye, is, in *The Birth of Tragedy*, the god of all plastic energies and the soothsayer, the "shining one," a god of restraint, of freedom from the wilder emotions, and a god of philosophical calm. Here Nietzsche quotes from Schopenhauer on the man wrapped in the veil of Maya (W1: 352f.): this is the notion of a man swept by tempests in a small boat at sea, yet supported by his principles. In that case, Nietzsche argues, it is the way in which the individual knows things as phenomena, and knows his ephemeral person, his extensionless present and his momentary satisfaction. That alone has reality for him, and he does all to maintain this reality, so long as his eyes are not opened to *better knowledge*.

Yet, Nietzsche suggests, Schopenhauer has depicted for us a terrible awe that seizes us when man is suddenly bereft of reason to account for some phenomenon or phenomena. If we add to this the blissful awe that arises at the inability, if not the collapse, of reason, we gain insight into the Dionysian. The closest analogy is provided by the influence of drunkenness (BT: #1): it is a sense of frenzy or ecstasy or rapture in which one realizes that reality is a unity, a one, and not composed of individual objects individuated in space and time (BT, #1). In effect, this unity is the Schopenhauerean world of will—not that of individuals but the universal will (BT: #17). Essentially then, Nietzsche is introducing, under the guises of Apollo and Dionysus, the notions from Schopenhauer of the self as a pure representing subject and of the self as will. This is the central dichotomy of *The Birth of Tragedy* and a dichotomy some vestige of which Nietzsche never gave up (Janaway, 1989: 345).

However, there is no *necessary* connection between the Apollonian world as representation and the beautiful. The world as experienced is not obviously beautiful, for we experience ugly and cruel things. But for Nietzsche, adopting Schopenhauer's notion of "Platonic" ideas, the world as experienced by the Apollonian artist is not the everyday world as experienced, but a world that is mediated and raised to the form of the ideal. So there is a "move," as in Schopenhauer's account of aesthetic experience, from the world as perceived to an idealization of an aesthetic and beautiful world (Young, 1992: 32f). As in Schopenhauer, this "move" is highly questionable. Nietzsche also uses a dream metaphor to capture the simplicity and pleasurable aspects of aesthetic experience (BT: #1). This metaphor is to be contrasted sharply with the metaphors of the Dionysian world.

The artistic for the Dionysian bursts forth from nature itself and does not require the mediation of the human artist (in contrast to the Apollonian, BT: #2). But every artist is an imitator according to Nietzsche: the Apollonian of dreams and the Dionysian of ecstasies. He goes on to talk of the Dionysian festivals as involving a return to or a communing with nature, the overthrowing of Apollo and reason, and a return to nature and to the frenzy and daring of the world. Thus:

Under the charm of the Dionysian not only is the union between man and man reaffirmed, but Nature which has become alienated, hostile, or subjugated, celebrates once more her reconciliation with her lost son, man. Freely, earth offers her gifts, and peacefully the beasts of prey of the rocks and desert approach. The chariot of Dionysus is bedecked with flowers and garlands; panthers and tigers walk under its yoke. (BT: #1)

These two "approaches" are to be considered as artistic energies:

as energies which burst forth from nature herself without the mediation of the human artist—energies in which nature's art-impulses are satisfied in the most immediate and direct way—first in the image world of dreams . . . and then as drunken reality. (BT: #1)

Young (1992) argues that in *The Birth of Tragedy* there is a necessary independence between these two notions for the Greeks. This is because Nietzsche also recognizes a dark side to the Dionysian attitude. There is a dual nature. On the one hand, there is "the charm of the Dionysian," but there is also "a horrible witches brew" of "cruelty and sensuality" (BT: #2), for there is no reason why the Schopenhauerean self should act benevolently and morally. It *may* do so, but it may also act cruelly and barbarically (Young, 1992: 34). To this extent, the Dionysian needs to be tempered with the cooler, more rational and more majestic forms and attitudes of the Apollonian. This cruel and barbaric aspect must be reined in. But in art Nietzsche says the Apollonian lies, for it, too, has a barbaric aspect. Thus in great art the Greeks hid the barbaric side of their representations behind such things as the majesty or greatness of what is represented. There is a divorce between beauty and context, and thus it is possible in Apollonian art for the beautiful and the barbaric to coexist.

Young argues that in *The Birth of Tragedy* the Apollonian approach to art cannot be a solution to pessimism and that Nietzsche must be read as endorsing the Dionysian "as offering the best solution to the suffering of life" (Young, 1992: 48). But this reading is at considerable expense because it leaves us with a pessimistic account of human life, inasmuch as it requires one to identify with human being in general, with the world-will, and to deny the self (certainly not a position that is to be held by Foucault on the self). Thus escape from pessimism in the present, in intoxication with Dionysian art, is itself a pessimistic view of human life, according to Young. Indeed the very need for intoxication is itself a pessimistic view of human experience.

Schopenhauer and Nietzsche draw a distinction between music and the other arts. According to Young (1992: 35), music can attain the fullest Dionysian dimension because, unlike the other arts, which are copies or representations of phenomena, music can be an *immediate* copy of the will itself.

THE NEW PHILOSOPHER

If Young's pessimistic interpretation of art and human experience in *The Birth of Tragedy* is correct, and if Nietzsche's major comments on art are to be found there, it is not all that Nietzsche said. Nor is it necessarily the case that his legacy to us is a life-denying account of art and human experience. A more life-affirming account of art and human experience can be discerned from his other discussions of the Apollonian and the Dionysian. In particular we will now turn to *Thus Spake Zarathustra* and *Beyond Good and Evil* to consider his remarks on the new philosopher and the new philosopher as *educator*. Nietzsche has much to say on the role of the educator and the role of the new philosopher, and to have spent so much effort on such matters hardly seems compatible with a life-denying account of human experience. It is, however, compatible with a pessimistic view of *present* experience. Let us then turn to these two works and see how this life-affirming account can be developed.

THUS SPAKE ZARATHUSTRA: A BOOK FOR ALL AND NONE

According to Magnus and Higgins (1996b: 39), *Zarathustra* is "the work least popular among philosophers, at least in the Anglo-American tradition," though "probably his most famous work." It depends on a fictional form and on rhetoric. For example, there is a narrative biographical story about Zarathustra and his wanderings; the aphorism "Thus spake Zarathustra" ends many of the sections; and there are protracted philosophical speeches, which seem to be asides from the plot. According to Kaufmann, *Zarathustra* was Nietzsche's first attempt to enunciate his philosophy but

he still did not proceed systematically . . . it is less philosophic than ever. Rhapsody, satire and epigram predominate; but Nietzsche's mature thought is clouded and shrouded by an excess of adolescent emotion. Nevertheless . . . the book is full of fascinating ideas. (Kaufmann, 1976: 12)

Even Kaufmann seems to have problems, philosophically, with *Zarathustra*!

According to Heidegger, Zarathustra teaches the reader "by showing" (Magnus and Higgins, 1996b: 41). Magnus and Higgins suggest that *Zarathustra* stands in a tradition whereby an individual's development (in this case Zarathustra's development) toward spiritual maturity is chronicled. Zarathustra can be seen, in his talking "at" or instructing the crowds and herd, in his conversations with possible companions—the higher men—and in his periods of reflection as being not merely a critic of modern life, of culture and of fellow human beings. Instead he should be seen as someone who is grappling with the collapse of values as a consequence of the death of God and with nihilism generally. For Nietzsche there is no clear place for human beings in the world unless they "reunite" with the world.

The claim to be advanced here is that Zarathustra represents in his wanderings, including his descents and ascents of the mountain, and in his teachings, aspects of the Apollonian and Dionysian attitudes identified above. It is not just the message of *The Birth of Tragedy* that art can provide a way "out" of pessimism and provide a deep cognitive understanding. It is more than that, for just as the Apollonian and Dionysian attitudes are important in art and understanding art, so also are they important in living and in understanding human experience.

First, Zarathustra is a teacher, but a new type of teacher; second, he is a philosopher, but a new type of philosopher. In *Zarathustra* (Part I, #1–2), it is clear that Zarathustra is an educator who needs, and is expecting, hands outstretched to accept his wisdom, for he is "bringing gifts unto man" and not mere alms. The major initial message is that God is dead. At the nearest town after he descends the mountain, Zarathustra speaks to the assembled crowd, but he is entirely misunderstood. They take him to be a busker for a circus and his philosophical speech to be an introduction to a performance by a tightrope walker. In a speech that introduces the *Übermensch*, or Overman, as an ideal for humanity, Zarathustra is attempting to pass on his insights to the assembled crowd (Part I, #3): "I teach you the overman. Man is something that shall be overcome. What have you done to overcome him?" But he fails to teach the crowd, and, as one says: "Now we have heard enough about the tightrope walker: now let us see him too!" Zarathustra fails because of a problem between the language and concepts of the potentially new philosopher (i.e., Zarathustra) and those of common sense and the crowd. Nietzsche discusses this more fully in *Beyond Good and Evil*, and the *Übermensch* is rarely mentioned in *Zarathustra* after Part I.

But what does this opening speech by Zarathustra "teach" us, the readers, about the Overman? He continues:

Let your will say: The Overman *shall be* the meaning of the earth! . . . I beseech you my brothers, *remain faithful to the earth*, and do not believe those who speak to you of otherworldly hopes! Poison mixers are they, whether they know it or not. Despisers of life are they, decaying and poisoned themselves, of whom the earth is weary: so let them go. (Part I, #3)

The relationship of the Overman to the earth is emphasized immediately (Part I, #3,) in an attack upon souls and God, and any notions of a future world. Because God is dead: "To sin against the earth is now the most dreadful thing, and to esteem the entrails of the unknowable higher than the meaning of the earth!"

Then he moves to reinstate the body over the unknowable soul (ibid.), for the body is to be the ground of all meaning and knowledge:

Once the soul looked contemptuously on the body, and then this contempt was the highest:—she wanted the body meagre, ghastly and starved. Thus she hoped to escape it and the earth. . . . what doth your body proclaim of your soul? Is not your soul poverty and filth and wretched contentment . . . Verily a polluted stream is man. One must be a sea, to be able to receive a polluted stream without becoming unclean. . . . the overman: he is this sea; in him your great contempt can go under. (Part I, #3)

In a repeated emphasis on the earth and the body, Nietzsche introduces the notion of Dionysian frenzy:

Where is the lightning to lick you with its tongue? Where is the frenzy with which you should be inoculated? Behold I teach you the Overman: he is this lightning, he is this frenzy. (Part I, #3)

And later (Part I, #5): "I tell you: one must still have the chaos in one, to give birth to a dancing star. I tell you: ye still have chaos in you."

This seems to indicate a stronger point on the role of the Dionsyian in considerations of the self, and hence of art, than the conclusion reached at the end of the discussion of *The Birth of Tragedy*. As the crowd demands that the rope walker commence his act, Zarathustra speaks again about man as a rope stretched over the abyss between man and the Overman (Part I, #4). Man must walk the rope. But Zarathustra in extolling the Overman makes it very clear that he is only the herald of the lightning, or the Overman.

When the rope walker falls and is dying, Zarathustra says to him: "You have made danger your vocation; there is nothing contemptible in that. Now you perish of your vocation: for that I will bury you with mine own hands." (Part I, #6). The importance to Nietzsche here of living a life of challenge and danger is clear from his use of the rope walker example and the metaphor of man, rope and abyss. The Overman must be willing to risk all in the service of humanity. He must, it would almost seem, be Dionysian.

After his initial speech to the crowd awaiting the rope walker, however, Zarathustra realizes that he has not communicated with them: "they do not understand me; I am not the mouth for these ears . . . do they believe only the stammerer" (Part I, #5: 128). Nietzsche sees this as a pedagogical problem, as the story shows us. His solution, which ends the Prologue, is not to speak to the people or the herd. Rather, he will seek *companions* who will understand him, for Zarathustra "shall not become the shepherd and the dog of a herd" for he must now "lure many away from the herd" and find fellow-creators (Part I, #9: 135).

There is not much more said about the Overman in *Zarathustra*, but he is contrasted with the last man and the higher man. These are examples of the companions that Zarathustra seeks to lure away from the herd. The last man is Apollonian, tied down by a lack of desire, seeking security, comfort and happiness. Then there are the higher men, Apollonian in that they adopt aspects of Zarathustra's teachings but in fundamental and differing ways between one another, thus distorting Zararthustra's more holistic perspective. If for Zarathustra the "way out" was to return to the earth, to a drunken frenzy and to laughter in a parody of the Last Supper and of Plato's cave, he realizes that they do not possess the Dionysian spirit, and they have not understood him. (To a certain extent they epitomize the fundamental differences that arise between academic philosophers in relation to perennial philosophical problems.)

They still sleep, these higher men, whilst I am awake: these are not my proper companions! It is not for them that I wait here in my mountains . . . I want to go to my work, to my day but they do not understand the signs of my morning; my stride is for them no summons to awaken. They still sleep in my cave . . . the heedful ear is lacking in their limbs. (Part IV, #The Sign)

Zarathustra sets off down the mountain again. What is clear is that he could not talk to the herd, nor does he find his companions in the higher men. "Fellow suffering with the higher men! . . . Well! That—hath had its time!" What he still lacks is a pedagogy for man to bridge the abyss from animal to Overman. He is not the Overman, but only the herald, and he does not have a pedagogy in Zarathustra. But as the ugliest man says to Zarathustra in the cave:

But one thing I do know,—it was from you that I learned it once, O Zarathustra: whoever would kill most thoroughly, laughs. "Not by wrath does one kill, but by laughter"—thus you once spoke, O Zarathustra, you hidden one, you annihilator without wrath, you dangerous saint,—you are a rogue! (Part IV, The Ass Festival, #1)

BEYOND GOOD AND EVIL

According to Nietzsche, *Beyond Good and Evil* says "the same things as my *Zarathustra*, but differently, very differently" (Letter to Jacob Burckhardt, quoted in Kaufmann's 1966 preface to *Beyond Good and Evil*). Certainly *Beyond Good and Evil* pursues the theme of a new philosopher and a new philosophy: "I insist that people should stop confounding philosophical labourers, and scientific men generally, with philosophers; precisely at this point we should be strict about giving 'each his due.' " But whereas in *Zarathustra* there seems to be a balancing between the Apollonian and the Dionysian spirits, in *Beyond Good and Evil* he is trying to go *beyond* such polarized and binary categories. The title uses the word "Beyond" and it is subtitled "Prelude to a Philosophy of the Future."

Nietzsche begins by attacking the very notion of truth—"Supposing truth is a woman—what then" (BGE: Preface). "Suppose we want truth," he continues; *"why not rather* untruth?"* In other words, philosophers assume that truth is valuable, without systematically pursuing that fundamental question, and they dogmatically provide a number of answers. Indeed, Nietzsche sees every great philosophy so far as:

the personal confession of its author and a kind of involuntary and unconscious memoir; also that the moral (or immoral) intentions in every philosophy constituted the real germ of life from which the whole plant has grown . . . for every drive wants to be master—and it attempts to philosophise in that spirit. (BGE: #6)

Thus Nietzsche is casting doubt on the intentions and motives of philosophers and on their claims to have arrived at objective conclusions.

Instead Nietzsche proposes a new approach to philosophy based on a "proper" physiopsychology:

All psychology so far has got stuck in moral prejudices and fears; it has not dared to descend into the depths. To understand it as morphology and *the doctrine of the development of the will to power*, as I do—nobody has yet come close to doing this even in thought . . . The power of moral prejudices has penetrated deeply into the most spiritual world . . . and has obviously operated in an injurious, inhibiting, blinding and distorting manner. (BGE: #23)

Nietzsche makes the point that such a physiopsychology must take account of hatred, envy, covetousness and the lust to rule as conditions of life, that is, as factors that must be present in any attempt to ground this new philosophy in an economy of life (BGE: #23). This naturalistic turn, however, "reproduces in naturalistic terms the original opposition between Apollo and Dionysus" (Conway, 1995: 32). This is therefore an important move by Nietzsche (see below).

But the new philosopher is not be an academic philosopher or, as Nietzsche calls him, a philosophical laborer or scientist (BGE: #211). In Part Six of *Beyond Good and Evil* he is scathing of accepted notions of the scholar and scientist: of "the self glorification and self exaltation of scholars" (BGE: #204); science now aims "to lay down laws for philosophy and to play the 'master' herself" (ibid.): "those hodgepodge philosophers who call themselves philosophers of reality . . . they are all losers who have been brought back under the hegemony of science" (ibid.), or "positivists." Nietzsche is therefore concerned about the dangers of the development of a philosopher, who is seen as living wisely and prudently. But the genuine philosopher will live unwisely, imprudently and "unphilosophically," for "he risks himself constantly" (BGE: #205). This is similar to the account of the tightrope walker and the metaphor of the rope across the abyss of life in *Zarathustra*.

Nietzsche returns to the pedagogical problem that in *Zarathustra* seemed incapable of resolution—Zarathustra's inability to communicate with the herd. But now:

I insist that people should finally stop confounding philosophical labourers, and scientific men generally, with philosophers . . . It may be necessary for the education of a genuine philosopher that he himself has also once stood on all these steps on which his servants, the scientific labourers of philosophy, remain standing—*have* to remain standing. Perhaps he himself must have been critic and sceptic and dogmatist and historian and also poet and collector and traveller and solver of riddles and moralist and seer and "free spirit" and almost everything in order to pass through the whole range of human values and value feelings and to be *able* to see with many different eyes and consciences, from a height and into every expanse. But all these are merely preconditions of his task: this task itself demands something different—it demands that he *create* values. (BGE: #211)

Nietzsche immediately classifies Kant and Hegel as philosophical laborers. He sees them as positing values and truths that were for a time called "truths," making them easy to think over and to *overcome* the entire past. But in so doing they differ from genuine philosophers, for they are "commanders and legislators: they say, 'thus it shall be' . . . their knowing is *creating*, their creating is a legislation, their will to truth is—*will to power*."

The new philosopher, being of necessity a man of tomorrow, had to find himself in contradiction with the present: "his enemy was the ideal of today." They were "the bad conscience of their time" (BGE: #212). But what a philosopher *is* is hard to learn because it cannot be taught, as "one must 'know' it from experience," as "all popular opinions about them are false" (BGE: #213). Indeed, artists are said "to have more sensitive noses in these matters" when they seem to do everything of "necessity" from the Dionysian forces welling up inside them. This seems to be a different position from *Zarathustra*, where Nietzsche talks of a balance between the Apollonian and the Dionysian forces in relation to the artist. Here it is more as if the Dionysian spirit is necessary for the new philosopher to "emerge" or develop. But if the Dionysian and Apollonian metaphors are not so explicit or prominent in Nietzsche's works after *The Birth of Tragedy*, there is a reincarnated or transformed version of Dionysus (Conway, 1955: 2). This, with its talk of the artist and the necessities welling up inside the artist, ready to erupt and burst forth, seems to place a higher emphasis on the Dionysian than Nietzsche did in *Zarathustra*.

Nietzsche has another attempt at "the philosopher," who is said to be:

A human being who constantly experiences, sees, hears, suspects, hopes, and dreams extraordinary things: who is struck by his own thoughts as from outside, as from above and below, as by *his* type of experiences and lightning bolts: who is perhaps himself a storm pregnant with new rumblings: a fatal human being around whom there are constant rumblings and growlings, crevices and uncanny things. A philosopher—alas, a being that often runs away from itself, often is afraid of itself—but too inquisitive not to "come to" again—always back to itself. (BGE: #292)

CONCLUSION

A number of educational issues remain unresolved: the nature of the self and the new philosopher; the education of the new philosopher; and the form of pedagogy for the new philosopher to communicate with the herd. We will address them in that order.

As both Janaway and Young point out, Nietzsche did not abandon Schopenhauer's metaphysics concerning the self. They were necessary for his account of art as the Apollonian/Dionysian distinction mirrors the notions of the world as representation and the world as will. On the latter Schopenhauer held an anti-dualist position to the effect that there were not two "things" when the body moved—will and movement—but only one as will *was* movement. This is retained by Nietzsche (e.g., BGE: #213), as the self essentially was the willing body and not the mysterious "I" (eye) of representation.

Nietzsche's contribution here is to ground the self in what he calls a proper physiopsychology (BGE: #23). In *Zarathustra* such a self must reunite with animals and the earth (Part IV, et passim). Thus the forces of the earth which erupt, bubble and destroy can be seen as similar, if not "causes" of the Dionysian forces that erupt in the artist, who possibly is more sensitive than other humans to such matters. But as these eruptions are controlled by stable forces, the Apollonian/Dionysian distinction is raised again in relation to this physiopsychological nature of human beings. It is clear, however, that if we are to go beyond good and evil, then the new philosopher must be more Dionysian than in the account of art in *The Birth of Tragedy*. It is no longer a question of some balance between the two but of going beyond, not of balancing old values (Apollo and Dionysus in *The Birth of Tragedy*) but of creating new ones, not of legislating on old values but of legislating *new* values.

But where does this new philosopher come from? Who is to educate the new philosopher? If Nietzsche is serious (BGE: #211) that the new philosopher must have stood among the herd and come up "all those steps on which his servants, the scientific labourers of philosophy, remain standing," then it is difficult to see how one emerges from the herd. The new philosopher is "a man of tomorrow" and must find himself "in contradiction to his today" (BGE: #212). He must be "the bad conscience of their time." Nietzsche continues:

He shall be greatest who can be loneliest, the most concealed, the most deviant, the human being beyond good and evil, the master of his virtues, he that is over rich in will. Precisely this shall be called greatness: being capable of being as manifold as a whole, as ample as full. (BGE: #212)

But this cannot be taught, and it must be known from experience (BGE: #213). All popular opinions about them are false, and artists seem to have a more sensitive nose on such matters, as "necessity" and "freedom of the will" then become one in them (cf. Schopenhauer).

From *Zarathustra* and *Beyond Good and Evil* the form of pedagogy is reasonably clear. The new philosopher must communicate with the herd and not shift concepts and values too markedly. Otherwise they will not be understood, as in the case of Zarathustra being taken as a circus busker. In order to communicate with the herd, the new philosopher must stand on all those steps below, but he must insert new ideas and values—not a new philosophical problem for those like Heidegger and Dewey who have tried to shift thought, understanding and experience in a language that is common and shared, and in which marked shifts in the meaning of concepts might not be, or are not always, understood. Here Dewey's concept of experience is an excellent example. Nietzsche realizes the pedagogical problem but does not offer a solution here.

Finally, it would seem then that Nietzsche can be interpreted in Magnus and Higgins' terminology not only as a positive and constructive reconstructionist. But he has indeed left us with a *prelude* to a new philosophy and the new philosopher, as the descriptions offered of the new philosopher (e.g., BGE: #213) may well fit a modern philosophical laborer. How does that description go *beyond*? Although new philosophers are to go beyond good and evil and create new values, and legislate so, we have no examples on these sources of what they might be, and thus of how "they" might pass on the new philosophy to the herd. How then are we to know that we are hearing a new philosopher rather than a busker?

Chapter 8

Nietzsche and the Limits of Academic Life

Peter Roberts

Falling, chronologically speaking, between *Thus Spake Zarathustra* and *On the Genealogy of Morals, Beyond Good and Evil* provides some of Nietzsche's most incisive observations on morality, culture and intellectual life. The sixth part ("We Scholars") sets out Nietzsche's views on the scholars of his day, contrasting their activities with those of philosophers—the new, "true" "philosophers of the future." This chapter summarizes this account, discusses some of the conditions Nietzsche saw as necessary for a philosophical life and considers the relevance of his ideas for the contemporary university. I argue that in a world characterized by frenetic activity (both within and outside the academy), *neither* scholars *nor* philosophers are likely to flourish. Serious reading and reflection are discouraged in a culture of consumerism, and in bureaucratic and marketized universities few have the time, space and material resources necessary for creative, critical intellectual work. I conclude by noting that if intellectuals are to exert any significant influence in the twenty-first century, they may have to dwell outside institutions, and will almost certainly have to become "philosophers of technology"—making "untimely" observations via "timely" (computerized) means.

SCHOLARS AND PHILOSOPHERS

Under the heading "scholars" Nietzsche includes scientists, philologists, schoolmen, specialists of various kinds, (almost all) academics and most of his philosophical contemporaries.[1] Nietzsche sees the emergence of "men of science" (scholars) as an after-effect of the evolution of democracy. Having successfully shaken the shackles of theology, science has taken it upon itself to lay down laws for philosophy—indeed, to play the role of philosopher (BGE: §204). Science is, however, undeserving of this role, though many who want to call themselves philosophers by profession are no more worthy of it. In fact, it is the poverty of recent philosophy (promulgated, in particular, by positivists and "philosophers of reality") that has opened the gates for any and all to claim the name "philosophers" for themselves (BGE: §§204, 205). Unsure of whether a path is still open for the genuine philosopher to emerge, Nietzsche nonetheless sets out some of the characteristics of such a figure by way of a series of striking contrasts with scholarly beings.

Philosophy, Nietzsche makes plain, is a lordly undertaking for which only very few will be suited. The philosopher demands of him- or herself a judgment ("a Yes or a No") not in relation to the sciences but in regard to "life and the value of life." It is from "the most comprehensive—perhaps most disturbing and destructive—experiences" that philosophers develop a sense of having a right or a duty to make such judgments. Genuine philosophers play a dangerous game, risking themselves, facing life's burdens and temptations (BGE: §205). The philosophers of the future will be critics and experimenters. They will possess certainty in standards of value, consciously employ a unity of method, and have courage, independence and the ability to justify themselves.

By contrast, the scholar is an ignoble character, bearing some resemblance to "an old maid." Subservience, industriousness, moderation, the desire for honor and recognition, insecurity born of an inner distrust, a lack of independence and a tendency to conformity are some of the distinguishing characteristics of scholarly beings. The diseases and ill breeding of an ignoble species are evident, with scholars often "rich in petty envy" for those who attain heights beyond their reach. Worst of all, scholars have an instinct for *mediocrity*—for that which destroys "uncommon man" and tries to break or straighten every "bent bow" (BGE: §206). The scholar is only an instrument for, or a mirror to, those who are mightier—"he is no 'end in himself.'" Unable to take proper care of themselves or to deal with their troubles, scholars can become "inauthentic, fragile, questionable, and wormeaten" (BGE: §207). The scholar neither affirms nor denies and cannot lead or follow or take sides between good and evil.

While genuine philosophers must be carefully distinguished from philosophical laborers, the education of the former may, Nietzsche suggests, involve prior experience of being the latter. In the path to becoming a philosopher of the future, someone might first be a critic, a dogmatist, an historian, a poet, a traveler, a moralist—in fact, "almost everything in order to pass through the whole range of human values and value feelings and to be *able* to see with many different eyes and consciences, from a height and into every distance." (BGE: §211). As Nietzsche observes in *Ecce Homo*, "I was many things and in many places in order to be able to become one thing—to be able to attain one thing. I *had* to be a scholar, too, for some time" ("The Untimely Ones": §3).

Nietzsche was fond of calling himself an "immoralist" and often saw himself as a man against his time—as an outsider. Indeed, this is an important element in his definition of the philosopher. The task of the philosopher, Nietzsche maintains, lies in being the "bad conscience" of one's age. The task is "hard, unwanted, inescapable," and those called to it would, Nietzsche suggests, bear witness to the greatness of humankind through strength of the will—exemplified, in part, by their hardness and capacity for protracted decisions. Nietzsche sees the emphasis on equality of rights as consistent with herdlike behavior. Such a doctrine, he cautions, could easily lead to equality in the *violation* of rights, working against "everything that is rare, strange, privileged, the higher man, the higher soul, the higher duty, the higher responsibility, and the abundance of creative power and masterfulness." Those who uphold the ideal of greatness are lonely, concealed and deviant, with an abundance of will and a mastery over their own virtues (BGE: §212).

ON THE REQUIREMENTS FOR A PHILOSOPHICAL LIFE

This section sets out some of the conditions Nietzsche saw as necessary for an authentic philosophical life.[2] Hayman (1980: 231) claims that Nietzsche was "not immune to [the] desire for power," but that it is "power over himself that he lusted." Why did Nietzsche write? In large part, it seems, his motivation sprang from a deep inner commitment to a certain mode of reflective activity—from his desire to *think*, to philosophize. Yet, he did not write merely for himself. Believing his work was of supreme importance, Nietzsche hoped some compensation for the physical pain he suffered would be found in the difference he made to other people. With a hint of vulnerability, Nietzsche confesses:

Every philosopher has probably had bad moments of asking: "What do I matter unless they accept even my bad arguments?" And then a malicious little bird flew by, twittering: "What do you matter? What do you matter?" (cited in Hayman, 1980: 241)

In 1882, however, it was still possible for Nietzsche to "entertain more heroic fantasies." "If only the masses would once again become respectfully involved with ideas as they had been during the religious wars, they would need leaders like him" (cited in Hayman, 1980: 241).

Nietzsche's attitude to academic life was at first ambivalent, and later openly hostile. When on his teacher Ritschl's recommendation, he was offered the chair in Classical Philology at Basel University at the extraordinarily

young age of 24, Nietzsche took his new responsibilities very seriously, believing his teaching could make an important difference in students' lives.
Yet while others were, to use Nietzsche's own descriptor, "dazzled" by the
title "Professor," he never was (Hayman, 1980: 103). Wearied by hard
work, he was nonetheless able to claim in mid-1869: "The whole thing [his
new academic job] could not suit, me better. It fits like a glove. Yes, I am
quite obviously in my natural element . . . Though it will take a while for
my nature to accustom itself fully to this activity" (cited in Hayman, 1980:
111). He was however already beginning to distinguish himself from many
of his colleagues, declaring that "amongst them I feel as I used to amongst
students. On the whole I feel no need to concern myself more closely with
them, but I feel no envy. To be precise, I am aware of a small grain of
contempt for them" (ibid.: 112).

Desperate to make philosophy his life's work, Nietzsche expressed an interest in a vacancy created by Gustav Teichmuller's resignation from his post
at Basel in the early 1870s. Writing a letter of application in 1871, Nietzsche
claimed it was "in the interests of the university" that he was making the
suggestion. He explained his ill health as a product of the excessive strain
caused by dividing himself between philology and philosophy for so long.
Nietzsche's efforts were in vain. Both his poor health and his support for
Schopenhauer would have acted as "strong deterrents" against appointing
him to the chair in philosophy (Hayman, 1980: 137–138).

While still holding his university post, Nietzsche had started to cast himself in what was later to become one of his favorite roles: the outsider, at
odds with the spirit of the times. His friendships with people like Erwin
Rohde (a philologist) and Paul Deussen (a philosopher) were based, in part,
on a mutual appreciation of both the need for solitude and the longing to
overcome it. "It is our lot," he would say in 1870, "to be intellectual hermits
and occasionally to have a conversation with someone like-minded" (cited
in Hayman, 1980: 119). At one time, Nietzsche entertained thoughts of
bringing such like-minded people together into a small monastic and artistic
community in which all members could "love, work, enjoy for each other."
While this remained nothing but a vaguely formulated ideal, the impulses
behind it were clear. Nietzsche was seeking an environment within which
genuine philosophical work could be undertaken. Early on, he saw the limits
of academic life and felt an eventual break with the university was inevitable,
for nothing revolutionary could start there. His ideal was the creation of a
new Greek Academy (ibid.: 132). Nietzsche was not unrealistic about the
material prerequisites for such a move, noting that he'd started keeping his
needs in check in the interests of accumulating some capital. He even placed
some hope in lotteries as a potential source of money for getting the ideal
off the ground (ibid.).

As Hayman (1980: 231) points out, Nietzsche's writing can be regarded
as a formulation of how he wanted to live—"a sketch for a critical biography

of his anti-social soul." Nietzsche captures some of the key elements of such a life in this passage:

Where is this whole philosophy going, with all its deviations? Does it do any more than, as it were, rationalize a steady, powerful craving for mild sunlight, a bright and bracing atmosphere, Mediterranean vegetation, sea breezes, quick snacks of meat, eggs, fruit and glasses of hot water, quiet walks that last all day, a paucity of conversation, occasional careful reading, solitary living, hygienic, simple and almost military habits—in short all the things I find most enjoyable and most wholesome? (Cited in Hayman, 1980: 231)

These ideas find further expression in *Human, All Too Human*, where Nietzsche speaks of the necessary conditions for people to live as true free spirits. Such people, who live for knowledge alone, do not desire state power or riches but rather will "easily be content with . . . a minor office or an income that just enables them to live." Prone to annoyance and irritation at anything that takes them away from the quest for knowledge, Nietzsche's free spirits will set themselves up to live in such a way that political upheaval and changes in external circumstances will not deter them from their path. The goal is to expend as little energy as possible on such matters, "so that they may dive down into the element of knowledge with all their accumulated strength and as it were with a deep breath" (HH: §291).

In "Schopenhauer as Educator," Nietzsche expresses his admiration for Montaigne and Schopenhauer, and laments the impoverishment of philosophy in German universities. For Nietzsche, philosophy is *life*. To live a philosophical life takes great courage. It involves setting oneself apart from one's fellow human beings—from the herd—and carries its own unique form of solitude. Philosophy is not defined by the studying of books or the recollection of theories; nor is it something housed within often arbitrary disciplinary boundaries imposed by a university curriculum. As Nietzsche puts it,

I profit from a philosopher only insofar as he can be an example. That he is capable of drawing whole nations after him through this example is beyond doubt; the history of India, which is almost the history of Indian philosophy, proves it. But this example must be supplied by his outward life and not merely in his books—in the way, that is, in which the philosophers of Greece taught, through their bearing, what they wore and ate, and their morals, rather than by what they said, let alone what they wrote. ("Schopenhauer as Educator," §3)

NIETZSCHE AND THE CONTEMPORARY UNIVERSITY

The university has historically been granted the responsibility of acting as a "critic and conscience of society." In New Zealand, this role is enshrined in law. The extent to which the critic and conscience function has been upheld in practice is, of course, a matter for considerable debate. The university has always been an "imagined" as well as a "real" community in its defense of academic freedom and other ideals (Smith and Webster, 1997). Even so, there is, some believe, still much to be gained in fighting for universities as unique sites for "cultural exploration and engagement" (Kumar, 1997: 31). But what forms of cultural engagement do we find in the academy? One response to this question is that academics assume a distinctive role in contemporary society as *intellectual* laborers. Yet this begs further questions about the mode of intellectual activity prevalent in universities. Are academics "scholars" or "philosophers," or might neither of these labels be appropriate in the twenty-first century?

Jacoby (1987) argues that intellectuals—much like Nietzsche's philosophers—should, in a certain sense, stand apart from the rest of society while at the same time having something important to say to that society. To be a public intellectual is to speak from the margins—from, or beyond, the periphery—to the "center" in a manner that is both comprehensible and challenging. It entails sharpness in perception and clarity in expression. Public intellectuals write not just for themselves but for a wider, intelligent but not specialized, reading public. Such intellectuals have, according to Jacoby, disappeared. In their place we find academics writing—in tortured and deliberately obscurantist prose—for each other: either directly, as exemplified by the professional association conference, or indirectly, through journals accessible to only a narrow range of disciplinary experts. There may be debates over matters of theory—or even theories *about* theory (Lemert, 1991)—but such battles often remain circumscribed by the limits of narrow academic specialisms. Jacoby (1997) views those who assume the role of "outsiders" while drawing generous salaries as tenured academics with a measure of contempt: such people are very much *insiders*, a world removed from earlier generations of intellectuals who were separated from—and sometimes deliberately eschewed—the comforts of a university post.

Care needs to be taken in drawing a parallel between Jacoby's account of public intellectuals and Nietzsche's portrait of philosophers of the future. The differences between the two ideals are probably as great as their similarities. Jacoby is concerned with a group of people who, for the most part, wrote for a living and secured an audience by addressing the social and public policy issues of the day. Nietzsche's philosophers have the larger task of reexamining past and present values, rising above the affairs of the day and creating a new direction for humanity. Nonetheless, there is at least one significant point of overlap between the two ideals: both speak of "outsiders" engaging in forms of critical intellectual activity that *make a difference*— a difference that *matters*—in their world or one in the future.

In the marketized world of early twentieth-first-century global capitalism, it is difficult to imagine either philosophers or public intellectuals having such an impact on the lives of others. The role of the critic—as philosopher, public intellectual or academic—is, for many people, *irrelevant* in the current age. Capitalism has proven—recently more than ever before—that it can contain its contradictions. Criticism in the era of the New Right is suppressed when necessary but on the whole is given an apparently "free" rein. Intellectual critiques of neo-liberalism fail not because they are lacking in philosophical or scholarly terms, but because they never make it on to the debating table. For the most part, they circulate among like-minded critics, while New Right political zealots and influential businesspeople maintain a relentless grip over the process of economic and social change.

Nietzsche sees philosophers as creators of values—as "*commanders and legislators,*" people who say "*thus* it *shall* be!" and determine the "Whither and For What" of humankind (BGE: §211). But how will the philosophers of the future do this? Exerting such an influence requires a medium through which one's ideas might be conveyed. The process demands both some sort of audience receptive to new ideas and a context in which these ideas might be carried forth, "promoted" and rendered intelligible (or sensible or reasonable). What does this mean in a marketized world—in a world dominated by new media, a world in which fewer people read seriously and in which there is less and less time for the reflection so necessary if one is to read well? What will it mean as we move into the realm of cyberspace?

In Nietzsche's time, the written text provided the prime vehicle for conveying philosophical ideas. Today, print competes with a host of other media, and the rules through which ideas are circulated have changed. More printed matter than ever before is produced, and "consumed" (this *is* the right word here), yet few people take, or have, the time to engage in the sort of serious reading Nietzsche wanted to encourage. How many citizens read—*really* read—Nietzsche? Many have *heard* about him but have read nothing of his work. This is symptomatic of the spirit of the times. Texts are produced in order to be "devoured," barely digested, and "spat out" at regular intervals, in a painless (read "entertaining") way. Surface-level understandings—sometimes, we should not be afraid to say, these will be *mis*-understandings—are actively encouraged.

Nietzsche's own views on the process of reading provide a direct contrast here. In the preface to *Daybreak*, he suggests that reading *well* means reading "slowly, deeply, looking cautiously before and aft, with reservations, with doors left open, with delicate eyes and fingers" (D: §5). Writers and thinkers he admired were accorded the respect of Nietzsche's closest possible attention. Nietzsche read his copy of Emerson's *Essays* time and time again, wrote extensively on the margins of the book and recorded dozens of passages in his own notebooks (Kaufmann, 1974: 7, 9). While acknowledging the necessity of reading for scholarly purposes, Nietzsche believed philosophical activity demanded a different approach. At one point he was moved to comment: "Our whole way of working is quite ghastly. The hundred books in front of me on the table are like fire-tongs for overheating the nerve of independent thinking" (cited in Hayman, 1980: 85). Nietzsche notes in *The Gay Science* that one of the marks of the scholar, the person for whom bending over books in order to gain ideas is essential, is cramped intestines. His preferred environment for philosophical thought is effectively captured in this passage:

We do not belong to those who have ideas only among books, when stimulated by books. It is our habit to think outdoors—walking, leaping, climbing, dancing, preferably on lonely mountains or near the sea where even the trails become thoughtful. Our first questions about the value of a book, of a human being, or a musical composition are: Can they walk? Even more, can they dance? (GS: §366)

In introducing *On the Genealogy of Morals*, Nietzsche admits that the book may be incomprehensible for some. He makes no apology for this—one commentator (Simons, 1988: 344) claims that Nietzsche "seems almost to have rejoiced in being misunderstood"—and notes that this book should be read in conjunction with his earlier writings. This is not meant to be an easy process. The art of reading (and for Nietzsche it *is* an art: Ridley, 1998: 241) demands a form of intellectual activity owing much, by way of analogy, to cows: rumination. But this process has been "unlearned," and—Nietzsche implies—needs to be "relearned" before his books might become "readable" (GM, "Preface": §8). Lyotard (1988: xvi) has advanced a not-dissimilar view in his comments on reflection near the beginning of *The Differend*. Reflection, he observes, requires *time*, and anything that takes time is, given the finality of today's economic genre, thrust aside. Philosophy—as a mode of reflective uncertainty—has always stood in opposition to the calculable and accountable uses of time demanded by this genre.

What hope is there for reflection or rumination in the current historical moment? Hearing *about* something or someone, from any source, rather than actually reading an original work or engaging ideas in detail, has become the order of the day. This is one dimension of a marketized world, where the image—the shimmering veneer—is everything. In-depth analysis takes too much time, is too wearying, and, above all, does not *sell*. Reducing discussion to the 20-second sound byte serves the imperatives of entertainment, advertising and the maximization of profit. Media executives laugh all the way to the bank, and those who participate as viewers, listeners or readers in such exercises find fewer and fewer opportunities for genuine thought (the thought Nietzsche demands of his new philosophers and strived to achieve himself), convinced this is "as good as it gets" in a digitized world. Walter Kaufmann, who was so essential in bringing Nietzsche's work to the attention of the English-speaking world, often complained about the manner in which Nietzschean texts were dealt with. As he notes at the beginning of his introduction to *The Will to Power*, a book can be famous and interesting, but "its stature and its reputation are two very different things." "Indeed," Kaufmann continues, "the nature and contents of the book are as little known as its title is familiar." Hegel's insightful comment in the preface to his first book is apposite here: "What is well-known is not necessarily known merely because it is well-known" (cited in Kaufmann, 1968: xiii). If Heidegger is right that we Westerners are in many senses unprepared for Nietzsche, *listening* to what he has to say in his texts becomes doubly difficult (see Heidegger, 1977: 58–59).

There is a further question to be addressed if we are to take Nietzsche's challenge seriously. How will the material conditions necessary for the emergence of philosophers of the future (or their contemporary equivalent) be secured? To live a life of the kind Nietzsche describes—something like the life he lived during the 1880s—requires a means through which other responsibilities and burdens might be relinquished. It demands a certain level of material well-being, a freedom from some of the struggles that characterize many everyday lives. Nietzsche, to be sure, suffered terribly—enduring great pain and almost incessant illness—through much of his life. This, he makes plain, was not antithetical to, but rather *vital for*, his development as a thinker. Yet, he enjoyed the benefit of an income sufficient (modest though it was) to meet his needs—even if only barely—while he traveled, reflected and wrote during the years following his retirement from his university post. Few are so fortunate. Even in Nietzsche's time, this sort of life was a world removed from the day-to-day activities of the university. Today, as Foucault's biographer James Miller (1998: 871) has recently noted, the very idea of leading such a life—of making philosophy a *way of life* rather than merely a subject for study in a university—is likely to be seen by most as "misguided, immodest and self-aggrandizing."

Academics in today's universities inhabit intellectual spaces defined not so much by reflective tranquility as by frenetic, non-stop activity. Daily life involves not long walks in the hills or hours gazing contemplatively at "blue skies" (to use the rather derisive term employed by some bureaucrats in New Zealand), but constant demands to complete forms, respond to e-mail messages, teach more classes, undertake meaningless administrative tasks and so on. What sort of character, it might be asked, is likely to emerge under these conditions? There has been no shortage of critics eager to ascribe many of the negative characteristics Nietzsche sees in the figure of the scholar to academics in the second half of the twentieth century. The perception that academics are now "careerists," committed not to the pursuit of truth or preservation of cultural values but to personal advancement, is widespread. Some (e.g., Sykes, 1988) depict academics as nothing more than self-serving money-makers. Opponents of "political correctness" (Kimball, 1991; D'Souza, 1991) identify a new form of herd activity (academic conformity and intolerance) in attempts to make higher education curricula more inclusive of women and ethnic minorities. Others lament the rise of professionalism and the decline of moral responsibility in the university (Wilshire,

1990). At the same time, many stomachs continue to ache from long hours spent slumped over desks, and academics are falling ill in record numbers (cf. Morris, 1998). An unwillingness to critique state policy, when research funding depends on government support, is by no means uncommon.

In many respects, however, a scholarly mode of being has come to represent one of the strongest possible *alternatives* to contemporary academic life. The ideal of the scholar poring over books, with a strong commitment to canons of rigor developed over centuries and a recognizable and robust community of peers enjoying the same vocation, is virtually a relic of the past. This is one of the key shifts as we move from the modernity of the university in Nietzsche's day to the multiversity of our postmodern moment: the figure of the "scholar" now stands as an almost forgotten *ideal* to which many academics would adhere—if only they had the time. Time is arguably the forgotten ingredient in the sense of loss, disorientation and anxiety that Bauman (1988) speaks of in describing the role of intellectuals and the university in the postmodern condition. The preservation of a scholarly mode of existence relatively "untainted" by the ravages of the market is now almost exclusively confined to a few privileged private universities, where generous endowment funds allow academics to enjoy lower teaching loads, substantial resources for research, and the time necessary for reading, reflection and writing. I would argue, then, that it is possible for *neither* scholars nor philosophers, as Nietzsche described them, to flourish in most contemporary universities. In their place, bureaucratic and entrepreneurial forms of academic life have come to dominate.

The bureaucratization of the modern university was explored at length by a number of thinkers in the twentieth century. The metaphor of the "iron cage" of bureaucracy remains one of the most powerful we have in the social sciences, and Weber must be credited with inaugurating a new phase in the interrogation of not just the nature of Western institutions but also some of the most significant changes in human activity and relationships. The portrait of bureaucratic rationality painted by Weber still has currency today, but the specific forms bureaucracy takes in postmodern universities demand their own form of analysis. The bureaucrats of our time enjoy, in some circumstances at least, unprecedented power. They stand not in the service of an academic community but, in a certain sense, at the apex of the postmodern university. This is so in at least two senses. First, the head of the university—the vice-chancellor (in the New Zealand context, the chief executive officer)—is expected to assume administrative leadership above all else. Academic excellence is not irrelevant—at least not in some universities (though their number is declining)—but it is, in practice, secondary to the administrative function. More fundamentally, however, the distribution of bureaucratic leaders around the university is increasing. Contemporary universities are now awash with deputy vice-chancellors, pro vice-chancellors (often several in number), deans, sub-deans, associate deans, assistant deans (these can all coexist and have different functions), heads of schools, heads of departments, deputy heads of various kinds, directors of research and teaching centers, deputy directors and so on. These titles are placed before "career academics" (this notion will not be of use for much longer) as the ideals to which university intellectuals ought to aspire. A vice-chancellorship is described as the "career peak" (this is the terminology used in publications such as *Campus Review*, a weekly newspaper-style publication for academics in Australia and New Zealand), to which only the exalted few will climb.

The figure of the scholar also stands opposed to, or rather might be seen as the forgotten precursor to, the emerging academic *entrepreneur*. While Sykes (1988) locates the roots of this phenomenon in personal greed and a lack of commitment to teaching, it is also possible to see entrepreneurialism in the academy as a reflection of broader trends in the marketization of higher education. When "education" becomes a commodity to be sold, traded, franchised and consumed, all elements of university life tend to follow the logic of the market. Competition within and between institutions—for student enrollments and research dollars—intensifies. In this context, the nature of intellectual work changes. Academics now spend much of their time—or at least some academics do (and those who don't will find it more and more difficult to legitimate themselves as the imperatives of postmodern performativity begin to bite)—trying to secure the *conditions* for research and writing. *Doing* the research almost becomes secondary to the endless process of completing application forms, hustling agencies for money, sitting in interviews and gaining the necessary approval from a variety of committees. Being an effective academic today demands, in part, the ability to demonstrate one's superiority as a revenue-generating unit. Indeed, it is not uncommon for job applications to involve a tallying up of research grants, allowing academics to specify their value in the most precise terms possible (by today's standards): dollars. The new criterion for success is not excellence in teaching or scholarship but the bottom line.

In analyzing Nietzsche's account of scholars and philosophers, it is important to consider his view of nineteenth-century German culture and education and to be aware of the significance and purpose of style in his writing.[3] Nietzsche was appalled by what he saw around him—both within and outside universities—in Germany, and referred often to the existence of widespread cultural impoverishment in Europe. Figures such as Goethe were, in Nietzsche's view, exceptional characters: free spirits who stood out when compared with the rest of "the herd." In *Twilight of the Idols* Nietzsche speaks of Schopenhauer, Goethe, Hegel and Heine as European *events* (TI, "Skirmishes of an Untimely Man": §21). Of the education system in Germany, Nietzsche had virtually nothing kind to say. Secondary schools, he claimed, were overcrowded, with overworked and stupefied teachers, while higher education had lost the end as well as the means to the end. Instead of supplying "higher wet nurses," what is needed is educators who have themselves become educated (TI, "What the Germans Lack": §5). Nietzsche's wider philosophical project was, in large part, an attempt to reclaim what had been lost under Christianity and other life-denying forces. Understood in these terms, statements that otherwise appear harsh and exaggerated in Nietzsche's discussion of scholarly life can be properly contextualized and reappraised.

It seems conceivable that any new philosophers of the twenty-first century might well be philosophers of *technology*—beings who work, in some way, with the machines and structures and social relations of cyberspace (cf. Kellner, 1995). It may not, in a literal sense, be a case of "giving Nietzsche a modem" (Kroker and Weinstein, 1994), but it seems almost certain that the thinkers of the future will make increasing use of a wide range of media for conveying their ideas. The ability to work effectively with information in its myriad complexities—to participate in, intercept, disrupt, and reroute its flows, relays and circular formations—is already creating new spaces for creative and critical work. Ultimately, the question of what it means to be a "philosopher" in postmodern times cannot be answered with words alone: it must be addressed, played out and tested by the lives people lead. As Nietzsche (BGE: §213) says, "What a philosopher is, that is hard to learn because it cannot be taught: one must 'know' it from experience—or one should have the pride *not* to know it." To live the sort of philosophical life Nietzsche envisaged probably demands an existence outside the confines of institutions. Universities, against their origins and the best instincts of many within them, have—under conditions of marketization—become profoundly *anti*-intellectual institutions, discouraging both scholarly and philosophical work. The same oppressive atmosphere prevails in many other contemporary institutions. (In the New Zealand context, we might name hospitals and government agencies as prime examples.) Institutions in a neoliberal world might be said to suffer from a form of sickness: a chronic illness that infects all who work within them.

Seeing the problem in this light shifts the focus away from individuals—some of whom bear many of the nastier features of the scholars described by Nietzsche—to institutional cultures, structural constraints and the wider fabric of social relations within which institutions have to operate. Making a move away from institutions to other intellectual spaces requires a certain level of material well-being and/or a high degree of commitment to ideals beyond personal advancement. For those who endeavor to make such a break under less than ideal (or even sufficient) material conditions, one quality Nietzsche admired greatly—*courage*—will be essential. That Nietzsche himself possessed this quality of character is abundantly clear. As Wicks (1997: 11) observes, the fact that Nietzsche "was able to write so prolifically and profoundly for years, while remaining in a condition of ill-health and often intense physical pain, is a testament to his spectacular mental capacities and willpower." It will be instructive to see how many academics take up

Nietzsche's challenge should the ideology of neo-liberalism become more deeply entrenched in social and institutional life during the twenty-first century.

NOTES

1. Kaufmann notes in his translation of *Beyond Good and Evil* that the term "science" could have been rendered as "scholarship." In Nietzsche's work, "the term does not have primary reference to the natural sciences as it does in twentieth-century English" (BGE: §204, translator's note 3).

2. I am indebted to Hayman (1980) for many of the biographical details. All quotations from Nietzsche in this section are from Hayman unless otherwise noted.

3. On the question of style, see Bingham's (1998) discussion of language and rhetoric in Nietzsche's writings.

Chapter 9

Revaluing the Self: Nietzsche's Critique of Liberal Education

Patrick Fitzsimons

To educate educators! But the first ones must educate themselves! And for these I write.
— Nietzsche, cited in Schact, 1990: 223

To evaluate = to create.
— Deleuze, 1983: 205

Evaluations are the "modes of existence of those who judge and evaluate, serving as principles for the values on the basis of which they judge" (Deleuze, 1983: 1). The values, then, are the symptoms of the principles. Since we select the evaluators from within the social system, any evaluation merely exposes the tables of values already embedded. This process cannot provide a revaluing of the worth of those values. For revaluation, the values themselves must be critiqued: that critique exposes their worth. The liberal self is one such social system that, through a critique of the values of liberal education, is the object of revaluation in this chapter.

In liberal societies, education is generally defined in terms of development of the (liberal) self. Nietzsche presents us with a critical genealogy of Western philosophy as the philosophy of self and, therefore, provides us with a critique of the liberal self. Nietzsche's genealogies (along with Schopenhauer's theorization of the will, the development of psychoanalysis, surrealism, existentialism, structuralism and poststructuralism) have problematized the self. For Nietzsche, the self is valued for its creations and its changing forms rather than as an eternal essential substance based on an ultimate appeal to reason under liberalism. This "self as creation and creator" suggests that there are ethical issues beyond the liberal value of reason. Rather than adopting the Cartesian *cogito* of liberal education, Nietzsche (GM: 15) asserts that, in an important sense, "we knowers are unknown to ourselves, we men of knowledge" and claims that as strangers to ourselves we do not understand our own existence. This is not a claim for the negation of self, nor does it mean that the self can be merely anything; it requires interpretation. Because Nietzsche derives social value from a new scale of values that are located on a continuum that has health and sickness at its poles (rather than, for example, truth/falsity and rational/unrational dichotomies), it is inconceivable that any particular interpretation offered would be definitive. The general direction, however, is clear; value lies in practices that promote survival, health and life. On this basis he asks us to revalue our heritage, for it is that which defines for us what is thinkable; for Nietzsche that is a genealogical task.

This chapter begins by providing an overview of some recent interpretations of Nietzsche. It proceeds with a brief genealogy of the liberal self of Western philosophy from which a particular philosophy of self derived from Nietzsche can be identified. Following Nietzsche, the chapter then critiques the idea of liberalism as belief in reason. Finally, a Nietzschean critique of liberal education is outlined. The conclusion is that liberal education is in need of a radical revaluation because of the inadequacies of its underpinning value of reason as its ultimate court of appeal for discovering value.

INTERPRETATIONS OF NIETZSCHE

The significance of Nietzsche's work is being rethought. As Shapiro (1989: 124) points out, early interpreters of Nietzsche such as Walter Kaufmann and Arthur Danto had argued that Nietzsche was "wanting in order and style (and they) aimed at articulating the internal order of Nietzsche's thought which the stylistic fireworks of the texts obscure." Koelb (1990: 305) cites Hollingdale as saying cynically that Zarathustra "does possess a plot of sorts." Nietzsche seems to have been written out of sections of philosophy because, as Koelb (1990: 300) notes

Nietzsche's name is almost completely absent from the genealogy . . . that Stephen Toulmin and Alan Janick have sketched in *Wittgenstein's Vienna* . . . yet Nietzsche's name and writings were inescapable in the Vienna in which Wittgenstein lived.

In the wake of the "death of the subject," contemporary ethical and political debate has been polarized by disputes over absolutism versus relativism and foundationalism versus fragmentation. The legacy of Nietzsche has played a role in these debates, even though his work is sometimes erroneously denigrated as a fragmentary, postmodern politics (see e.g., Higgins, 1990: 213).

As a way out of such inadequate interpretations of Nietzsche, Schrift

(1990: 171) offers a Derridean insight that a good Nietschean interpretative practice "requires both attentiveness to textual detail and creativity of engagement with the text." Schacht (1990: 247) regards Nietzsche's *Zarathustra* as a "truly remarkable accomplishment . . . it is almost in a class by itself among efforts of this kind in the philosophical literature after Plato." Shapiro (1989: 127) reminds us that "Nietzsche's strategy of interpretation, hermeneutics and semiotics ought not to be written off as mere rhetoric." Koelb (1990: 305) cites three instances of the acceptance of Nietzsche's idiosyncratic but valuable style by prominent commentators: he says that Alan Megill maintains positively that "Zarathustra simply will not fit into a critical or analytical framework"; Rosen argues that since Zarathustra "is a revelation rather than a treatise . . . we may expect a certain oddity of language with concomitant problems of interpretation"; and "Derrida . . . attributes to Nietzsche a style designed to render 'undecipherable' the traditional constituent values of philosophy and literature." Of all Nietzsche's interpreters, however, Foucault has probably come the closest to capturing the spirit of genealogy when he opposes the search for origins and for a coherent identity. Under genealogy, Foucault's (1977: 145–146) "numberless beginnings" negate the idea of a single origin and recognize its displacement as an empty synthesis, in liberating a profusion of lost events.

A GENEALOGY OF THE LIBERAL SELF

As a source of possibilities for addressing the question of the self, philosophy is constrained by the ontologies available at various times in history. In order to examine these possibilities, a lineage of philosophers and their implications of philosophy for the self are now outlined. The following brief genealogy of Western philosophy of the self—from the Cartesian pure reasoner to Kant's represented self, through Schopenhaeur to Nietzsche where the self is its own creation—suggests that the self is a function of human practices and, therefore, there are no essential human qualities. It is rather, practices that engage with the world, which create the temporary forms. For Nietzsche these human practices are to be evaluated on the basis of their contribution to survival and health (as metaphors for life) rather than their contribution to abstract notions of truth and rationality. However, certain redundant metaphors for the tradition of "self as truth" have carried over into the present as historical remnants in the form of reified practices. The particular practices in question within the history of philosophy are those predicated on the underpinning assumptions of the autonomous, individualistic, transparent and self-interested, rational subject.

Since Descartes, philosophy has been committed to the self as subject—a notion that requires the individual to build an order of thought in the first-person singular based on universal criteria; the individual reasons as anyone and everyone. This radical disengagement from ordinary experience began with the internalization of a modern identity where we come to think that we "have" selves as we have arms and legs. We lose our understanding of our self-experience through disengagement from the world. But this idea of human agency defined as "the self" independent of practices, is a linguistic reflection of our modern understanding. To the extent that this form of self-exploration becomes central to our culture, radical reflexivity assumes crucial importance alongside disengagement. Reflexivity refers to the idea of a continual monitoring of modern society, a kind of chronic revision in the light of new knowledge. Rather than objectifying our own nature and hence classing it as external to the self and, therefore, irrelevant to our identity, it consists in exploring what we are in order to reestablish this identity. Because the assumption behind modern self-exploration is, as Nietzsche (GM: 15) suggests, that we know not who we are, reflexivity engages us in a continual search to find out. Prior to Nietzsche, Kant argued for the transcendental conditions under which experience of an objective world was possible. On the basis of this Kantian architecture, we could know ourselves only through representation, which itself was a mental construction. This process implied an autonomous, individualistic, transparent, rational subject.

Kant's transcendental architecture did not hold for Nietzsche, nor did it appeal to Schopenhauer, who rejected Kant's interdependence of concepts and perceptions. Schopenhauer offered an account of perception in which the human intellect created the world of ordinary material things by applying the principle of cause and effect to bodily sensations. The human intellect projected, as the cause of sensation, a material object "outside" in space, and this projection was the object, which we perceived. Thus the principle of causation was important to Schopenhauer because it governed all interaction between material things and was responsible for how the empirical world was perceived. By distinguishing the world as appearance and as a "thing-in-itself," Kant paved the way for Schopenhauer to formulate a concept of *will*—the thing-in-itself, which included the self. In a metaphysical move, a move that is both life denying and nihilist, Schopenhauer transcended the will. For Schopenhauer the knowing subject appeared as an individual only through identity with the body. This body was presented in two different ways: one was in the perception of the intellect as representation, and the other was denoted by the word *will*. For Schopenhauer, the subject that was doing the representation and the object that was represented were both illusory because, for him, in the "world in itself," the division between subject and object did not exist.

An extension of this concept was that the whole world—including the self—was will and, therefore, subsumed rationality. This perspective was a symptom of, and a factor in, a radical shift in epistemology where knowledge was a derivative feature of what we are. Schopenhauer's idea was that the body was a manifestation of the will to life, a kind of blind striving, at a level beneath that of conscious thought and action, which was directed toward revaluing life. The *will* determined everything, though it, in turn, was not determined, and in this sense the will was free. In Schopenhauer's system, there was no room for the liberal notion of freedom of the will, since whatever we did as individuals was not the result of choice but of our own character, and this lack of human agency was determined by the will from birth. Our desires are only the will's unconscious strategies to perpetuate itself, and our willing choices are merely manifestations of the will, and not under our control. Schopenhauer even insisted that reason was a self-interested manifestation of the will. Although Schopenhauer's doctrine of the will is now considered flawed for many reasons, including its diminution of human agency, it has value in that it explains the effects of unconscious drives and feelings on the intellect. It also suggests a picture of a self-interested, and (partially) rational subject under the control of the will.

NIETZSCHE'S NOTION OF THE SELF

Despite his criticism of Schopenhauer's pessimism, Nietzsche was convinced of the soundness of Schopenhauer's conviction of an irrational world, full of senseless conflict and with no teleological justification for what the individual is destined to endure. But Nietzsche was unsettled by Schopenhauer's dark conclusions with respect to the value of existence in a world where the only deliverance is that of death and oblivion. In his *Nietzsche and Philosophy*, Deleuze (1983: 195) points out that Nietzsche withdrew from philosophy to evaluate the value of all values through an historical process termed genealogy. Nietzsche offers a totally new concept of life, which included innate urge, and the essential affirmation of increase, enrichment and value perfection; life itself is the goal of life. For affirmation of life, Nietzsche looks back nostalgically (perhaps a little too romantically) to the Greeks, whom he saw as not having any myth of historical progress and human perfectibility and yet who did not succumb to Schopenhauerian pessimism because they turned to art as a way of healing. In this view there is no rationale for transcendent explanations and, since God is dead, man is all there is to value. The ways in which we conduct our lives—our practices—are, therefore, of the utmost importance. He suggests, therefore, that we should re-create ourselves. His methodology for the examination of practices was genealogical.

The term *genealogy* refers to the joining of erudite knowledge and local memories, which leads to the establishment and tactical use of an historical knowledge of struggles. A genealogical analysis establishes and preserves the singularity of events, turning away from the spectacular in favor of the discredited, the neglected and the range of phenomena denied a history. The focus is on local, discontinuous, disqualified, illegitimate knowledges against the claims of a unitary body of theory that filters, hierarchizes and orders them in the name of "true" knowledge. When the technologies of power of the past are elaborated in detail, present-day assumptions, which posit the past as "irrational," are undermined. It is this gap between the past and the present which underlines the principle of difference at the center of Nietzsche's historiography. Discontinuities can remain unexplained, and hence the role of "cause" is reduced because it leads to closure and defeats the purpose of a genealogy of difference. By contrast, history seeks to place events into grand explanatory systems and linear processes, to celebrate moments and individuals and to document a point of origin.

Nietzsche's genealogical methodology addresses two important problems: the authority of a "perspectival" approach to the past, and the endowment of the past with meaning in relation to present practices. Nietzsche employs perspectivism to explain the world, but he does not accept that any perspective will necessarily do. We know an object (and, therefore, ourselves) from the standpoint of certain interests that direct our attention to only certain aspects of the object of knowledge. Perspectivism emphasizes that knowledge is always interested (and thus partial) and, although different interests may increase the knowledge, does not imply that knowledge lacks objectivity or that there is no truth about the matters known. When Nietzsche says there are only interpretations, he ought not to be understood as meaning any logically possible interpretation but, rather, that each meaning or change of meaning is an exercise of power. This is his justification for genealogy. Because it acknowledges a people's aesthetic responses as their truths, genealogy can be regarded as an adequate theory for making assumptions. Since aesthetic responses are not under rational control, many perspectives develop and we cannot, therefore, argue convincingly for a universal morality in the face of infinitely differing situations in life. The method affirms this epistemology, even as it deconstructs teleological, deterministic and legalistic approaches to history.

Through genealogy, Nietzsche explains a rank ordering of human desires, a review of the standards of history, art, morality, and religion, and new views of human excellence. The affirmation of perspectivism emerges as the life-enhancing alternative sufficient to go beyond the reactive decadence of binary morality. It is a productive style of reading that "opens" texts to new interpretive possibilities. What we are dealing with in these interpretations of texts is what has been said by specific people on specific occasions, perhaps gathering force through being respected and reprinted. As opposed to conceptual analysis, this genealogical style refuses to grant that its objects are part of an impersonal world of ideas to be assessed on their own merit—a kind of textual politics.

It is important to recognize, as Deleuze (1983) points out, that Nietzsche wanted to go beyond metaphysics and oppose the Hegelian dialectic where mystifications find a final refuge. Deleuze (1983: 195) argues that three ideas define the dialectic:

the idea of a power of the negative as a theoretical principle manifested in opposition and contradiction; the idea that suffering and sadness have inherent value, the valorization of the "sad passions", as a practical principle manifested in splitting and tearing apart; the idea of positivity as its theoretical and practical product of negation itself.

As he suggests, it might be "no exaggeration to say that the whole of Nietzsche's philosophy is the attack on these three ideas" (Deleuze, 1983: 195). As a criticism of rule by reason, he adds that consciousness is but a symptom of non-spiritual forces in which "perhaps the body is the only factor" (Deleuze, 1983: 39). Nietzsche argues that consciousness is only a means of communication in that "there is no such thing as 'willing' but only a willing something" (1968: 353). This is a non-dualist philosophy insofar as our body movements are acts of will. "What defines a body is this relation between dominant and dominated forces. . . . In a body the superior or dominant forces are known as *active* and the inferior or dominated forces are known as *reactive*" (Deleuze, 1983: 40). The goal of life (and of education) is the "discovery of active forces without which the reactions themselves would not be forces. What makes the body superior to all reactions . . . is the activity of necessarily unconscious forces: . . . the body is . . . superior to our consciousness" (Deleuze, 1983: 41–42). Active forces reach out for power, whereas reactive forces resist power. Nietzsche wants to define the active force as an affectivity, a sensibility and a sensation of the *feeling of power*. "This capacity measures the force of a body or expresses its power" (Deleuze, 1983: 62). "All sensibility is only a becoming of forces" (Deleuze, 1983: 63). In the sense that, for Nietzsche, there is no essential space, time or cause inherent in us, we are the result of such forces.

Despite the claims of reason, human excellence has never been anything more than a fortunate accident. Nietzsche says that humankind is not evolving toward a better or stronger or higher levels, as these terms are understood today. Progress is merely a modern idea, not a fact of life; even our survival is problematic in that:

It is Nietzsche's general view that, while the eventual outcome is still very much in doubt, nature is making a unique experiment in us. In our social and conscious life, a complex alternative to the general kind of instinct structure operative in other forms of life has emerged. Indeed, he considers certain aspects of the conditions imposed upon us by our social life to have played an important role in breaking down or our former instinct structure, as well as in the filling of the resulting void. (Schacht, 1995: 217)

Because we are alive, we are able to seize hold of our existence and to redeem it from the mindless accident of chance. As Nietzsche says, "[T]here exists in the world a single path along which no one can go except you: whither does it lead? Do not ask, go along it" (A: 129). For Nietzsche the self can only justify itself by refusing all ease and contentment and willing its own higher law. For Kant, this suggested an ideal of autonomy that was prior to all particular moral valuations, where the autonomy of the individual became the basis of morality and the highest expression of willing. There was a sense in which the whole of Kant's system depended on the possibility of autonomy, which first called the subject into being. Nietzsche rejects this account of free will but still retains a "vision" of individual autonomy which suggests, in his discussion of Apollo and Dionysus and in *Ecce Homo*, how the individual can take charge of existence to become what he or she is. In opposition to Kant, he refuses to legislate autonomy, or to prescribe any universally binding precepts, for he understands that autonomy is effectively destroyed once it is reduced to a set of rules (as, for example, in liberal education). Through genealogy what Nietzsche has done is to show that individuals are actually a product and a construction of forces that lie outside themselves. Neitzsche's account of individual will and the will to power does not promote or celebrate domination over others. His genealogy shows that individuals are not self-contained but integral to the forces of life that produce them. To provoke the individual will is thus to effect a counterforce against nihilism and a celebration of life.

For Nietzsche, the self could be revealed and its weakness overcome, not by introspection or from the learning of formulas, but through genealogy about our revered objects and educators of the past. In other words, by evaluating how we have become who we are. Nietzsche has indicated how an active education would allow the self to transform itself, to go to its limits, to appropriate its own powers, to impose form, to subjugate and to experience the forces of life as inevitable. It would involve the Dionysian in conjunction with the Apollonian spirit. This education includes the will, the sublime as well as the absurd, and, therefore, it transcends rationality. It undermines our picture of ourselves as autonomous, individualistic, transparent and self-interested, rational subjects. Nietzsche does not fully reject the Enlightenment or classical traditions in view of their place in Western genealogy. He sees them as the place to begin the revaluation rather than as the final product. Neither does he fall into solipsism; his subject is involved in clarifying its personal commitment through narrative in the form of intersubjective practical reasoning, the value of which is open for continual revaluation. This individualism requires more rather than less discipline, hence the requirement to build on what has gone before.

Nietzsche's view is problematic for the current liberal educational agenda limits us through a reified, ahistorical and universal table of values abstracted unproblematically from a particular version of history on which a particular view of the self depends.

LIBERALISM AS BELIEF IN REASON

Liberalism is the major public discourse that underpins education systems in many modern Western countries. Its tenets are freedom, rationality, equality and individualism. At the "progressive" end of the liberal spectrum, legitimate authority is seen as central, and society is thought of as a liberal democratic framework. At the "conservative" end of the liberal spectrum is a philosophy that wants government out of the lives of individual citizens. In all versions of liberalism, there are claims about the rights of individuals in preference to authoritarian rule. Rationality is fundamental to liberalism on the basis of two notions: first, humans are essentially rational by nature, and, second, all beliefs should be open to rational scrutiny. Consequently, the structures, the social institutions and even the idea of authority itself are contingent upon rationality.

Under liberal notions of education, the self is unproblematically assumed as humanistic, rational, autonomous, individuated and assured of progress that transcends nature through enlightenment that itself produced an epistemological revolution with anthropological consequences. Enlightenment humanism takes humanity to be a function of the ways in which we know things, and it provides us with our modern understanding of subjectivity. The humanist valorization of *man* implies that humans can be located on a scale of value with degrees of enlightenment as the measures. On this scale some humans are better than others, depending on their degree of enlightenment. Since on this view some humans are more "human" than others, they are seen as more substantially the measure of things. The historical logic of this view leads to the assumed superiority of so-called enlightened liberal education.

With its negation of difference, the enlightenment project held that the "unenlightened" world contained much error, superstition, darkness and barbarism. In the interests of progress through reason, liberal education has been proselytized to the far reaches of the world to strip the "premodern" world of its magic and "enlighten" it in its own image. Enlightenment is thus reduced to rationality. This is not to suggest that such education is merely or only an illusion. Rather, it is to say that many deployments of "enlightenment" draw heavily on an unreconstructed subjectivity such that it is possible to believe in progress under the name of enlightenment that actually produces an oppressive outcome. It could be argued that this subjectivity forms an important element of legitimacy for the anti-democratic dimensions of capitalism. The more oppressive capitalism becomes, the stronger the requirement for the oppressed to "turn the other cheek" (to use the Christian idiom) and derive satisfaction from the kingdom of God within through the internalization of explanations for their conditions. The "reason" for the oppression is then said to lie within the subjectivities of the oppressed and not in the liberal institutions.

Perhaps this is why Nietzsche observes the oppressive nature of liberal institutions. In some versions of liberal education, even the emotions can (it is said) be brought under reason because they have an object and hence are part of the subject who, it is said, is rational. On the basis of a fundamental distinction between negative and positive notions of freedom, Marshall (1996: 56) suggests that it "may be better to see liberalism, not as a set of basic ideas or principles, but, rather, as an attitude of mind." However it, it seems that that this "attitude of mind" is the liberal leap of faith into reason as the ultimate source of value. The problem with reason for Nietzsche (WP: 58–65) is that it conceals four great errors: it confuses causes with effects; it attributes false causes; it attributes imaginary causes; and it mistakes the nature of free will in that it assumes that through reasoning, man has arrogated to himself an unattainable level of control over the world.

Liberalism does not value human practices as the ultimate source of value. Rather, it avoids the empirical world through its appeal to transcendental reason, which, by definition, is unattainable as a source of value and verification. If "faith is not wanting to know that something is true" (WP: 181), this appeal to faith represents the denial of life that Nietzsche calls nihilism. Such a transcendent theory of values protects the established order insofar as it loses sight of the principle stated in the epigraph at the beginning of this chapter: "to evaluate = to create" (Deleuze, 1983: 205). For Nietzsche, evaluation is based on the results of the practices of people in the world. Creation is an idea that "finds its principle in the will. The lightness of that which affirms against the weight of the negative; the games of the will to power against the labour of the dialectic; the affirmation of affirmation against that famous negation of the negation" (Deleuze, 1983: 197).

The "rational" liberal individual is a recent creation. Nietzsche argues that people either create values that are derived from life's conditions or invert current values to make them their own. In both cases, these values are not developed from *a priori* reason, and since values existed prior to the historical development of the notion of the liberal individual, it cannot be that individual who creates the value; it must be the practices of people in their attempts at survival and health. We must, then, discover values within social practices. These practices include reasoning but are not governed by it.

For an example of the limitations of reason, we can point to Nietzsche's description of the awe that seizes us in our experience of the world outside rationality—what he calls a Dionysian experience. In the modern world, we attribute to our rational thinking our capacity to control nature. But this attribution is of limited value because we are unable to comprehend the lack of control even though we think we can. As Nietzsche (BT: 22) illustrates, "even as on an immense, raging sea, assailed by huge wave crests, a man sits in a little rowboat trusting his frail craft, so, amidst the furious torments of this world, the individual sits tranquilly, supported by the *principium individuationis* and relying on it." Like the man in the boat, we believe we are individually in control of our destiny through our reasoned inquiry into causes. Although we are involved in agency in some small sense, much of life is outside our control. This may be why Nietzsche (1956: 4) asks *contra* rational philosophy, "might it be that the 'inquiring mind' was simply the human mind terrified by pessimism and trying to escape from it, a clever bulwark erected against the truth." Such self-justified rationality cannot even see its own predicament as the following quotation reveals: "these benighted souls have no idea how cadaverous and ghostly their 'sanity' appears as the intense throng of Dionysian revelers sweeps past them" (BT: 23). Rationality as the ultimate liberal explanation for value excludes Dionysian life forces by redefining the will as under the control of reason. By excluding such a life force through its leap of faith into reason, liberalism is inadequate for an education for survival, health and vitality.

A NIETZSCHEAN CRITIQUE OF LIBERAL EDUCATION

A Nietzschean critique of liberal education shows that practices create value. Support for such a critique comes from Wittgenstein, who argues for deriving meaning from the practices of ordinary life and who rejects the reference to mental activities but creates a much larger discursive domain for interpretation and meaning where the meaning of a word is in its use in the context of a "language game" or discourse. Wittgenstein (1953: #83) says at one point: "a rule stands there like a sign-post." At another point he adds (Wittgenstein, 1953: #87): "the sign-post is in order—if, under normal circumstances, it fulfils its purposes." Where regularity is perceived, then, if the present situation is sufficiently like previous situations, there is warrant for following the rule. If we apply such notions to liberal education systems, we can show that where their policy rhetoric is applied in a consistent manner different from traditional practices, new value is created.

Liberal education is the bureaucratic product of reason as the ultimate source of value. Such education is directed at the total mobilization of human capital in the interests of global financial capital. These education systems are increasingly governed by globally influenced, nation-state control of standardized curriculum, managerialized administration under neo-liberal moral explanations for humanity. They are defended under a rhetorical notion of the "public good" because they promote the idea that the "public" is also the "private." This is a problematic idea because public policy is ordinarily thought of as public provision as well as public ownership, which is not the case under government policies of privatization. This shift in language represents a change in practice in education, the meaning of which, according to Wittgenstein, is defined by common practice. The meaning of public education then, is to be found in its practices of privatization. Public now means private; that is, the historical meaning has been reversed.

Such education systems, which combine total mobilization with maximum economic productivity as the ultimate source of economic rationalist value, are more reminiscent of an economy at war than an education focused on survival, health and vitality. This economic value takes precedence and is marketed directly to individuals who are also redefined as *homo economicus* (what Sen [1987] calls the self-interested, rational, utility, maximizer) a form of subjectivity that makes its appeal to individual autonomy in the market. But this autonomy is more apparent than real; it merely reacts to the limits and features of the market. That market can be changed infinitely as required within the limits of financial capital's influence over governments. The market demands a new subjectivity—the self-interested, rational, utility, maximizer—that could also be called the "autonomous chooser." The autonomous chooser presumes new practices of self. It is not just that human beings are autonomous or that their autonomy can be developed, but instead there seems to be a new constituent faculty of choice which necessarily is continuously exercised on commodities. Through the rationality of the market, neo-liberal doctrine implies for the individual an imperative of continuous choice, which introduces an element of behaviorism. Here the chooser must be continually responsive to the environment, which at the same time structures the choices of the individual. In this world, the individual's self-formulated purposes are governed insofar as their choices can be manipulated. And in a discourse of choice, the less visible those manipulations are to the chooser, the more free and responsible they will regard their choices.

The invisibility of the manipulative market conditions surrounding the choice increases the chances that an individual will make an enterprise out of the capacity to choose because on the surface at least, the ability to make choices is promoted as autonomy, which, in turn, has been attributed a positive value within the discourse of choice. The conditions are largely unconscious to the chooser, and there is a consequent imperative of choosing that is required in order to be fully human. Education systems are markets nested inside, and modeled on, the economic rationalist market, itself requiring a socially constructed legislative form (although in some radical versions of neo-liberalism—see for example, the work of F. A. Hayek quoted in Gray [1984: 31]—the market is said to arise spontaneously from human interaction and thus not require social control).

Under this rubric of economic rationalism, there are no spaces for questions about the value of liberal values. Since information in the market (the primary allocative mechanism of the distribution of rationality) has replaced education, what matters is increasing the levels of rationality so that information exchange is maximally effective. Since rationality is said to depend on information, we are thus in the iron grip of rationality. This type of education is not a creative venture, since rationality is the solution always—and already—supplied. Because the solution is available, there is nothing of value to create. Therefore, insofar as creation is associated with life, there is no "life" in the system; it is nihilistic in that it is based on "faith" in the transcendent principle of reason, manifested in personal autonomy derived from the economic metaphors of efficiency, growth, national security and standardization. With economic rationalism as the guiding explanation for education, with reason as the ultimate value in liberal education, with *homo economicus* as the fundamental explanation for human functioning, with the market as the primary allocative device in society and with economics explained through high-status disciplines such as science and mathematics, the circle is closed.

Economic rationality has captured higher education. Under state participation policies, education is increasingly funded through privatized student loan debts. A key mechanism employed to structure students' willing acceptance of such debt is the government-sponsored, and increasingly privatized marketing campaign that extols and appropriates certain historic virtues such as life-long education (or, as Deleuze [1995] would have it, "perpetual training"), as the key to future happiness and prosperity. However, despite expectations to the contrary based on egalitarian education ideology, such happiness and prosperity are not evenly distributed: predictable categories of students gain a disproportionate share of material value under the competitive meritocracy (the societal hierarchy that results from the factorization of higher intelligence and higher levels of effort, i.e., rationality). This is an appropriation of education (under the rubric of reason) to the current interests of the state—an appropriation that was well understood by Nietzsche (WP: 75) who, when speaking for his time, remarked,

what the "higher schools" of Germany in fact achieve is a brutal breaking-in with the aim of making, in the least possible time, numberless young men fit to be utilised, *utilised to the full and used up*, in the state service . . . (and although) one may have *motives* for defending this state of things, as the professors of Heidelberg recently did—there are no *grounds* for doing so.

Certain interest groups today have motives too, but likewise they probably have very few grounds—when judged in terms of survival, health, and vitality—for the current state of education. Such major order systems of education are seen as decadent by Nietzsche (GM: 136), who observed the venality of the liberal condition (in its attempts to bureaucratize the will) in that "the whole of history teaches us that every oligarchy conceals the lust for tyranny; every oligarchy constantly trembles with the tension each member feels in maintaining control over this lust."

As Nietzsche saw it, the problem with Kantian notions of rational autonomy is that they must presuppose effort on the part of the individual will,

since all social arrangements—and this includes state-mandated "disciplinary" education—are directed at the suppression of the individual and the
constitution of a subject as the efficient tool of the state. On this basis,
Nietzsche would want to revalue the present arrangements of liberal education, including its moral ideals. Regardless of their particular notion of
"justice," these ideals are precisely the forms in which the individuals lose
themselves, become part of the herd and are deflected from their proper
task. Clearly, creativity is not available in formulas such as are marketed in
liberal education or its recent mutation, the neo-liberal information-
dispensing retail outlets that rely on accreditation of standardized products
and systems as their rationale for quality. So for the sake of the individual
living within such a culture, the educator must become a critic of what is
considered moral. He or she will necessarily be "untimely," for the task is
to educate against our age. As the second of the two opening epigraphs
suggests, Nietzsche writes for those who would educate themselves and not
for those who would pursue infinitely more fine-grained systems of rational
control. A Nietzschean education, then, is oppositional rather than recip-
rocal.

CONCLUSION

This Nietzschean critique suggests that liberal education leads to the
emergence of a rational, autonomous subject and has actually achieved the
opposite of true individualism. What emerges are individuals identical with
each other. Nietzsche recognizes that contemporary society can no longer
be relied on to provide a framework for individual fulfillment. As he sees it,
disciplinary education transforms the individual into a docile and obedient
subject as it presents a small range of possibilities limited by reason. What
Nietzsche suggests is a way of dealing with such education in order to go
beyond it: to destroy the domination of the past by forgetting it, incorporating it and redeeming it within a horizon of the individual life. Here the
task of the educator is to articulate critiques about the value of the values
behind liberal education. "He who wants to shatter this education, has to
help youth to speak out, he has to light the path [that] their unconscious
resistance has hitherto taken with the radiance of concepts and transform it
to a conscious and loudly vocal awareness" (A: 117–118).

Nietzsche's position is that life is not governed totally by rational principles—as the assumptions behind a liberal education would have it; it is,
rather, full of cruelty, injustice, uncertainty and absurdity. He argues there
are no absolute standards of good and evil that can be demonstrated by
reason. Accordingly, we are victims of the excessive development of the
rational faculties at the expense of the human will and instinct. He stressed
that we ought to recognize the dark and mysterious world of will and instinct—the true life force. Otherwise we will smother the spontaneity nec-

essary for creativity. Any expectation then that education could have value through interpreting experience by reason alone would be a denial of existence of the Apollonian-Dionysian spirit. In his promotion of the idea of a revaluation of all values, Nietzsche has provided us with a view of what it means to be human that is more generous than the more limited dominant liberal tradition of transcendent rational idealism. With such arguments the rational foundations of liberal education have been eroded: without reason as the governing idea, faith in liberal education systems cannot be sustained.

For Nietzsche, the question of values must drive education, which itself must be a continual revaluation of all values, a process of self-overcoming through the radical creation of the self under the Dionysian-Apollonian spirit. This notion of education, however, does not mean its valorization over liberal education: Education is no mere intellectual play of practices; it is integrally engaged with revaluation of political and material practices, which includes liberal education. The liberal leap of faith into reason as the ultimate source of value, then, is the problem and is the agenda for revaluation within a Nietzschean education.

Chapter 10

Subjectivism and Beyond:
On the Embeddedness of the
Nietzschean Individual

Stefan Ramaekers

In philosophical discussions, assuming a problematizing attitude toward tradition can be said to have taken a start from Nietzsche. By decidedly de(con)structing modernity's pride—reason as the unquestionable ground for truth and value—Nietzsche provided outlines of what we now call postmodernity. What has been in this respect, educationally speaking, exercising many minds is Nietzsche's Overman: that particular individual who razes to the ground the predominant values and meanings (hence breaking with tradition) and puts her own values and meanings in their place (favorably radical alternatives). In a recent article in *Educational Theory*, Johnston argues that Nietzsche's task is not to reconstruct culture, but "to point the way to the possibility of a new individual, a self-overcoming individual, one able to create and live within his or her own valuations" (Johnston, 1998: 79). The educational attractiveness of this argument is obvious: the child who asserts her own self by this guarantees renewal. However, when one doesn't elucidate what is meant by such appealing utterances as creating one's own values and meanings, and how one is to understand the concept of the self, this particular use of Nietzsche can be very problematical. For solipsism, subjectivism and interpretations *ex nihilo* are never far away.

This chapter argues that a subjectivistic understanding of Nietzsche and of education from a Nietzschean point of view is incorrect, because it does not fit with Nietzsche's view on the importance of being embedded in and being entangled with the cultural and historical background. The first section examines this proposition by giving an account of what he means by obedience and by lying. It will also be necessary to deal with his perspectivism (in the second section). From an educational point of view, the importance of being embedded means that the self-development and self-education of the child, or the path she has to follow to become a true individual, can be properly understood only by starting from that cultural and historical embeddedness. This idea will be explored in the third section. In the fourth section this exploration will be extended and nuanced by giving an account of Nietzsche's anti-essentialistic conception of human being. Finally, it will be argued that an important lesson to learn from Nietzsche is to adopt a serious engagement for what one stands for.

OBEDIENCE, OR THE IMPORTANCE OF EMBEDDEDNESS

Much as one values Nietzsche for his criticism on culture and, following from that, for his culturally innovative ideas, it would be a mistake to overlook the importance he attaches to obedience. Johnston argues that one cannot just infer an anarchistic account of education from Nietzsche's writings because of his emphasis on obedience and discipline in primary school (cf. Johnston, 1998: 71–72). However, Johnston doesn't give obedience its rightful place. In Nietzsche's account of morals (particularly in *Beyond Good and Evil*, more specifically in the chapter "The Natural History of Morals"), it becomes clear that obedience is not just about keeping pupils in line and hence not just a didactical aid in primary school, but it means obedience to the cultural and historical rules, and as such is a moral imperative to all of humankind. The most important feature about every system of morals for Nietzsche is that it is "a long constraint," a "tyranny of arbitrary laws" (BGE: #188). For such cultural and historical phenomena as virtue, art, music, dancing, reason, spirituality, philosophy, and politics to originate, it is not absolute freedom or spontaneous unconstrained development that is required but subordination to something "arbitrary" (to what appears as arbitrary), a long bondage of the spirit; one is supposed to obey what doesn't change for a long period:

The singular fact remains . . . that everything of the nature of freedom, elegance, boldness, dance, and masterly certainty, which exists or has existed, whether it be in thought itself, or in administration, or in speaking and persuading, in art just as in conduct, has only developed by means of the tyranny of such arbitrary law; and in all seriousness, it is not at all improbable that precisely this is "nature" and "natural"—and *not laisser-aller*! (BGE: #188)

The "nature" of morality inspires us to stay far from an all-too-pervasive freedom and cultivate the need for restricted horizons, and it narrows the human being's perspective to a restricted view. This narrowing of perspective is for Nietzsche even a condition of life and growth (BGE: 188). Subordinating to (the rules of) a system of morals should not be understood as a deplorable restriction of a person's possibilities and creative freedom because, on the contrary, it is the necessary determination and limitation of the conditions under which something can be conceived at all as possibility and as creative freedom. Only from within a particular framework of (arbitrary) determinations can freedom itself be interpreted *as* freedom. In other words, Nietzsche points to the necessity of being embedded in a particular cultural and historical frame. The pervasiveness of this embeddedness can be shown in at least four aspects of Nietzsche's writings.

First, *in the way Nietzsche criticizes morality.* Nietzsche realizes all too well that it is impossible to criticize a system of morals from outside, as if it were a view from nowhere. Instead, it demands a particular concretization. *Beyond Good and Evil* may very well, as a prelude to a philosophy of the future, excite dreams about unlooked-for horizons and unknown possibilities. In *On the Genealogy of Morals,* however, written by Nietzsche as further elaboration and elucidation of the former (cf., in the German editions, the subtitle of this work: "Dem letztveröffentlichten '*Jenseits von Gut und Böse*' zur Ergänzung und Verdeutlichung beigegeben"), he explicitly states that *Beyond Good and Evil* does not imply beyond good and bad (GM: I, 17). Criticizing a system of morals inevitably means judging from a particular point of view.

Second, *in the way Nietzsche represents the true philospher.* Nietzsche insists on not confounding philosophers with philosophical workers and, in general scientific men, for the philosopher's task is the most noble of all tasks: to create values. "*The real philosophers* [. . .] *are commanders and lawgivers;* they say: 'Thus *shall* it be!' "(BGE: #211). The true philosopher's inspiration to determine the wither and the why of humankind does not, however, emerge out of nothing. Nietzsche makes it unambiguously clear that in order to "grasp at the future with a creative hand" (BGE: #211), the philosopher must himself have stood upon the steps of the scientist, of the critic, of the dogmatic, of the moralist, and so on. These steps are the preliminary labor that has to be done in order to be able to create; they are the means, the instruments, the hammer (cf. BGE: #211), in short "a foundation and scaffolding" (BGE: #258). The real philosopher hammers decidedly on the prevailant bastion of values but nontheless needs the pieces to create his own bastion.

Third, *in the role language plays in constituting truth.* As early as "On Truth and Lies in a Nonmoral Sense," one of Nietzsche's earliest philosophical writings, he premises that what one normally understands by truth is essentially constituted by language: "[the] legislation of language likewise establishes the first laws of truth" (OTaL: p. 81). For Nietzsche, speaking a language is using certain images and metaphors. Hence, speaking a language is a kind of subordination of the strictly individual to the general. "Speaking the truth" then means using the customary metaphors, thus signifying a certain kind of convention, a particular commonness, which one has to subordinate oneself to—language is constraint (cf. BGE: #188)—the penalty of which is being incomprehensible. In *Beyond Good and Evil*, Nietzsche specifies this commonness as a conformity in "groups of sensations." In order to understand each other, it is not sufficient just to use the same words; one also needs "to employ the same words for the same kind of internal experiences," that is to say, one "must in the end have experiences *in common*" (BGE: #268). In other words, individuals understand each other, "speak the truth" when, having lived together for a fairly long time under similar conditions, as a consequence they "speak the same language."

Fourth, *in the fact that a human being undergoes difficulties in giving an appropriate place to what is not yet "given" in her embeddedness*. A human being always first lets the familiar, the (well-)known world affect her, and only later, slowly and cautiously, what is unfamiliar to her, the (to her) unknown world. Nietzsche puts this in an unsurpassable manner:

Our eyes find it easier on any given occasion to produce a picture already often produced, than to seize upon the divergence and novelty of an impression: the latter requires more force, more "morality". It is difficult and painful for the ear to listen to anything new; we hear strange music badly. (BGE: #192)

When confronted with something unfamiliar, a human being typically reacts in a reserved manner, maybe even with a little aversion, since it "is painful" seeing and hearing things that are hard to conceive of or that go against everything one is accustomed to. "(F)rom our fundamental nature and from remote ages we have been—*accustomed to lying*" (BGE: #192), Nietzsche says, that this "lying" should not be understood as "not speaking the truth," but as pointing to the constellation of a particular cultural and historical frame that constitutes the human being's narrowed perspective. One should not deplore this "lying," that is, the fact that "lying" is taken for granted. On the contrary, from the observation that our eyes "are hurt" when seeing the unfamiliar and that we can only hear new music with great difficulty, it follows that "lying" is always presupposed in order that the unfamiliar can hurt us at all. To explain this it will be necessary to elaborate on Nietzsche's perspectivism.

PERSPECTIVISM, OR THE IMPORTANCE OF EMBEDDEDNESS

For Nietzsche the perspectival is the fundamental condition of life (cf., e.g., BGE: Preface; HH: I, Preface, 6). It is, however, of the utmost importance not to interpret this perspectival in a traditional metaphysical manner in which reality is understood as an invariant essence, ready "out there" to be put in perspective by a human being. Human perspectives, on the other hand are conceived as particular variations of that fixed background. No more does Nietzsche's perspectivism mean that the multiplicity of perspectives should be combined to form a kind of universal insight of the world or a universally valid perspective. Nietzsche makes it unambiguously clear that *there are only perspectives* (cf. GM: III, #12). Put differently, Nietzsche makes an attempt to surpass the opposition between "background" and "foreground," between "text" and "interpretation"(cf. BGE: #22; KSA: 12, 7[60]¹), between "absolute knowing" and "relative knowing" (KSA: 11, 38[14]), between the "true world" and the "seeming world" (BGE: #34; KSA: 12, 3[106]). Consequently, criticizing the conception of an absolute truth means that there is no sense anymore in bringing these distinctions forward. "We have done away with the true world: which world remains then? the seeming one maybe? . . . But of course not! *together with the true world we have also done away with the seeming one!*" (KSA: 6, *Götzendämmerung*, TI—my translation).

The difficulty is that Nietzsche's way of putting this mostly reminds us of the traditional metaphysical terminology and hence suggests a background lying behind a foreground. The point however is that all these expressions— "perspectival," "seeming world," "interpretation," as well as "lie," "exploitation," "mistake" (cf., e.g., BGE: #34, 230, 259; GM: II, #11; KSA: 11, 25[505])—should not be understood in the traditional manner. There is nothing there to be interpreted; there is no "something" one can lie or be mistaken about. Rather, Nietzsche means that there is no distinction at all between the true world and the seeming one. "The opposition between seeming world and true world converts into the opposition between "world" and 'nothing' " (KSA: 13, 14[84]—my translation).

Consequently, Nietzsche argues that there is something wrong with the customary *searching* for the truth, since it supposes one has to break through the seeming world in order to attain the real one. Attempting to free oneself from the seeming world, however, brings to ruin truth itself: "if, with the virtuous enthusiasm and stupidity of many philosophers, one wished to do away altogether with the 'seeming world'—well, granted that *you* could do that,—at least nothing of your 'truth' would thereby remain!" (BGE: #34). In other words, attempting to dispose of the perspectival is tantamount to giving up the world itself: "As if there would remain a world, when one would set aside the perspectival!"(KSA: 13, 14[134]—my translation).

A similar reasoning obtains when Nietzsche speaks of the constitution of the world by language. When he states that because of language "the way seems barred against certain other possibilities of world-interpretation" (BGE: #20), that expression in language limits the formulability of the world (cf. KSA: 12, 9[91]), this doesn't mean that there's a background "out there" waiting to be nominated by language. That language has become an autonomous force doesn't mean human beings aspire to something outside the distinctions put forward by language. Rather it means that language, human beings and world are entangled with one another in such a manner that it is impossible to dispense with language (e.g., in the typically traditional "searching" for truth), for one would at the same time dispense with human being (OTaL: 88f).

In summary, the emphasis Nietzsche puts on "obedience" leads us to the importance of human beings and world being embedded, which also means—put in terms of his perspectivism—that it is impossible not to see reality from within a framework, the penalty of which is seeing nothing at all. The perspectival outlook of the world—human beings and world as constituted by language even by "lying"—is the precondition in order to be able to see anything at all, to be able to differentiate between things. At the moral level, this means that being in the world neutrally is tantamount to not being in the world at all.

EDUCATION AND THE IMPORTANCE OF BEING EMBEDDED

Having elaborated on the importance of being embedded in Nietzsche's writings, one can now understand the value of what he says about education (childrearing and schooling) *Beyond Good and Evil*:

Parents involuntarily make something like themselves out of their children—they call that "education"; no mother doubts at the bottom of her heart that the child she has borne is thereby her property, no father hesitates about his right to subject it to *his own* ideas and notions of worth. (BGE: 194)

In view of the importance Nietzsche attaches to "obedience," to being embedded, one should not be surprised that he considers initiating the child into a particular constellation of "arbitrary laws" to be a natural part of her education. For the child, education means, at least in the early stages, to be subordinated to a particular view of what is worth living for; to be introduced into a system of beliefs. Education is teaching the child to see and to value particular things, to handle a perspective—to "lie." The argument goes even further. In view of Nietzsche's perspectivism, one must now say that not initiating the child into a perspective, not teaching to "lie" is, educationally speaking, not even an option: The child makes herself familiar with a perspective she cannot ignore since it is the precondition for making sense of anything and exploring the unfamiliar. Put differently, because of the necessity of being embedded, a human being is molded into a particular shape she cannot do without.

My understanding of Nietzsche is consequently at variance with any understanding that argues for a radical individualism and takes the individual to be the point of reference of all values and thruths. Johnston (1998), for example, turns the scale too strongly toward the individual as a self-affirming autonomy. Hence he disregards the epistemological and ethical constitutive importance of the individual's embeddedness for what the individual affirms as true and valuable. He even argues that the individual put forward by Nietzsche is the antipode of the social realm. For Nietzsche, dixit Johnston, "there is no question of a reconciliation between the realms of the individual and the social" (1998: 81). Referring to Dewey, he makes it look as if the Nietzschean individual can withdraw from the social embeddedness since there apparently is in no need to refer action to that of others (1998: 68). Adopting a thoroughly Nietzschean stand on education therefore requires, in Johnston's opinion, a break with education conceived as a making familiar with and being initiated in a cultural inheritance, that is, as socialization. The magic word here consequently becomes self-education.

It is not hard to understand that focusing in this manner on the individual is greatly welcomed by "progressive" educational movements such as child-centered pedagogies. In their critique of the traditional educational model characterized simply as a bestowal of values from the educator, they show their concern with the child's personal identity. It is said that initiating the child into a particular view of life does injustice to her personal identity, for her "true self" is being suppressed, suffocated and not given the opportunity to develop into what it really is. Education should, instead, create room for the self-development of the child's true self. This seems to be the educational lesson to be learned from Rousseau, Rogers, Steiner and Freinet, among others. A particular kind of experiential learning, supported by a particular conception of what experience is, warrants the child to give meaning to her life.

Now there's nothing wrong with the notion that socialization in some sense resembles "indoctrination" and is, from a particular point of view, a kind of injustice, for there is no longer a problem with the concern for the child's personal identity. The problem, however, is that the way in which the Nietzschean individual is accounted for only allows a subjectivistic interpretation of self-education (even inclining to solipsistic). Johnston rightly argues that Nietzsche's critique of the conception of absolute truth and universal values gives rise to perspectivism. However, he treads on dangerous ground when he claims that, for Nietzsche, from an epistemological point of view, all truths, and from a moral point of view, all values exist only "as a matter of individual perspective," that for Nietzsche "truths are reducible in the last to the individual" and that "[t]he new system of values provided by and for this individual takes its point of reference from the individual, and not the outward society, church, state, nation, or culture" (Johnston, 1998: 68, 69, 78).

NIETZSCHE'S ANTI-ESSENTIALISTIC CONCEPTION OF MAN

Putting such a strong emphasis on the constitutive importance of being embedded does not mean that one cannot give any meaningful sense to self-education. The fact that every human being, because of her being embedded, is affected with a particular perspective or molded into a particular shape, doesn't necessarily mean for Nietzsche that she is limited to that particular perspective or shape. The child's self is not constituted *permanently* by her being embedded. Alteration, development—in short, "self-education"—remains possible. Nietzsche does indeed argue that the merit of every system of morals lies in narrowing the human being's perspective, yet he is quite bold in his critique on the *particular* moral interpretation of human beings and world. To be more precise, the thorn in his (philosophical) side is not that the system of morals molds human beings and world into a particular shape, but that it *absolutizes* that particular shape. Nietzsche thus criticizes the fossilization of the moral interpretation of human beings and world in the name of their multi-interpretability and manifoldedness.

For Nietzsche, a human being is "the *animal not yet determined*" (BGE: 63—my translation). She is an animal, that is, embodied and driven by instincts. At the same time, she is distinguished from the animal because her instincts don't limit her to one particular model (cf. KSA: 11, § 107; Van Tongeren, 1994: 145). Nietzsche lets Zarathustra say that a human being is "a rope, fastened between animal and Superman"; she is a bridge, not a goal, her destiny is to go "up and beyond" (Z: 4, 43). Indefiniteness, not reasonableness, is the crucial distinction between human beings and animals. Following from this, Nietzsche sets himself the task of placing humankind back into nature:

In effect, to translate man back again into nature; to master the many vain and visionary interpretations and subordinate meanings which have hitherto been scratched and daubed over the eternal original text, *homo natura*. (BGE: 230)

In a certain sense, one can therefore argue that, although Nietzsche's view of human beings is of a naturalistic kind, this is not to be understood in an essentialistic or reductionistic way. The "nature" of a human being is to have no essence; particular historical manifestations are only an exemplification of this. Rather, this "nature" can be understood as an empty place from which a multiplicity of possibilities can arise. It's important, however, to notice that "empty place" and "nature" merely act as metaphors to criticize the prevailing uniformity with which a human being is represented. *De facto* she is never an empty place, she is never indefinite, but she is always already a particular possibility, without reduction to which there is no sense at all in speaking about other potential possibilities. The *homo natura* is the original text scratched upon with interpretations and meanings, about which one cannot speak at all without those interpretations and meanings. In this sense, every human being is unique, and irreducible to a basic pattern, since that pattern doesn't exist.

EDUCATION AS THE EVERLASTING TASK OF
SELF-OVERCOMING

Nietzsche's view of human being sheds additional light on the concept of education. In view of the importance Nietzsche attaches to being embedded and in view of his perspectivism, it has been argued here that education cannot but be understood as teaching to "lie," that is, as initiating the child in a particular view of what is valuable and worth living for. Mindful of Nietzsche's view of human being, one should now say that any particular molding of the child is detrimental to what it really is: not yet determined, unique, irreducible to a basic pattern. Therefore, the preeminently educational task—expressed by Nietzsche in the powerful dictum "become what you are" (cf. Nietzsche's subtitle for *Ecce Homo*: "How to Become What You Are")—can be defined as a never-ending process of self-overcoming. In other words, a human being's tragic fate is to live her life in the twofoldedness of, on the one hand, always being of a particular kind without, on the other hand, being allowed to be reduced to that particularisation (cf. Van Tongeren, 1994: 147).

It is of the utmost importance to understand that the child's educational task "to become what you are" should be understood as a process that can not get started unless a molding is "forced upon" her. Put otherwise, the child's true self is not of some sort of nucleus of essential characteristic features. Already there are germs waiting to be unfolded. It arises from within with thanks to the molding that is offered. In this respect, Cooper rightly argues that there is no child-centered pedagogy to be found with Nietzsche because of the importance of obedience and because there is no nucleus one should not counteract (Cooper, 1983b: 122–123). The child's true self lies not deep within herself but is rightly understood as being above her.

An important question that arises here is how exactly the child proceeds to self-overcoming—in other words how she discovers the (possibility to) transgress and thus succeeds to surpass the "herd." In view of the importance of being embedded, the only answer to this question can be that the impetus to self-overcome arises from the embeddedness itself. Education as teaching to "lie," the necessary precondition for the child to find her own path, means education must realize that it is *merely* a "lie." Education as "making something like themselves out of their children," as teaching the child to put things into perspective, means passing through what is worth living for without pretending that the perspective that the child is initiated into is universal and is absolute in nature. "I think, nowadays we're at least far away from the ridiculous immodesty, to ordain from our corner, that one only *can* have perspectives from a particular corner" (GS: V, 374—my translation). Education as *merely* "teaching to lie" then points to evoking the disposition of self-overcoming[2]—whereby evoking means arousing as well as provoking.

From the child's point of view, she then discovers that the cultural and historical shape of the world and the socialized and culturalized molding of her own self are "lies." It is important to notice that this doesn't lead her toward THE TRUTH, as should now be clear from Nietzsche's perspectivism; rather, room is made for the appreciation of "lying" *as* "lying." For Nietzsche the only possible truth is precisely this notion of the "lying" *as* "lying." "I was the first to *discover* the truth, through the fact that I was the first to experience the lie as lie" (KSA: 6, EH, § 1 of "Why I Am a Destiny"—my translation). Alteration, renewal, personal interpretation of the world, freeing oneself from the sociocultural straitjacket, and so forth, are not enacted against the background of a "true world" or on the ground of an essential nucleus, but should be understood as "a continuously shifting falseness" (KSA: 12, 2 [108]—my translation): The child must make her own "lies," again and again. She shall be most "herself" when continuously acknowledging her own indefiniteness—that is to say when showing herself to be open for a multiplicity of possibilities:

It is always more obvious to me that the philosopher, as a man *indispensable* for the morrow and the day after the morrow, has ever found himself, and *has been obliged* to find himself, in contradiction to the day in which he lives; his enemy has always been the ideal of his day. (BGE: 212)

In a certain sense, one should therefore say that the true individual never shall *be* but always *shall* be.

However difficult this task may be, the arrival of the higher human being is more than welcomed by Nietzsche. For Nietzsche's analysis of his time leads him to conclude that human beings are living in the mentality of the herd: "*Morality in Europa at present is herding-animal morality*" (BGE: 202). Human beings become dull, under the impulse of, among other things, the typical modern ideas and Christianity (BGE: 203), They degenerate into mediocrity and superficiality and please themselves with dullifying repetition of what they have been spoonfed—which for Nietzsche is the greatest danger for humankind.

The leveling and diminution of European man is our greatest danger; because the sight of him makes us despond. . . . We no longer see anything these days that aspires to grow greater; instead, we have a suspicion that things will continue to go downhill, becoming even thinner, more placid, smarter, cosier, more ordinary, more indifferent, more Chinese, more Christian—without doubt man is getting "better" all the time. . . . This is Europe's true predicament: together with the fear of man we have also lost the love of man, reverence for man, confidence in man, indeed the *will to man*. Now the sight of man makes us despond. What is nihilism today if not that? (GM: I, 12)

That's why, according to Nietzsche, every culture needs individuals who consciously commit themselves to that culture's values, (re)valuate them and thus revitalize them. The true individual *speaks* where the herd fails to speak; she eases the tightness of the chains with which the herd is enchained. This individual, "anti-christ and anti-nihilist," frees human beings from her will to nothing, to nihilism (cf. GM: II, 24).

RELATIVISM VERSUS DELIBERATE COMMITMENT

Are we at this point obliged to conclude than that it doesn't matter what exactly the individual does? In other words, is relativism the inevitable outcome? One could answer this question in a strictly philosophical way and argue that the question of relativism doesn't arise at all with Nietzsche because of his perspectivism. Nietzsche explicitly intends to settle for once and for all the business with the opposition "absolute" versus "relative": for want of absolute knowledge and truth—of a world which is not mediated through object representations—there is no sense at all to speak about relative knowledge and truth. Hence the problem of relativism dissolves naturally with Nietzsche. This answer, however, may not be very convincing for some. Because the matter of relativism is too complex to be fully developed here, I shall conclude by indicating some highly relevant issues.

As indicated in the introduction to this chapter, Nietzsche can be seen as the founding designer of postmodernism since he decidedly de(con)structs the foundational conceptual frameworks of modernity and, consequently, of education along modernity's lines. However, that there are no objectively justifiable grounds for an educator's action anymore doesn't tempt Nietzsche to say that everyone is correct. Nor does he shift the pith of the matter to the child (in a final attempt to provide education with a firm foundation again), for as has been made clear, even for Nietzsche, meaning does not arise from within the individual itself. Nietzsche's perspectivism, the outcome of the lack of objective foundations, can be understood as an incentive to stop looking for justifications and instead to articulate clearly what one stands for. For one could say that it is precisely the belief in objectively justifiable standards in education that can give rise to "dullifying" repetition, which Nietzsche so feared. If what one envisages to represent is THE TRUTH, then in the long run a clear articulation is not needed, so one could say, for in the end, the truth will prevail. Because there are no objective foundations but only perspectives, it is necessary for the educator, and later on for the child, to articulate what he or she stands for. So when Nietzsche says "My opinion is *my* opinion: another person has not easily a right to it" (BGE: 43), he is not making a plea for a subjectivist point of view or for relativism: Rather, he is emphasizing the importance of taking up a serious engagement to what one stands for. Making moral decisions— and what is education if not this—is not a matter of plain and simple re-enactment of what lies in the purportedly justified logical line of one's culture's expectations, but is in the end a highly personal matter. " 'Good' is no longer good when one's neighbour takes it into his mouth" (BGE: 43).

NOTES

I am grateful to Paul Smeyers for reading previous versions of this chapter and for commenting on both the philosophical argument and the language.

1. Cf. Nietzsche, BGE: § 22; cf. also *Kritische Studienausgabe in 15 Bänden* (KSA): 12, 7[60]. (The translation of his unpublished fragments was not available: therefore the references to these passages refer to the German text. The first figure refers to the volume, the next to a period of time delimited in that volume and the number between brackets to the section of that delimited part.)

2. I am indebted to Paul Smeyers for this particular way of putting it.

Chapter 11

Luce Irigaray Celebrates Friedrich Nietzsche—and Teaches Sexual Difference

Betsan Martin

One repays a teacher badly if one always remains nothing but a pupil.
And why do you not want to pluck at my wreath? You revere me; but
what if your reverence tumbles one day? Beware lest a statue slay you.
—Nietzsche, Z: On the Gift Giving Voucher, 3

INTRODUCTION

"Western" education could be regarded as split between the state agenda
maintaining a supply of workers for the (capitalist) economy and a more
idealistic agenda of being a conduit for life enhancement through access to
knowledge and cultural history. In both cases there is a component of social
reproduction. The aspect of supply of labor and economic continuity has
been well documented by analysts of the Marxist tradition. The aspect of
reproduction that is embedded in cultural knowledge, often at the level of
"higher learning" or more abstract knowledge (see Young, 1971), is not so
often scrutinized. An exposé of the values embedded in knowledge and
philosophy was the subject of Nietzsche's philosophical corpus, an exposé
that isolated him and made him out of time with his philosophical peers. It
was precisely Nietzsche's purpose to challenge many of the prevailing ide-
ologies of liberal thought, such as the illusory sovereignty of individuals and
utilitarian economic theory which dictated an economic imperative to human life. He despised stifling social conformity, which reproduced values
associated with ascetic ideals. It could be said that one of his main purposes
was to intervene against social and cultural reproduction, and to generate
the conditions for cultural recreation. Equality has been a spearhead for

many movements for change and emancipation in the liberal tradition—and nowhere more so than in education. In Nietzsche's analysis, equality is a trap—a mechanism for reproduction and continuity of values that deny artistic creativity. To state the case simply, equality as a framework for life enhancement and justice, philosophically for Nietzsche, is no more than aspiration confined within the metaphysics of a binary, oppositional system. Difference can be regarded as the endeavor to break meaning and values out of the confines of a binary system.

Nietzsche's work is a major legacy for the French philosopher of our time, Luce Irigaray, for her philosophical oeuvre of making a break with the phallic tradition of Western philosophy—a tradition of only one (masculine) sex. Like Nietzsche, Irigaray observes major problems with equality as a focus for aspiration and change because it does not lead beyond a system of patriarchal, or phallocracy: equality belongs to a system that violates the "other." Irigaray, like Nietzsche, seeks a break in the Western tradition in order to make space for a new paradigm, in her case, of sexual difference. The educational focus of this chapter is Nietzsche's and Irigaray's critiques of equality, and beyond that some of the philosophical conditions for knowledge constructed on sexual difference. The intent is to highlight a critical approach to knowledge for counteracting more of the same; this means investigating values that are embedded in knowledge and culture, which may not be readily discernible. Beyond critical analysis, this chapter will present aspects of *difference* that lead out of enclosure in thought which is premised on the values of one sex. The concept of "difference" as a critique of "equality" has its inheritance, or its genealogy, in the work of Nietzsche, even though it has perhaps become best known in the work of Jacques Derrida, through his notion of *différance*. This chapter will interpret Nietzsche's work as leading the way beyond metaphysics governed by enclosure within a binary system, which he framed as constituted on the relation between master and slave. Consideration will be given to Irigaray's movement beyond the horizon of opposition, opening space for the feminine as instrumental in culture.

The binary construction of knowledge is based on a mechanism of splitting—the masculine from the feminine, reason from passion, mind from body. Nietzsche's critique of moral values constructed on Truth and the binary oppositions good and bad brings the challenge for a constant review of "taught" values, scrutinizing their "truth" and inviting reexamination of the world or culture we know—reexamination that leads to re-creation. Irigaray's work on sexual difference is constituted by an analysis of the binary system as constructed on mastery, with the masculine as the definer of the binary terms, and the binary system itself represents a phallic structure. Irigaray contends that the aspirations to equality that have been largely the guiding force of the Western feminist movements will not deliver "liberation" for women because equality is limited to a system of mastery and a phallic framework that precludes the values of the feminine. The most that women will achieve under the star of equality will be a shift in position within the binary. It will not shift the system which is constructed fundamentally on the negation of the "other," which for Irigaray, is the feminine.

This chapter will begin with Nietzsche's critique of binary opposition— the Hegelian system of negation of the "other." Nietzsche's genealogical methodology exposes the operations of the binary as serving the purposes of mastery exercised as dominating power. Genealogical critique leads Nietzsche to language, and to the binary structure of (European) languages, as the wind which drives the ship of culture. For Irigaray, that ship is premised on phallic mastery, with a corresponding suppression of creativity and responsibility of women. Nietzschean genealogy enables Irigaray to expose the operations of the binary construction of the sexes and to develop her views of sexual difference. In her major text on Nietzsche, *Marine Lover of Friedrich Nietzsche* (1991), Irigaray undertakes a complex celebration of Nietzsche's philosophy, while at the same time exposing his work as a repetition of the negation of the feminine. For her, Nietzsche fails to articulate the "difference" that he claims to open up because he does not engage with shifting the feminine from the negated place in metaphysics. Failure to account for sexual difference constitutes a repetition of phallic mastery. Zarathustra, Nietzsche's spokesman for "man" as *different*—as beyond "man," the master of negation, who expresses his potency and creativity through affirmation—cannot be ethical because his pursuit of artistic creation is essentially solitary; it is not constituted through relation with the feminine. *Marine Lover* will be the major reference for Irigaray in this chapter for examining her notions of sexual difference and symbolic representation of the feminine.

NIETZSCHE'S CRITIQUE OF BINARY OPPOSITION

Nietzsche's genealogical critique of knowledge and morality shows the limitations of confining knowledge within rationality: rationality is an attribute of Western philosophy (in particular), constructed in *opposition* to passion or intuition. Rationality and knowledge are closely tied to the notion of "Truth"—and Truth, whether appropriated by theology, philosophy, science or linguistics, is a major target of Nietzsche's critique. In metaphysics Truth is equated with certainty, verifiability, unity and self-presence, and it has been regarded in philosophy as of transcendent and universal value, as having abiding value regardless of the concrete circumstances of time and space.

The Cartesian subject is transcendental—what he transcends is, precisely, his material basis, and he expels matter-earth. But at the time of Descartes—and this is what distinguishes him from his predecessors—the idea that the site is necessarily the site of Being and Knowledge has become so essential to the order of discourse that it was indispensable to the Cartesian validation of the universal. (Braidotti, 1996: 254)

The Fontana Dictionary of Modern Thought (Bullock et al., 1977) explains transcendence as the state of being beyond the reach of experience and mentions that its opposite is *immanence*. *On the Genealogy of Morals* accuses "knowers" of not ever taking time for experience. The *Dictionary* distinguishes the transcendent and the transcendental. The transcendent is unknowable by our minds because minds are dependent on the senses for their knowing. The transcendental, which is the basis of Kantian philosophy, is the logical hardware comprised of concepts and principles that organize experience. Nietzsche exposes logic as an insubstantial basis for truth; Truth for him is an idea that serves to camouflage the assertion of power and control:

What, then, is truth? A movable host of metaphors, metonymies, and anthropomorphisms—in short, a sum of human relations, which have been poetically and rhetorically intensified, transferred and embellished, and which, after long usage seem firm, seem to a people to be fixed, canonical and binding. Truths are illusions which we have forgotten are illusions; they are metaphors that have become worn out and have been drained of their sensuous force, coins which have lost their embossing and are now considered as metal and no longer as coins. (OTaL: 84)

The purpose of transcendental philosophy was to provide "universal knowledge" which must have the character of inner necessity, independent of experience, being clear and certain before itself (Krell, 1996: 11). It attempted to postulate a scientific basis for human knowledge that was consistent with the requirements of logic and that would signify a unified system of knowledge. Transcendental philosophy is an endeavor to find the essence, to find "access to things in themselves" (Krell 1996: 15). Kant's aim was to establish metaphysics as a science, the fundamental science of reason. Nietzsche objects to Kant's transcendentalism because it is an ideal of the scientific truth of rationality. The scientific ideal is the child of idealistic metaphysics and morals, and both of these ideals stem from a kind of asceticism. "Both science and the ascetic ideal stand on one ground . . . namely on the same overestimation of truth (more correctly, on the same belief in the inestimability, the uncriticizability of truth" (GM: 111).

The metaphysical ideal of Truth is part of the metaphysical structure of binary opposition, which is a focus of the penetrating critique of Nietzsche's *Genealogy*. This text is addressed to philosophers as "knowers" whose discipline is focused on truth—but Nietzsche opens his inquiry into the origin of the moral value of truth with the query that knowing does not take account of experience:

Our treasure is where the hives of our knowledge are. As born winged insects and intellectual honey gatherers we are constantly making for them, concerned at heart with only one thing—"to bring something home." As far as the rest of life is concerned the so called "experiences"—whoever of us ever have enough seriousness for them? Or enough time? (GM: 149)

Nietzsche interrogated the prerogative assumed by philosophers to promulgate the ideals of morality:

I went down to the deepest depths; . . . I started to investigate and unearth an old faith which for thousands of years we philosophers used to build on as the safest of all foundations—which we built on again and again although every previous structure fell in: I began to undermine our *faith in morals.* (Nietzsche, cited in Mahon, 1992: 92)

Nietzsche's attention, then, must be turned to the consideration of good and evil because this dichotomy is the basis for the construction of Christian morality and the moral norm of Western cultures. The ideal of Truth was equated with the logos, which was sanctioned as divine:

And in India, as in Greece, the same mistake was made "we must have been divine, for we have reason!" Indeed nothing has yet possessed a more naive power of persuasion than the error concerning being as it has been formulated by the Eleatics. After all, every word we say and sentence we speak [are] in its favour. "Reason" in language—oh what an old deceptive female she is! I am afraid we are not rid of God because we still have faith in grammar. (Nietzsche, 1982: 483)

Here, Nietzsche draws attention to language as the underlying means through which oppositional forces are perpetuated and cultural life is regulated. In *On the Genealogy of Morals* Nietzsche diagnosed the pathology of the dominant morality of "good" and "evil," which is governed by *ressentiment,* to have its roots in language: the division between "good" and "evil" is determined through the binary structure of linguistics and its deployment in the service of mastery. Nietzsche opens the way for Luce Irigaray to scrutinize the oppositional construction of the masculine and the feminine, and to propose language as central to shifting the feminine from an object to representation of the feminine as a subject in language.

Nietzsche's arguments for the danger of the moral evaluations of good and evil are based on his critique that this is productive of nihilism. The binary system is dangerous because it operates as an enclosed system, and the only movement possible within this structure is the movement of reversal of the terms. In this analysis reversal produces rancorous dynamics, driven by *ressentiment,* or fear of the other. The possibility of affirmative creativity is precluded by fear. The danger for Irigaray is that the binary is a system of mastery in which the masculine is the defining term. The masculine functions as the universal and therefore precludes the presence of the feminine in her capacity as a subject. The attributes of male subjectivity, such as rationality, the exercise of phallic power, autonomy, identity and the author of desire, function as a *universal* notion of subjectivity. Irigaray, among many other theorists and feminists, contends that this is an alienating conception of subjectivity for women because it is referenced morphologically to the *male* as a subject (see Irigaray, 1995). Irigaray's concern with fecundity and regeneration deepens Nietzsche's diagnosis of nihilism, to engage sexual difference for regeneration.

CRITIQUE OF EQUALITY IN EDUCATION

As Nietzsche's "pupil," Irigaray acclaims the treasures of his work: without idolizing him, she takes his arrows and redirects them with her own bow. Through her encounters with Nietzsche and *Zarathustra*, Irigaray opens the way for symbolic representations for feminine subjectivity and for new formations for ethical interchange between the two sexes, with temporality that accords with the feminine. Her encounter with Nietzsche models an ethic of sexual difference and represents her endeavor to bring Western culture toward regeneration of life. It is her perception that Western culture (in the desire for immortality) is preoccupied with the denial of death and therefore with the denial of birth (and the feminine).

The primacy that Irigaray accords to sexual difference is an intervention against the sexual indifference of the universal logic that is represented as mastery by Nietzsche, as the logic of the Same by Emmanuel Levinas and as the metaphysics of presence by Derrida (see Spivak, 1976: xxi). Naomi Schor, who identifies the universal in processes of "othering" and "saming," writes:

If othering assumes the other is knowable, saming precludes any knowledge of the other in her otherness. Exposing the logic of othering—whether it be of women, Jews, or any other victims of demeaning stereotyping—is a necessary step in achieving equality, exposing the logic of saming is a necessary step in toppling the universal from his/(her) pedestal. Since othering and saming conspire in the oppression of women, the oppression of *both* processes needs to be exposed. (Schor and Weed, 1994: 48)

(In this passage, Schor does not engage with a critique of equality as set out in this chapter.) If othering assumes that the other is knowable, saming, within which the notion of equality is embedded, precludes any capacity for difference. In *Marine Lover*, Irigaray, while exposing the processes of othering and saming as the negation of the feminine, builds an argument for sexual difference. Irigaray articulates sexual difference as a new universal—a universal of two sexes. It is articulated in a critique of a patriarchal universal of one subject, with reference to a broadly conceptualized "Western" linguistic structure and cultural/historical framework.

From Nietzsche and Irigaray's critique of equality, it can be deduced that girls' participation in education on the basis of equality runs the risk of leaving the universal intact: a universal of sexual *indifference*. Irigaray specifically scrutinizes equality for its basis in the universal, which is masculine and therefore inadequate for women. As she explains:

To demand equality as women is, it seems to me a mistaken expression of the real objective. The demand to be equal presupposes a point of comparison. To whom or to what do women want to be equalised? To men? To a salary? To a public office? To what standard? Why not to themselves? (Irigaray, 1993c: 12)

In "A Personal Note: Equal or Different?" Irigaray is explicit about her claim that sexual *indifference* has been the basis for the exploitation of women, and sexual subordination will only be solved through a strategy that deploys the notion of sexual difference. Irigaray interprets the "neutralization" of sex, for example, in the language that is "unisex," as a denial of sex. She says that the much more important work is to represent sexual difference by articulating the values of the female sex, as well as the male sex. Historically, the significant achievements on the basis of equality in many areas—the franchise for women, equal pay, human rights legislation for the prevention of child labor, legislation against abuse—in its myriad forms, has included sexual rights as well as cultural/ethnic rights, such as citizenship rights for indigenous people and affirmative action programs. Irigaray observes that often these are unstable gains.

The universal functions in such a way that women have to "sacrifice" their sexed identity. In Irigaray's analysis, specifically developed in *Marine Lover*, the universal is governed by the mastery of death. She identifies an economy which under the pall of death prevents the renewal of life that is only possible through birth—and, symbolically, through the valuing of birth. She specifies that regenerative love is possible only through the values of two sexes. The condition for regenerative love is ethical subjectivity—as "becoming" rather than "being"—in resistance to ontological subjectivity in which notions of masculine and feminine identity are embedded. Irigaray's critique of the universal is not a basis for the universal to be abandoned. Rather, it must become articulated with reference to two sexual subjects. A woman should not "[renounce] her natural identity" but should instead recognize the value of a "culture" of and for women. "She should not comply with a model of identity imposed upon her by anyone, neither her parents, her lover, her children, the State, religion or culture in general" (Irigaray, 1996a: 27).

In Irigaray's analysis, the phallic economy functions to separate; separations that might be identified in education are those separating practice from theory, the material and the symbolic. In *Marine Lover*, the continuity between language, subjectivity, relation to land and sea, mythologies, economic production and the distribution of goods is elucidated and reflects the continuity between symbolic economies and material economies that Nietzsche and Irigaray made explicit. Throughout *Marine Lover*, Irigaray sustains a critique of separation and distancing as a symbolic and material symptom of the phallic will to power. Sexual difference in education is to be addressed in language. The neutrality of the universal is untenable because it is a cover for the reinstitution of the masculine paradigm. Irigaray claims that there is no neutrality in language.[1]

Sexual difference cannot therefore be reduced to a simple extralinguistic fact of nature. It conditions language and is conditioned by it. . . . This accounts for the fact that women find it so difficult to speak and be heard as women. They are excluded and denied by the patriarchal linguistic order. (Irigaray, 1993c: 21)

Language is a key to repositioning women in culture. Education that espouses equality premised on the values of autonomy, rationality and freedom constructed as masculine attributes, without cognizance of passion, intuition and the body, means that a phallogocentric economy is reproduced.

LUCE IRIGARAY: SEXUAL DIFFERENCE AS A CRITIQUE OF NIETZSCHE

In *Marine Lover*, Irigaray examines the conditions of time and space in Nietzsche's endeavor to overcome the ascendance of ascetic ideals through the "eternal return" and "at a distance" for overcoming "man." Irigaray discerns a fault in Nietzsche's overcoming of man, that he in fact, continues to be governed by *ressentiment* through his fear of death. Fear of death in the binary economy correlates with denial of birth and the relation to the mother. The remembering of birth and the replacing (in representation) of the mother are major temporal and spatial conditions for new subjectivities—the overcoming of man. Irigaray's role as a teacher is to suggest spatial and temporal conditions for sexual difference for the inauguration of new history. Preparation for new history requires both analysis and imagining the conditions for sexual difference that will inaugurate new history. Time and space are the major motifs through which Irigaray's proposes the conditions for sexual difference.

Irigaray refers specifically to her writing of *Marine Lover* as a text in a series that will deal with the elements earth, air, fire and water. "I was anxious to go back to those natural matters that constitute the origin of our bodies, of our life, of our environment, the flesh of our passions. I was obeying a deep, dark and necessary intuition, dark, even when it is shared by other thoughts" (Irigaray, 1993b: 57). She reflects on the ways in which these natural elements are often presented as alien, and our relationship to them is fearful because we do not relate to them as part of ourselves; we do not see ourselves as intrinsic to the natural world but as masters of it. Where we cannot position ourselves as masters, fear dictates that nature is seen as monstrous. We deny our own elemental makeup in not recognizing our relationship to these elements:

We still pass our daily lives in a universe that is composed and is known to be composed of four elements: air, water, fire and earth. We are made up of those elements and we live in them. They determine, more or less freely, our attractions, our affects, our passions, our limits, our aspirations. (Irigaray, 1993b: 57)

Irigaray chooses the sea to represent the feminine and to engage with Nietzsche/Zarathustra from the "position" or point of view of water. Water represents amniotic fluids and feminine *jouissance* (joy) in sexual pleasure.[2] Amniotic fluids suggest the pre-oedipal time in the psychoanalytic structure, before the phallic symbolic intervenes to define the mother as castrated and therefore as impotent—an impotence represented as the denial of representation of the mother, in her own terms, in language. In this context of thought, the "waters" represent immemorial time that is anterior to positioning in the oedipal and phallic symbolic order.

The elemental, specifically the sea, provides Irigaray with different symbolics for speaking and for articulating notions of space and place. Irigaray signals that she is speaking to "him," Zarathustra/Nietzsche, from a different position, a space outside of which he is accustomed to relating to her:

You have always trapped me in your web and, if I no longer serve as your passage from back to front, from front to back, your time will let another day dawn. Your world will unravel. It will flood out to other places. To that outside you have not wanted. (Irigaray, 1991: 4)

Irigaray/the Marine Lover is speaking from a new place outside his system of the same, and she is speaking in a new language. She will not be captive to his definitions of her and support for his self-affirmation, "amplifying his speech with an endless resonance" (Irigaray, 1991: 3). "I am no longer the lining of your coat, your—faithful—understudy. Voicing your joys and sorrows, your fears and *ressentiments*" (Irigaray, 1991: 4).

In *The Gay Science*, Nietzsche celebrates the horizon as a new dimension of space—a horizon that is not blocked with the metaphysics of Truth—a new space for philosophy. The open horizon is the new vista across the sea that has been cleared of the philosophical and theological quest for truth.

At last the horizon appears free again to us, even granted that it is not bright; at last our ships may venture out again, venture out to face any danger; all the daring of the lover of knowledge is permitted again; the sea, *our* sea, lies open again; perhaps there has never yet been such an "open sea." (Nietzsche, 1974: 448)

It is into the new horizon on the sea that Irigaray sails with the fresh wind of sexual difference. Her venture into this new unchartered space has textually begun to be charted in *Marine Lover*.

The text is inflected with rhythms of the sea. Tidal rhythms suggest rhythmic time—a different approach to time than that of Nietzsche's eternal return. Tidal time evokes rhythms of daily time and the governance of the moon with monthly cycles. Phonemically, in the text, the *sea* becomes associated with *she*. The immemorial waters suggest the beyond, the unfathomable place that must be encountered to some extent as mystery because women have not yet or have barely begun the work of representing themselves from a place that is referenced to women. Nor has there yet been a time or space of positive sexual difference. Difference/distance is represented in *Marine Lover* as the space between (Zarathustra of the) mountain heights and the sea. The reader of Irigaray, however, must take care to avoid a monolithic view of these representations of difference; they are not symbols that can be used as fixed or set in concrete because the masculine and the feminine are not fixed in identities. They are identities in flux; Irigaray's writing is from a position of difference *and* critique, for which she employs a strategy of representing masculine values in terms of solids—ice, mountain peaks, gold—signifying as she has in other texts, enclosure and masculine, or more precisely phallic attempts to enclose otherness (in this case the feminine) within a system over which *he* can exercise propriety: this is the realm of mastery in which the master exercises power as ownership, as property.

The style of *Marine Lover* is not only a vehicle for conveying the qualities of fluidity. It is written in a poetic, lyrical style that intimates love for Nietzsche—and the shared focus of their projects—yet expresses the need for interrogation about how different subjectivity and a new paradigm might be achieved. Nietzsche's *Zarathustra* is written as philosophy *and* poetry, both fiction *and* theory, literature *and* analysis, a style that confounds these terms as opposites. Similarly, Irigaray writes philosophy in poetry, narrative and aphorism and employs polyvocality, reflecting Nietzsche's styles, to appeal to discourses beyond rationality's limitations—to bring passion to rationality. Irigaray's symbolic invitations to Nietzsche/Zarathustra to engage with her, and her challenges to Nietzsche, are textually played out in fragments, in repetitions, in suggestive nuances, returning again and again like waves of varying intensity, sometimes crashing, sometimes washing softly and rhythmically on the shore. Nietzsche's "eternal return" recurs to be played out in new terms by Irigaray.

The feminine voices are symbolic, at times the sea, at times a narrator, at times "a woman." The men whom she addresses can be men in general (more noticeable in the French with the use of "vous") or a specific man, with whom she chooses "tu" as the mode of intimacy: "between you (tu) and me, will there not always be this film that keeps us apart?" (Irigaray, 1991: 5).

A feminine voice, "speaking as a woman," cannot be articulated authoritatively, or prescriptively, because it has not been lived. Furthermore, to capture the feminine definitively would be to confine it within being, whereas Irigaray approaches the feminine in terms of becoming. However, a *place* from which to speak is the major condition for being able to speak. It is a place beyond that which positions her as supporting man's identity, to an economy where each might speak for themselves *and* be other for the other, in the horizontal and asymmetrical relations between the sexes:

If you were to gaze at yourself in me, and if in you also I could find my reflection, then those dreams would unlimit our spaces. But if I keep your images and you refuse to give me back mine, your self-same (ton même) is but a prison. (Irigaray, 1991: 5–6)

Throughout the section "Speaking of Immemorial Waters," Irigaray returns again and again to themes of opposition and to metaphors of space, signifying the ontological distance of the feminine from the masculine as oppositional distance, or as a further distance—a distance from which she speaks to him in a voice that is not his other. If "he" will respond, then the conditions will be created for intimacy and for proximity as a basis for conceiving spatial boundaries, and will allow for non-assimilative exchanges mediated with respect and generosity.

ZARATHUSTRA IS GOVERNED BY *RESSENTIMENT*, IN RELATION TO THE FEMININE

Both Nietzsche and Irigaray are engaged in an endeavor to "overcome man"—in the sense of overcoming subjectivity constituted on the negation of the other.

The most concerned ask today: "How is man to be preserved?" But Zarathustra is the first and only one to ask "How is man to be overcome?" I have the overman at heart, *that* is my first and only concern—and *not* man: not the neighbour, not the poorest, not the most ailing, not the best. (Z: IV, On the Higher Man, 3)

When Nietzsche proclaims "Yes, life is a woman!" (cited in Irigaray, 1991: 93), he may be desirous of appropriating her artistic qualities for his re-creative endeavors:

Woman is the veil, or sail which captures and secures man's self-affirming flight across her surface. Possession of her veil of beautiful possibilities guarantees his own infinite becoming. Becoming woman, becoming the mother who gives birth to himself. (GS: 87)

Woman is the life-affirming principle of endless becoming. "Woman" does not fit neatly into man's placement of her; she is in excess of it. In Nietzschean terms she is not silent; she makes a noise. In his maritime metaphor,

even on the most beautiful sailboat there is a lot of noise and unfortunately a lot of noise. The magic and most powerful effect of woman is, in philosophical language, actio in distans; but this requires first and above all—distance. (GS: 123)

Nietzsche's philosophy of the *übermensch* for overcoming man is articulated through the possibility of exceeding the confines of the truth of metaphysics by appropriating the elusive "excessive" women. If Nietzsche's project were the overcoming of "man" (as in the Enlightenment philosophical project of man as a rational subject), then overcoming the system that produces man is implicated.

Irigaray goes a long way with Nietzsche in his diagnostic approach of negative referencing to the other. In her analysis, *ressentiment* governs subjectivity, which is referenced to the feminine as other. Irigaray's interest in overcoming man is directed against subjectivity expressed as phallocratic mastery, by which identity is secured for man alone, and toward an economy of subject-to-subject relations: an economy of sexual difference. Nietzsche's notion of *ressentiment* as the governing of reactive forces of the slave is one that Irigaray employs to expose an operation of *ressentiment* in *Zarathustra*. *Ressentiment* is an expression of slave morality:

Slave morality says No to what is "outside," what is "different," what is "not itself"; and *this* no is its creative deed. This inversion of the value positing eye—this *need* to direct one's view outward instead of back to oneself—is the essence of *ressentiment*; in order to exist slave morality always needs a hostile external world; it needs physiologically speaking, external stimuli in order to act at all—its action is fundamentally reaction. (GM: 171)

Ressentiment suggests the dynamics of good and evil to be in play—and therefore ascetic ideals, which deny sensuousness and are motivated by fear (in contrast to the self-affirming strength of the masters). Irigaray's suggestion that Zarathustra is governed by *ressentiment* is startling, to say the least, and requires careful analysis. It positions Zarathustra as governed by opposition as a slave. Zarathustra is not the self-affirming, active master but a slave in the form of master. He therefore represents the rule of the ascetic ideal and, in Nietzsche's own terms, becomes the purveyor of evil:

The more you aim for height and light, the more powerfully you are rooted in evil. That is how your world was built—the good in it always assumes evil. Whoever rises up turns away from and towards evil. And there is no end to that eternal coupling. (Irigaray, 1991: 23)

This is a most surprising reversal, which compels the question of who, then, is his opposite? his master? To whom is he in debt?

ZARATHUSTRA'S *RESSENTIMENT* AS FEAR OF DEATH AND DENIAL OF BIRTH

Irigaray examines Zarathustra's joyful response to awakening and his impetus to escape to eternity—expressed in his litany "joy wants the eternity of *all* things, wants deep, wants deep deep eternity" (Z, IV: The Drunken Song, 11), which is often repeated. Announcing his desire for eternity is tantamount to a desire to escape—to transcend. The desire to transcend replays the motif of ascent (and glory) that Irigaray identified as characterizing the making of the gods. In the desire for ascent, Irigaray exposes the distancing operation of the pathos of distance, which leads her to expose the mastery in play. As a genealogist, Irigaray examines the quality of the forces on which Zarathustra's mastery is premised. Irigaray's evaluation is that Zarathustra's desire for eternity is a denial and fear of death; this observation lead to her assessment that he is governed by death. In wanting to leave behind the material and physiological limitations of man, he is, in effect, saying no to these attributes of life, and he is implicated in the ascetic ideal and *ressentiment* (the dominance of the forces of weakness and passivity, the negative) is the "other." Zarathustra is found to be contradicting Nietzsche's challenge to philosophers to engage with experience and with life.

It is the phallocratic *system* that is under scrutiny by the Marine Lover—not as the voice of the feminine as "other"—This would be a scrutiny from within that system and therefore would be an expression of *ressentiment*. Love is not possible from *ressentiment*. The lover of *Marine Lover* is the feminine as a lover of herself, she who values *her* life enough to leave the captivity of functioning in compassionate support for him. Compassion has effectively kept her enclosed within his system. In leaving his system, the Marine Lover is not only taking the responsibility of love for herself (and for women), but she maintains a love for him as well. It is a quality of love that encompasses responsibility for the future. The question is whether he is able or willing to listen.

The Marine Lover sees that Zarathustra, in spite of his wish to be the spokesperson of the place beyond good and evil, represents the overcoming of man, and she finds him still implicated within the system that Nietzsche wishes to transcend. He is still man and, furthermore, he is man in the position of a slave. His will to power is not active but reactive—driven by a desire for eternity, which, in Irigaray's analysis means fear of death. In functioning from fear, and therefore from *ressentiment*, then he is the slave, "one who is ruled by the morality of others" (Vasseleu, 1993: 82). The genealogical question, then, is Who is the master in this economy of Zarathustra?

In the first section of part one of *Marine Lover*, "Baptism in the Shadow," Irigaray refers to Zarathustra's appropriation to himself of the sun at noon, suggesting that the height of the day is analogous to the height of Zarathustra's, the wanderer's, aspirations/pleasure/attainments—a time and place where he revels with pleasure. "Still, still, did not the world become perfect just now?" (Z, IV: At Noon). To revel in the noon hour and dream of this as eternity, as if stealing time, is to ignore the shadows of the sun— the midnight on the other side, and the deepest depths of the sea where the sun does not reach. The sun illuminates his circle, his sphere:

The sun? the sun? and why should it hide the sun from us unless it is the same sun that you have taken as your projector of your circle? But this torch, your lamp, makes shadow. Even (meme) at noon. . . . Your noon leaves in the darkness the other side of the earth, and in its inside, and the depths of the sea. Does your noon itself not have another side? Do you see behind your sun? (Irigaray, 1991: 6)

Irigaray reminds him of other spheres that he does not represent in his circle. She perceives *ressentiment* in Zarathustra when he ecstatically wishes, in this noon hour, for eternity to be his wife. Nietzsche's challenge to philosophers who are genealogists had been to develop the discernment to ascertain active and reactive forces. Here Irigaray, the genealogist, signals the reactive forces in Zarathustra's longing for eternity:

Eternity, that is the music of one who senses and fears decline. And for passing beyond life and death, see how busily he is at work at this moment. To leave the body behind and fly away unburdened, isn't this always and forever the point of his creation. (Irigaray 1991:27)

In his desire to transcend death, Irigaray recognizes a corresponding denial of death, which betrays death's mastery of him. What she does is to remind him that death, destruction and decay are intrinsically tied to earth and to life:

But if your only love is for eternity, why stay on this earth? If pleasures and mortifications, for you are perpetually bound together, why don't you give up living? If birth amounts to a beginning of death, why drag out the agony? (Irigaray, 1991: 24)

In his desire for eternity, Zarathustra seeks to escape death, and in the escape from death, an escape from birth is implicated. Irigaray (and the

Italian philosopher Adriana Cavarero [1995]) diagnoses the denial of death and birth as symptomatic of Western culture. The way in which Irigaray and Cavarero link death with birth provides a major means to the project of revaluing birth and the representation of the mother in these philosophers of the feminine. She takes him even more deeply into material and feminine reality, in her reminder that death is tied to birth and that birth must remind him of the mother, of she who gives life. Embedded in the mastery of death are the denial of birth and the negation of the feminine.

The rhythms of birth and death, of decay and regeneration, are recurring processes to be honored if life is to be respected, both human life and natural life, linking Irigaray's and Nietzsche's claims for becoming as a mode of life and linking respect for the earth with respect for the feminine. The love of the earth that Nietzsche claims through Zarathustra is subjected to critique by the Marine Lover as Zarathustra's misrecognition of the processes that maintain the energy and vitality of the earth. He forgets that for man to become he must be engaged with material life. For Irigaray eternal return is the regenerating rhythm of birth and death. For Nietzsche it is the return of the possibility of joy and the affirmative will to power. Irigaray's interpretation is supported by the text in *Zarathustra* where Zarathustra wills the return of the ecstatic, joyful experience of the "noon" (Z, IV: The Drunken Song, 8). On the mountaintops, Zarathustra repeatedly celebrates the joy of solitude in soliloquies that suggest a play, theater, which are not life, but a stage. Solitude frees him from the compassion that ties him to his neighbor, leaving him free for self-affirming aesthetics—valuing the "I" but not the feminine/mother.

"An airy grave" (Irigaray, 1991: 28) is an elaboration of Zarathustra's adulation of the heights as a kind of death. His elevation is an escape: "And how he leaves you (vous) his other, in charge, in order to get as far away as he can" (Irigaray, 1991: 29). She lets him know that his quest for immortality is a passion that is often violent to her, so that she has learned to become passive and indifferent—experiencing a kind of living death, "a mourning veil" that keeps her from facing the reality of life and death because his claims to immortality depend on her position as "morte," as representing death. Irigaray's view is that he negates, or escapes pain, death and decay by "laying the burden on the other" (Irigaray, 1991: 29). His efforts to escape leave him in a precarious position: "as long as the other of himself appears to him only as a shadow to overcome, as a river to get over, he will miss his footing, tightrope walker that he is" (Irigaray, 1991: 29). A man who "resolves enigmas in himself" is one who starts to live in a world where the boundaries are not of place, of "geographical" boundaries, but only the limitations of his own body. When the other is not a shadow but a relationship, he will not have to walk the tightrope from which he fears to fall because he will be grounded in the reality of both of them—but also inspired by the fecundity that is generated in loving exchanges.

She turns to reflect on how it might be if a woman was not confined to the place he gives her—confined to the borders of flowerbeds, to use Irigaray's image, presenting a facade of beauty. She would come and go according to the times and seasons that suit her rhythms. She wants to disentangle herself from her role of providing a mirror image—to leave his projections so that she can find her own life. But she poignantly asks whether, if she leaves, he will just replace her with another who will function as other for him, refusing the opportunity for life.

THE MARINE LOVER MIMING ZARATHUSTRA AND EXCEEDING HIS HORIZONS

The motif of withdrawal (and of return) of the woman in Marine Lover mimes Zarathustra's withdrawal from the world of man and reinterprets Nietzsche's major theme of eternal return. In this case, as Irigaray explains in *This Sex Which Is Not One*, mimesis brings into play the place to which women have been assigned in a patriarchal economy, and it also creates a place to explore woman-referenced interpretations of subjectivity, values and ethics. Explaining the problematic of this place, Irigaray writes of "the aporia of discourse as to the female sex":

the articulation of the reality of my sex is impossible in discourse, and for a structural eidetic reason. My sex is removed, at least as the property of a subject, from the predicative mechanism that assures discursive coherence. (Irigaray, 1985b: 149)

Both Zarathustra and the Marine Lover return—Zarathustra to preach the way of the *übermensch* and the Lover (of the feminine and of "man") to engage him in a relationship with her that enacts a different economy, in other words, to teach sexual difference. She will no longer be in the position of supporting his subjectivity at the expense of her own: "You have always trapped me in your web and, if I no longer serve as your passage from back to front, from front to back, your time will let another day dawn" (Irigaray, 1991: 4). Zarathustra has been away for ten years. The return of the Marine Lover has very different connotations: she is "coming back from far, far away" (Irigaray, 1991: 4), suggesting, with reference to the title of the section "Speaking of Immemorial Waters," that she is coming back from time immemorial, from beyond the time of women's positioning as other, as his echo, his shadow. This suggests that she brings a message, as a woman, from another realm, a realm not governed by his ownership of her, where her body is not inscribed with his meanings:

I have washed off your masks and make up, scrubbed away your multicoloured projections and designs, stripped off your veils and wraps that hid the shame of your nudity. I have even had to scrape my woman's flesh clean of the insignia and marks you had left upon it. (Irigaray, 1991: 4)

The interlocutor of *Marine Lover* is a woman from whom these inscriptions of male possession have been washed away in a baptismal ritual that signifies a spiritual cleansing in preparation for a new life that is not governed by the weight of men's meanings. This is not a new coming. It is a return. Women have lived their fullness, their subjectivity, before. She therefore has access to a memory of what this might mean, memories that are retained in fragments of mythologies and theogonies, which can serve as genealogical sources of inspiration for aspirations to the meaning of the sexually specific feminine subject:

I know of no society that has lived from market exchanges amongst women. Perhaps such a one existed long ago? Perhaps such a one exists very far away? But where are the traces of a *currency* among women? And of a God *among* women? (Irigaray, 1993b: 80)

In this and other texts, Irigaray is calling out for ethical life between the sexes. Such an apocalyptic event would engage a new economy of the interval, the space between them as a necessary, separating space—necessary to signify the preservation of their differences. These differences could no longer be conceived as opposing differences, in which difference is repressed in order to sustain his self-enclosed subjectivity which imposes his propriety on her; in which identity is sustained by ownership. A rhythmic refrain is heard in *Marine Lover*, when the Lover laments: "for I love to share whereas you want to keep everything for yourself" (Irigaray, 1991: 19).

Irigaray engages markers of boundaries that are permeable and yet also signify difference. The membrane and similar terms such as the "film," the hymen and the cord or rope of the placenta, indicate proximity between the different terms *and* suggest (Levinasian) relational qualities in terms of the feminine. The feminine thus becomes distance in new terms, as an affirmation of difference, and retains the guardianship of relations as an attribute of the feminine:

His first mistake, from her point of view, was his mastery of the membrane that separated him from his mother—his refusal to be separated, in effect. His seeking to destroy the source of nothingness, once he perceives it as "nothingness", rather than God, by turning inward on himself, will hasten his own destruction. Here Irigaray agrees with Nietzsche in *On the Genealogy of Morals* (1968: 19) that nihilism, the will to nothingness, is a supreme danger. (Oppel, 1993: 101)

The membrane is no longer to be destroyed and feared but preserved, the film to be retained. The membrane is regarded as a feminine separating space that is not governed by phallocratic binary opposition of forces or dominating assertion of will to power as hierarchical distancing. Irigaray explores the membrane in various representations, including the hymen and the placenta. The placental economy in "On the Maternal Order" (Irigaray, 1993c)[4] is an example of various modalities of mediation that might be possible to respect sexual difference in knowledge and culture.[5]

Loving *Life* means engaging with birth *and* death, which are the unavoidable rhythms of life and the renewal of life, the only means to return. Claims to eternal life that are premised on transcendence and avoidance of the feminine will face men with the death that is nihilism. The death of his dominating subjectivity and the death of illusory self-identity would be signs of life. From this death, "she"—the feminine, the marine lover—offers him the opportunity of eternal return to life—again mimetic of Nietzsche—by exercising the power of affirmation of negation. It has been "she" who has been negated. If he now affirms her, exercising his will in the revaluation of the feminine (a task in which she is already engaged), he thereby *will*(s) not the return of the Same but another kind of rhythmic (erotic suggestion intended) return of the opportunities for relationship and the guardianship of the future. This is not the repetitive return of an enclosed circle. It is a new rhythm that has to remain open to what cannot be foreseen. Nietzsche has proved a wonderful educator: his student has in no way remained his or anyone else's pupil. Nor does she allow him to remain a master. In many ways, she has become his teacher. If they can be lovers, their creativity will bring the dawn of a *new* day.

NIETZSCHE AND IRIGARAY AS TEACHERS

Nietzsche does not expect an educator—such as himself—to participate in reproducing or carrying forward the conventions of a closed metaphysical system. A teacher or educator for him is the genealogist who disturbs enclosure, the philosopher with the hammer for destroying and building. Distance—action at a distance—is appropriated as the necessary space for change and free-spirited creativity. Irigaray breaks with the oneness of the universal to build a universal of two sexes. The power and distinctiveness of the discourse of sexual difference lie in the active positive creativity in the relation between the feminine and the masculine as the basis for a new social order. Whereas the ascetic ideal confines women's aspirations in opposition to that of men, within the limits of masculine desire, feminine jouissance leads to a horizon of a different future.

At the heart of the educational interest raised by philosophers such as Nietzsche, Irigaray and Levinas is a critique of the knowing subject whom Irigaray equates with the phallic subject and the phallogocentric economy. The knowing subject (the ontological subject) is constituted through language, which is structured on binary terms. Not only does this turn an educator-genealogist to linguistics, but it turns the teacher for new history to the creation of language that represents different modalities of subjectivity. If Irigaray has been educated by Nietzsche in her espousal of his philosophical approach to knowledge as genealogy and poetics, and thereby becomes, in her symbolic account, his lover, she also becomes his teacher and his critic in constructing knowledge for sexual difference.

NOTES

1. For essays on language, see "Women's Discourse and Men's Discourse," "Linguistic Sexes and Genders" and "The Cost of Words" in Irigaray (1993c) and "Love of the Other" in Irigaray (1993a).

2. In her essay *Corp-a-corp avec la mere*, Irigaray discusses *Marine Lover* extensively. As far as I know, the whole text has not been translated into English. I therefore rely to some extent on Oppel (1993).

3. Mimesis is a form of engagement with the discourse that imposes its shape on her by assigning her an opposing role—an imposition that effectively sustains the privilege of the attributes of rationality and unity as belonging to the male sex, so that in both a sociological and philosophical sense, they have become associated with the male gender. The challenge of mimesis is to mime and still retain that which is different, which cannot be absorbed back into the phallocratic system. In other words, to identify the feminine as exceeding that system is a task that is very much the text of *Marine Lover*. The Marine Lover wishes to speak heteronomously and beautifully to keep desire and pleasure alive.

4. For a very valuable discussion of this neglected area of Irigaray's work, see Schwab, "Mother's Body, Father's Tongue" in Burke, Schor and Whitford (1994).

5. In using the term "sexual difference," I do not wish to invoke the patriarchal mode of heterosexual relationships, nor do I agree with those who claim that Irigaray's project of an ethics of sexual difference reinscribes heterosexism. This interpretation can only come from a simplistic and careless reading of her work. "Sexual Difference" is referenced to the reality of two sexes and to an intervention into the enterprise of universality which recognizes only one sex.

Chapter 12

The Analytic/Continental Divide: Nietzsche, Nihilism and the Critique of Modernity

Michael Peters

All philosophers have the common failing of starting out from man as he is now and thinking they can reach their goal through an analysis of him. They involuntary think of "man" as an *aeterna veritas*, as something that remains constant in the midst of all flux, as a sure measure of things. Everything that the philosopher has declared about man is, however, at bottom no more than a testimony as to the man of a *very limited* period of time. Lack of historical sense is the family failing of all philosophers . . . what is needed from now on is *historical philosophizing*, and with it the virtue of modesty.
—Nietzsche, "Of First and Last Things," in HH: 12–13

INTRODUCTION

This chapter links up with themes pursued in the Introduction, for it too examines Nietzsche's place in the Western philosophy curriculum and asks why Nietzsche was all but ignored by English-speaking philosophers until very recently. This question, which is seen as central to philosophy of education, is explored in relation to a brief comparison between Nietzsche and Ludwig Wittgenstein and in relation to how each of them has been "made over" by analytic philosophers. The question is pursued further and to its ultimate source in relation to the so-called analytic/Continental divide. Nietzsche stands at the very heart of the separation of the two strands of contemporary philosophy and serves to emphasize the centrality of tradition and history for Continental philosophy. Nietzsche, through his concept of nihilism, continues the Kantian critique of metaphysics out of which Continental philosophy emerges, and it is this critique that is intimately tied up with Nietzsche's critique of Enlightenment humanism, modernity and liberalism. Accordingly, this chapter focuses on Nietzsche's critique of modernity, for it is this thematic that still decisively separates the problematic of Continental philosophy from that of analytic philosophy and determines the style and content of a post-Nietzschean philosophy of education. The final section traces the post-Nietzschean discourse concerning the critique of modernity in the writings of Jürgen Habermas and Michel Foucault.

NIETZSCHE, WITTGENSTEIN AND ANALYTIC PHILOSOPHY

In the Introduction to this collection, we commented on and documented the historical fact that, despite being a great educator and moralist, Nietzsche's educational thought largely has been ignored. Following David Cooper (1983a), we argued that this was true of his philosophy as a whole, especially its reception in the English-speaking world. Why Nietzsche's philosophy had been ignored in the English-speaking world, as we also remarked, is a complex question tied not only to the style and the ethical substance of his work but also to the legend of his character, his "madness" and the appropriation of his work by Nazi apologists. Nietzsche's place and status in the history of philosophy can never be an innocent question to be "read off" the reality of events. Indeed, similarly, the relation of any major thinker to the philosophical canon is open to the politics of interpretation, depending on the status of the interpreters, their philosophical training and cultural horizon (including national language and traditions), their institutional affiliation, the received biography of the thinker and the reception of the corpus of work of the thinker. In other words, the history of philosophy, which often follows the predictable "liberal" historical approach of focusing on *individuals*, at the expense of, say, *periods*, tends unwittingly to repeat, at a methodological level, assumptions concerning the philosopher as the author of his/her works or as intentional agent that are part of the liberal philosophical worldview. If anything, Nietzsche stood against any such simple worldview and the legitimation of the university based on it.

The question of why Nietzsche's educational thought has been consistently bypassed in the English-speaking world is part of this larger historical question. In the postwar period, the dominance of analytic philosophy and its status as *the* paradigm in the philosophy of education disqualified Nietzsche in a double sense: first, as a "real" philosopher who writes about anything recognizably philosophical, and second, as one who does not have or follow a distinct philosophical method. This first disqualification has operated in terms of a number of strategies: Nietzsche's work was seen to be of interest, if at all, to novelists or literary critics; his work was considered anything but philosophical. The second disqualification that insisted on method as a qualifying criterion for professional admission in the late modern period based on the emulation of the hard sciences tended to obscure in the English-speaking world anything that proceeded hermeneutically, symbolically or out of a combination of "psychological" and literary approaches. This double dismissal, implicit in the ruling assumptions of the analytic paradigm, bears a close resemblance to the charges made against Jacques Derrida in a letter to *The Times* by Barry Smith which was signed by thirteen other "analytic" philosophers. Both Nietzsche's and Derrida's cases demonstrate the *political* nature of the history of modern analytic philosophy and the Western curriculum in philosophy: of what is seen or allowed to count as philosophy and philosophical method, and of those who take it upon themselves to make such determinations.[1]

The ignoring of Nietzsche's philosophy and of his educational thought—his almost complete absence from the philosophical curriculum in English-speaking countries—is a question of considerable importance for the philosophy of education. How is it that someone of Nietzsche's philosophical stature could be systematically ignored and then become so fashionable beginning in the 1990s? This is both a historical question and a political question: it is a question concerning the *politics* of the history of philosophy. Nietzsche's exclusion from the philosophical curriculum and from contemporary philosophy of education by analytic philosophers is even more curious given his linguistic and philological orientation to philosophy. He was, after all, *the* philosopher, well before Ludwig Wittgenstein and postwar linguistic philosophy, who developed a philosophy of language based on a grammatical "method" with great respect for the concept. The similarities to the Wittgenstein of the *Investigations* are, at times, uncanny. Compare, for example, Nietzsche's remark, "The strange family resemblance of all Indian, Greek, and German philosophies is explained easily enough. Where there is affinity of languages, it cannot fail, owing to the common philosophy of grammar" (BGE: #20) with Wittgenstein's notion of "family resemblance" in the *Investigations* (Wittgenstein, 1953: #67).

Wittgenstein, like Nietzsche, speaks of a new way of philosophizing, of a new *style* of philosophy or of thinking that is therapeutic (Wittgenstein, 1953: #133) and designed to resolve puzzles that arise in our language through *grammatical* investigations. For instance, where Nietzsche proclaims "A philosophical mythology lies concealed in language which breaks out again at every moment, however careful one may be otherwise" (HH: 306), Wittgenstein suggests that "An entire mythology is laid down in our language" (Wittgenstein, 1993: 199). Both Nietzsche and Wittgenstein emphasize the importance of language—its powers to mystify us—and philosophy as the means by which we can undertake grammatical investigations to demystify metaphysical problems. Nietzsche, for example, writes in relation to the "I think" or the "I will": "I shall repeat a hundred times; we really ought to free ourselves from the seduction of words!" (BGE: #23).

Nietzsche, like Wittgenstein, responds to the dualisms inherent in the

Cartesian conception of the subject and, also like Wittgenstein, the "old philologist"—Nietzsche's self-description—tells us that we must become aware of and overcome grammatical *habits* (BGE: 24). He talks of the awkwardness of language, and he investigates, as does Wittgenstein, the misleading grammatical forms that produce a metaphysical illness. For Wittgenstein, too, philosophy can be likened to the "treatment of an illness" (1953: #254), and, in terms similar to Nietzsche, he suggests that metaphysical problems arise when we attempt to use scientific methods to investigate philosophical problems. He asserts that "We are engaged in a struggle with language" (Wittgenstein, 1980: 11e), and suggests that "Philosophy is a battle against the bewitchment of our intelligence by means of language" (1953: #109). Given these strong similarities between Nietzsche and Wittgenstein, and Nietzsche's overall linguistic orientation, it is perhaps even more curious why Nietzsche's work did not receive recognition or systematic treatment by analytic philosophers until very recently.[2]

Part of the reason for this neglect and deliberate overlooking of Nietzsche may be the ahistorical nature of analytic philosophy, which paradoxically, has also been naively historical in terms of its own self-description. The official story of its own inception, beginning with Frege and Russell, is described as a "revolution," a break with everything that went before. It is a story that is a self-invention, part of the preoccupation with its newly professionalized self-image in the academy and its "scientific" status. The official narrative is one that christens itself "Anglo-American," a nomenclature that is deceptive in terms of its linguistic and national beginnings and boundaries. Wittgenstein himself, it could be argued, was "denatured," domesticated and fabricated as a Cambridge philosopher—a makeover that largely stripped him of his Austrian identity and separated his thought from its Continental milieu and influences.[3] Analytic philosophy is also fiercely polemical in the self-assertion of its own identity, from the early days defining itself in opposition to Continental philosophy. This spurious distinction was defined in polemical terms. I am reminded, for instance, of the messianic ethos that originally characterized the *Wiener Kreis*'s manifesto with its Promethean faith in science, its extension of scientific method to philosophy itself, conceived in the form of a rigorous "verificationist" empiricism, and its underlying liberal worldview. Rudolph Carnap's "The Overcoming of Metaphysics through the Logical Analysis of Language," published in *Erkenntnis* in 1932, is the paradigm of the analytic attack on the Continental tradition. Carnap uses Heidegger's "What Is Metaphysics?" to demonstrate what he considers pseudo-statements.

Certainly, analytic philosophy, describing its own origins dating from Frege and Russell, was too ready to dismiss that which went before historically as of less significance. Yet the very stereotyping of the distinction has resulted in a kind of international bifurcation that has been intensely political and fiercely polemical to the extent of preventing a balanced and fair selection of the philosophical curriculum or a comprehensive portrayal of the history of modern philosophy. Moreover, this philosophically nuanced "culture war" has slowed down, if not prevented, interesting work that has and might have taken place at the interstices between so-called analytic and Continental philosophy (see, e.g., Dasenbrock, 1989). It has falsely divided philosophy in the West between a "scientific" philosophy based on a group style from a literary-historical philosophy turning on philosophers-as-writers and a philosophy comprised of texts rather than problems.

NIETZSCHE AND THE ANALYTIC/CONTINENTAL DIVIDE

Simon Critchley (1997: 347) has considered stereotypical representations of the analytic/Continental divide and attempted to redraw the distinction by focusing on a number of themes:

1. the centrality of tradition and history for Continental philosophy and the way it affects philosophical practices of argumentation and interpretation;

2. the way in which the concept of Continental philosophy emerges out of the German idealist reception of the Kantian critique of metaphysics and the significant way this is continued in Nietzsche with his concept of nihilism;

3. the centrality of the concepts of critique, emancipation and praxis of the Continental tradition;

4. the importance of the theme of crisis that runs through the Continental tradition;

5. an explanation and justification of the pervasive anti-scientism of the Continental tradition.[4]

Critchley concludes the abstract of his argument by "criticizing the professionalization of philosophy that has produced the analytic-Continental divide, insofar as this divide disguises a deeper possible debate about the identity of philosophy itself outside its professional confines" (1997: 348). One should observe that the *pedagogy of philosophy*—the drafting of courses, the selection of reading lists, the establishment of the philosophical curriculum, the standardization of teaching methods based on the lecture and the seminar and the introduction of common forms of assessment—along with recruitment and employment policies and the growth of philosophy journals and societies—are all a crucial part of the professionalization of the academy.

For Critchley (1997) Nietzsche stands at the crossroads that defines the difference between analytic and Continental philosophy. Critchley's (1997: 356) thesis at this point is worthy of brief summary. He suggests: "it is arguable that much of the difference between analytic and Continental philosophy simply turns on *how* one reads Kant and *how much* Kant one reads," that is, whether one is solely concerned with the epistemological issues of the First Critique, or whether one is prepared to entertain the systematic ambitions, in addition, of the Third Critique, and consider as worthy of study Kant's attempt to bridge Understanding and Reason through a critique of Judgment—the reconciliation of freedom and necessity. For Critchley, Nietzsche provides the critical response through his concept of nihilism, which is decisive for a whole generation of critical thinkers from Heidegger and Adorno to Lacan, Derrida and Foucault. He writes:

the recognition of the subject's freedom goes hand in hand with the collapse of moral certainty in the world, that the highest values have devalued themselves. Nihilism is the breakdown of the order of meaning, where all that was posited as a transcendent source of value in pre-Kantian metaphysics becomes null and void, where there are no cognitive skyhooks upon which to hang a meaning for life. All transcendent claims for a meaning to life have been reduced to mere values—in Kant the reduction of God and the immortality of the soul to the status of postulates of pure practical reason—and those values have become, for Nietzsche . . . standing in need of "transvaluation" or "revaluation." (Critchley, 1997: 357)

Critchley argues that it is the Christian *reactive* response to our all-too-human origin of our values in declaring existence or life meaningless that is the real source of nihilism. That is, once the transcendental guarantees of Christian morality and grand expectations based on them collapse or are exposed for what they really are, an active nihilism ensues. Yet the same genealogical critique, the loss of faith in the categories of reason, can also inspire a revolutionary demand for things to be different. Critchley retells the story of Continental philosophy by narratively crafting the importance of central notions of *practice*, *critique* of the present, the production of *crisis* (especially in relation to modernity), and *anti-scientism* (as a modernist metanarrative) in defining a tradition that recognizes the essential historicity of philosophy and, therefore, also the radical finitude of the human subject and the contingent character of human experience. This constitutes an important direction in post-Nietzschean philosophy of education: a philosophy of education based on central notions of practice, critique, and an understanding of nihilism. Post-Nietzschean philosophy of education not only provides a critique of the rational, autonomous subject but also directs our attention to sources of normativity that are both historical and embedded in cultures. In other words, it provides, a path for moral reconstruction after the so-called death of God—a way forward and a positive response to the question of nihilism that demands the revaluation of values. Most importantly, post-Nietzschean philosophy of education belongs to the counter-Enlightenment tradition of thought that asserts the historicity of human reason and experience on the basis of a radical questioning of the transcendental guarantee and moral authority of God, and all possible substitutes for God—Reason, Man, Science. On that basis, it is also fiercely anti-scientist.

The philosopher, in Nietzschean terms, is the one who provides an "unprecedented *knowledge of the preconditions of culture* as a scientific standard for ecumenical goals" (HH: 25). The philosopher, acting as a cultural physician, is not able to create culture but acts as a "solvent" or a "destroyer." Nietzsche was concerned to understand what it is and to develop knowledge of the conditions for the renewal of cultural in the age of science, and he wished to define the cultural significance of the philosopher. Above all, he wanted to signal the importance of the philosopher as a physician of culture, as one who could *prepare* the ground of culture, and, in the figure of the future philosopher-artist, *create* new values. The philosopher of the future is "the man of the most comprehensive responsibility who has the conscience for the over-all development of man—this philosopher will make use of religions for his project of cultivation and education just as he will make use of whatever political and economic states are at hand" (BGE: #61). Nietzsche talks of "genuine philosophers" in contrast to "philosophical laborers": "*Genuine philosophers, however, are commanders and legislators*: they say, '*thus* it *shall be!*' . . . Their 'knowing' is *creating*, their creating is a legislation, their will to truth is—*will to power*" (BGE: #211).

Nietzsche's "philosophy of the future" has essentially a de(con)structive task: to destroy dogmatism in all its forms—in religion and in science—and what he calls "blind secularism." In this role philosophy serves as the tribunal of education in an age without culture: schools must follow philosophy in destroying secularization and subduing the barbarizing effects of the knowledge drive. As part of secularization and with the promotion of a scientific worldview, education has lost its ability to confer unifying values. Philosophy, in terms of its own self-critique, must overturn the naive realism of science to undermine it from within by mastering the knowledge drive. Yet it must also move beyond the purely negative moment of skepticism if philosophy is to become an affirmative cultural force and philosophers are to become cultural legislators in the form of the philosopher-artist. Philosophy can pave the way or clear the ground for culture by showing the *anthropomorphic* character of all knowledge as well as by recognizing the power and necessity of illusion.

NIETZSCHE AND THE CRITIQUE OF MODERNITY

A post-Nietzschean philosophy of education draws its intellectual sustenance from Nietzsche's critique of modernity and Enlightenment values, especially liberalism (its construction of democracy) and secular humanism. The method, in part, is genealogical in the sense that it follows Nietzsche's exposure of the perspective from which Enlightenment valuations are made by analyzing the constitution of moral systems. By responding with a cultural perspectivism—implying a pluralism of moral systems—Nietzsche is simultaneously deconstructing universalist pretensions claimed by adherents of one system or another, and indicating that "truth" or "right" is a discursive result of a system that produces "right" or "wrong," "true" or "false" statements. He writes:

For one may doubt, first, whether there are any opposites at all, and, secondly whether these popular valuations and opposite values on which the metaphysicians put their seal are not perhaps merely foreground estimates, only provisional perspectives, perhaps even from some nook, perhaps from below, frog perspectives, as it were, to borrow an expression painters use. (BGE: #2, 10)

In *Ecce Homo* (1992, orig. 1888), having told the story of Zarathustra, in which he emphasizes the idea of eternal recurrence as the "highest formula of affirmation that can be attained" (p. 69), Nietzsche turns his attention to *Beyond Good and Evil*, which he says belongs to the "*No-saying* and *No-doing* part: the revaluation of existing values themselves"—"*the work of destruction*" (p. 82). He proceeds to comment:

This book (1886) [*Beyond Good and Evil*] is in all essentials a *critique of modernity*, the modern sciences, the modern arts, not even excluding modern politics, together with signposts to an antithetical type who is as little modern as possible, a noble, an affirmative type. In the latter sense the book is a *school for gentlemen*, that concept taken more spiritually *and radically* than it has ever been taken. (EC: 82; emphasis in original)

In *On the Genealogy of Morals* and *Twilight of the Idols*, Nietzsche continues the work of critique, first, through exposing the psychology of Christianity, based on the spirit of *ressentiment* as a preliminary study for the revaluation of all values, and, second, through an analysis of "modern ideas"—as he says, "the old truth is coming to an end" (p. 86). In the essay "Expeditions of an Untimely Man" (*Twilight of the Idols*), he writes a section entitled "Criticism of Modernity" beginning:

Our institutions are no longer fit for anything: everyone is unanimous about that. But the fault lies not with them but in *us*. Having lost all instincts out of which institutions grow, we are losing the institutions themselves, because *we* are no longer fit for them. . . . For institutions to exist there must exist the kind of will, instinct, imperative which is anti-liberal to the point of malice: the will to tradition, to authority, to centuries-long responsibility, to *solidarity* between succeeding generations backwards and forwards *in infinitum*. . . . The entire West has lost those instincts out of which institutions grow, out of which the future grows: perhaps nothing goes so much against the grain of its "modern" spirit as this. One lives for today, one lives very fast—one lives very irresponsibly: it is precisely this which one calls "freedom." (TI: 93–94)

For Nietzsche, then, the critique of modernity involves a critique of "modern" ideas and institutions: democracy, liberalism, humanism, "freedom," truth, equality, modern marriage, modern education and science. The critique of modernity above all involves crucially the critique of modern philosophy based on these concepts and its respect for their founding institutions. In opposition to modern philosophy, Nietzsche advocates an overcoming of the concepts of the "will" and the "soul," and, ultimately, of the morality that presupposes such notions.

Nietzsche, in passages like the one above in *Twilight of the Idols*, and in *Beyond Good and Evil* and *The Will to Power*, identifies the break with tradition as the defining feature of modernity, and he underscores its accompanying recognition that the sources of its values can no longer be based on appeals to the authority of the past. It is a situation that Nietzsche understands will bring about a kind of value reversal to traditionalism: traditionalism is understood in terms of the veneration of things past. Crudely speaking, "the older the better" because the further back in time we go, the closer we get to mystical first causes or origins, and the closer we get to the sacred books of revelation in the religious tradition. By contrast, modernity understood as a break with the past—an aesthetic, moral, political and epistemological break—encourages a self-consciousness of the present and an orientation to the future based on notions of change, progress, experiment, innovation and newness. Most importantly, modernity involves that myth it constructs about itself which is able to create its own values and normative orientations somehow out of its own historical force, movement and trajectory. Nietzsche rejects any simple-minded opposition and refuses to embrace one option or the other unreservedly. Rather, we might see him contemplating how and why "we moderns" want to draw up the historical stakes in terms of such an exhaustive dichotomy.

Alexander Nehamas depicts the Nietzschean diagnosis of modernity as one that involves a kind of impasse that can be called *nihilism*:

Reason has revealed the inadequacy of tradition: the putatively divine, or in some other way authoritative, origins of various institutions are not sufficient to justify them. The idea that such a justification might be provided by the existence of an inexorably progressive path toward final perfection is equally unacceptable: neither a single beginning nor a unitary end can provide a sense to the events that surround us. But in revealing the inadequacy of history, reason has also itself lost the ability to provide the means for the evaluation of our institutions because any such evaluation is bound to be circular. Reason can provide a rational evaluation of such institutions only if it can be rationally demonstrated that it has the ability to do so; but such a demonstration will inevitably have to be based on the very principles which need to be justified. (Nehamas, 1996: 227)

Nihilism, Nehamas suggests, interpreting Nietzsche, is brought about by a threefold realization. First, we relinquish the modernist belief in progressive historical change and the corresponding view that there is meaning to be found in events—"becoming aims at *nothing* and achieves *nothing*." Second, we come to understand that there is no coherent pattern for world history and no universal method or procedure for interpreting it. Third, we realize that the seemingly stable world of being to which we appeal in order to evaluate and judge the world of becoming is itself no more than a psychological concept constructed from our needs. Nehamas (1996: 228) cites Nietzsche's remark in *The Will to Power* (12): "the categories 'aim', 'unity', 'being', which we used to project some value into the world—we *pull out* again; so the world looks *valueless*."

Nietzsche's attitude to modernity is complex and cannot be identified with easy assessments as have been provided by a variety of contemporary philosophers who focus on one central feature of Nietzsche's critique: rationality or truth, or irony or relativism. Nehamas provides an interpretation of Nietzsche that disputes the readings offered by Heidegger, Habermas, Rorty and MacIntyre. In the eyes of Nehamas, Nietzsche is not the "last metaphysician," or the irrationalist and nostalgic romantic, or the playful ironist convinced of the contingency of our subjectivity and institutions or, finally, a radical relativist. According to Nehamas' interpretation, Nietzsche is to be characterized as a postmodernist. By this he means that for Nietzsche modernity does not designate a single thing, perhaps not even a distinct cultural-historical period and certainly not something that "we moderns" can somehow appreciate, justify or criticize *as a whole*. Yet this does not mean that specific institutions and values cannot be criticized or defended. Nietzsche entertains a complex and divided view of tradition as that which constitutes not only the past but also the present—a source of cultural continuity often underestimated by a reading of modernity characterized as essentially a break with and overcoming of tradition on the basis of radical progress in scientific understanding and socioeconomic change. Nietzsche's view, Nehamas argues, is more typical of what we now understand as modernism.

> In Modernism we find both the love of innovation and the rejection of the authority of tradition, but also, and at the same time, a questioning of the value of progress, a critique of rationality, a sense that premodern civilization involved a wholeness and unity that have been irreparably fragmented. (Nehamas, 1996: 224)

Where Nehamas "saves" Nietzsche from himself, from being consumed by his own critique by contrasting the twin competing notions of modernity and modernism, Gary Shapiro emphasizes the differences in interpretation between generations of Nietzsche scholars. Specifically, he suggests that the first generation of interpreters of Nietzsche, impressed with the nineteenth-century cult of progress, saw him as a philosopher of the future who radicalized and rewrote the modernist metanarrative. By contrast,

Now we read Nietzsche as the paradigmatic postmodern philosopher, providing a genealogy and a deconstruction of those modernist metanarratives. He does not offer simply one more transformation . . . of such grand stories of legitimation but rigorously and vigilantly undermines the claims to uniqueness and legitimation that one finds in the enlightenment tradition. . . . Our Nietzsche is the radical critic of such future oriented thinking. Above all he exposes that logic of *ressentiment* by which the future is laid under the obligation of redeeming the debts of the past. (Shapiro, 1991: 15)

In politics as in other areas of philosophy Nietzsche, once considered marginal, has now become part of the canon. This change of status is, in part, as Mark Warren (1998: 90) confirms, "a result of what it means to do political theory." His summary of Nietzsche's relevance to contemporary political theory is worth repeating here in its lengthy form because it prefigures Nietzsche as a thinker who, on the basis of his critique of modernity, anticipates many contemporary theoretical moves.

Where . . . political theory is driven by a quest for epistemological certainty . . . Nietzsche questions not just whether epistemological certainty is possible, but whether it ought to be a goal of thinking at all. Where political theorists are captivated by philosophical approaches to life . . . Nietzsche injects aesthetic, psychological and pragmatic perspectives. . . . Where political theory seeks universal principles or unitary designs, Nietzsche draws our attention to ways such principles and designs generate costly dismissals of the world with its plural possibilities. Where political theorists attend to judgements of the mind, Nietzsche reminds us that our embedded existence is more than a residue of life to be conquered by the mind. Where political theorists are attracted to big abstractions, Nietzsche shows how such attractions depend upon sacrificing honesty and disciplined analysis with respect to experience and history. Against those who define political philosophy as applied ethics, Nietzsche suggests ethical sensibilities may be part of life in ways not captured by the "application" of ethical rules. Where political theorists seek to insulate political life from contingency, Nietzsche points to the ways in which contingency makes us what we are. . . . When political theorists understand power as external forms of coercion that are polar opposites of thought, reason, and discussion, Nietzsche reminds us that ideas and judgments, cultures and interpretations, have effects as well, that there is an important (and relevant) sense in which they, too, are power. Where political theorists take capacities for political judgment, agency, and responsibility for granted, Nietzsche asks how such capacities could come into existence and what makes such individuals possible. And where political theorists become enamoured of language as the medium of public life, Nietzsche is there to show how language, however necessary, can also constrain and flatten the uniqueness, the extraordinariness, the particularity of individual experiences. (Warren, 1998: 91–92)

It is, perhaps, no wonder that Jürgen Habermas should identify Nietzsche's thinking as the decisive point of entry both into discussions of postmodernity and into the task of identifying what is necessary to reconstruct the philosophical discourse of modernity in order to preserve its emancipatory impulse. On Habermas' account, Nietzsche's critique of modernity engulfs the very norms of autonomy and rationality that constitutively define political modernity and thereby undermines the very possibility of critique. Habermas' view was very influential in shaping the debate during the 1980s and 1990s over the nature, scope and conditions of possibility of postmodernity, and he characterizes contemporary French philosophy, after Nietzsche, in a fierce polemic as an anti-modern irrationalism instituting a total break with Enlightenment values. Both Habermas' interpretation of Nietzsche and Nietzschean-inspired French philosophy are palpably false; neither seeks a total break with the Enlightenment, though this does not mean that they do not reject certain features of modernity or attempt to revalorize tradition, or, ultimately, inquire into the cultural conditions necessary for the creation of new values. On Warren's analysis we might picture Habermas as someone looking for a political solution to nihilism where there isn't one to be found. Ultimately, in Nietzsche's view there are only cultural solutions to nihilism, to which politics should be subordinated (Warren, 1998: 93).

HABERMAS, NIETZSCHE AND THE QUESTION OF POSTMODERNITY

In an early lecture—"Modernity versus Postmodernity"—delivered in 1980 as an acceptance speech for the Adorno Prize bestowed upon him by the city of Frankfurt, Jürgen Habermas (1981) casts himself as defender of what he calls "the project of modernity," which he traces back to Kant and Weber, against the "antimodern sentiments" of a variety of self-styled postmodernist thinkers. Habermas (1981) attributes the term *postmodernity* to the French current of thought, the tradition, as he says "running from Bataille to Derrida by way of Foucault," and he compares the critique of reason of these French philosophers to the "Young Conservatives" of the Weimar Republic:

The *Young Conservatives* recapitulate the basic experience of aesthetic modernity. They claim as their own the revelations of a decentered subjectivity, emancipated from the imperatives of work and usefulness, and with this experience they step outside the modern world. . . . To instrumental reason, they juxtapose in manichean fashion a principle only accessible through evocation, be it the will to power or sovereignty, Being or the dionysiac force of the poetical. (Habermas, 1981: 13)

Habermas' typology distinguishes the "anti-modernism" of the "Young Conservatives" from the "premodernism" of the "old conservatives" and from the "postmodernism" of the "neoconservatives" while hinting at a new ideological shift that focuses on an alliance of the postmodernists with premodernists. By contrast, Habermas (1981: 12) situates himself (and Adorno) in a relation to the "project of modernity" to learn "from the mistakes of these extravagant programs which have tried to negate modernity."

The issue between Habermas and the poststructuralists, as Habermas sees it at least, concerns their respective evaluations of modernity. Habermas, locating himself in the tradition of Marxist social criticism as reflected in the work of the Frankfurt school, argues that we should attempt to preserve the "emancipatory impulse" behind the Enlightenment:

The project aims at a differentiated relinking of modern culture with an everyday praxis that still depends on vital heritages . . . this new connection, however, can only be established under the conditions that societal modernization will also be steered in a different direction. The life-world has to become able to develop institutions out of itself which set limits to the internal dynamics and to the imperatives of an almost autonomous economic system and its administrative complements. (Habermas, 1981: 21)

In contrast, he sites so-called poststructuralist thinkers in a tradition of a line of thinkers, intellectually indebted to Nietzsche and Heidegger, who allegedly wish for a total break with the Enlightenment by criticizing the very constitutive norms of modernity that together make critique possible.

Habermas sees his work as a continuation of a philosophy of history that arose in the eighteenth century with the work of Kant, Herder, Condorcet and Hegel, whereas French poststructuralism specifically involves a rejection of the narrative of world history conceived of as the story of a single logical-temporal movement able to embrace and contain, without residue, all individual histories and cultural differences. This totalizing-world narrative is seen by poststructuralist thinkers as inherently ideological, serving only to legitimate certain views and values at the expense of others. From the vantage point of poststructuralist thought, this Hegelian philosophy of history, which since the Enlightenment has presented itself as the ultimate horizon of all interpretations, appears simply as *one* way of making sense of world events among others. It functions as myth to describe the progress of a universal subject and protects from criticism a specific set of cultural values that are deeply embedded in Western cultural modernity. From the viewpoint of poststructuralists, the rejection of the grand narrative is by no means a flight from understanding world history. Rather, it is an important first step toward comprehending the historicity of our values and institutions.

For example, Lyotard's *The Postmodern Condition* (1984) is, above all, a critique of Enlightenment metanarratives—*grand récits*—which in terms of their alleged totality, universality and absolutist status render themselves ahistorical, as though their formation took place outside of history, of language and of social practice. Lyotard wants to question the dogmatic basis of these metanarratives, their "terroristic" and violent nature, which in asserting certain "Truths" from the perspective of an authorized discourse, does so only by silencing or excluding statements from another. Lyotard, in a now-often-quoted passage, uses the term *modern*

to designate any science that legitimates itself with reference to a metadiscourse . . . making an explicit appeal to some grand narrative, such as the dialectics of the Spirit, the hermeneutics of meaning, the emancipation of the rational or working subject, or the creation of wealth. (Lyotard, 1984: xxiii)

In contrast, he defines "postmodern" elliptically as "incredulity toward metanarratives," by which he means to point to "the obsolescence of the metanarrative apparatus of legitimation" to which corresponds "the crisis of metaphysical philosophy and of the university institution" (Lyotard, 1984: xxiv).

Lyotard's (1984) work historically challenges the two grand Hegelian metanarratives—the emancipation of humanity and the speculative unity of knowledge—which underlie the philosophical tradition to which Habermas belongs. Lyotard's indirect assault is against the concept of "totality"—elsewhere he announces "a war against totality"—and the notion of autonomy as it underlies the sovereign subject. His line of argument, therefore, is an apparent confrontation with Habermas' notion of a rational society modeled on communicational processes where so-called validity claims immanent in ordinary conversation can be discursively redeemed at the level of discourse. In this realm and vision of a "transparent" communicational society, moral and practical claims are said to be resolved rationally and consensually without distortion or coercion—claims are said to be resolved through only the force of pure argumentation itself. For Lyotard, this conception represents the latest, perhaps last, attempt at building a "totalizing" philosophy: one that depends on driving together, albeit in an original way, the two grand Hegelian metanarratives, which, themselves, are under suspicion. The "totalizing," emancipatory vision of a "transparent" communication society, by invoking a quasi-transcendentalism and ideal of consensus, is both "terroristic" and exclusory.

Habermas' (1981) original and uncompromising stance as the defender of the radical traditions of the Enlightenment and as a fierce antagonist of poststructuralism has softened considerably as he has reevaluated his position (Habermas, 1987a). Although he is more charitable to Foucault than he is to Derrida, there is clearly less of a desire on Habermas' part to define or to treat them together as "Young Conservatives" and more of an effort to recognize the differences that characterize their work. Habermas (1987a) might even appear to be encouraged by aspects of Foucault's work, paying tribute to him especially for his genealogical research on the subject and his account of power. In more recent work still, Habermas (1990) openly acknowledges how his position and that of the poststructuralists are not as antithetical as they have often been commonly conceived. By contrast, other commentators (e.g., Lash and Boyne, 1990; White, 1988) have emphasized the kinds of affinity that exist between Habermas and the poststructuralists, commenting on the way they share certain characteristics, particularly in regard to their objects of criticism and their respective visions of viable contemporary political forms.

Some five years after the Adorno lecture, Habermas again turns to address "the philosophical discourse of modernity" in a book originally published in German under the title *Der Philosophische Diskurs der Moderne: Zwölf Vorlesungen* in 1985 and translated as *The Philosophical Discourse of Modernity* (1987a). Habermas (1987a: 74) does not merely wish to defend "the project of modernity" by explicating the concept of the subject and subjectivity in accordance with the model of unconstrained consensus formation in a communication community. He also wants to tell a story about the history of modern philosophy, which suggests that "the discourse of modernity took the wrong turn at that first crossroads before which the young Marx stood once again when he criticized Hegel."

To tell the story in this way enables Habermas to *agree* with the post-structuralists that the paradigm of the philosophy of consciousness is exhausted, but against the poststructuralists he attempts to preserve the impulse of the project of modernity by developing what he refers to as the "paradigm of mutual understanding"—the intersubjectivist paradigm of communicative action that first surfaces in *Knowledge and Human Interests* (1971) and is brought to fruition in *Theory of Communicative Action* (1984, 1987b). This paradigm, like the Nietzschean-inspired critique of Western *logos*, can similarly emphasize the embodiedness of reason in history and language against its universalist and ahistorical pretensions. Yet it can do so allegedly *without* undermining the capacity of reason to be critical.

Habermas emphasizes some common ground and agreement when he suggests that the paradigm of the Cartesian-Kantian philosophy of consciousness is exhausted. He identifies two paths of postmodernity that lead out of Nietzsche: one leads through Heidegger to Derrida, and the other through Bataille to Foucault. Nietzsche's work is the decisive point of entry into discussions of postmodernity and into reconstructing the philosophical discourse of modernity. Habermas (1987a: 97) comments:

Nietzsche's critique of modernity has been continued along both paths. The sceptical scholar who wants to unmask the perversion of the will to power, the revolt of reactionary forces, and the emergence of a subject-centered reason by using anthropological, psychological, and historical methods has successors in Bataille, Lacan and Foucault; the initiate-critic of metaphysics who pretends to a unique kind of knowledge and pursues the rise of the philosophy of the subject back to its pre-Socratic beginnings has successors in Heidegger and Derrida.

The Nietzschean-inspired critique of the Western *logos* proceeds destructively and eventually collapses in upon itself:

It demonstrates that the embodied, speaking and acting subject is not master in its own house; it draws from this conclusion that the subject positing itself in knowledge is in fact dependent upon something prior, anonymous, and transsubjective—be it the dispensation of Being, the accident of structure-formation, or the generative power of some discourse formation. (Habermas, 1987a: 310)

These insights are preserved, Habermas (1987a: 311) maintains, in his own "less dramatic" but "testable" critique of subject-centered reason, without being prone to the same destructive consequences:

It conceives of intersubjective understanding as the telos inscribed into communication in ordinary language, and of logocentrism of Western thought, heightened by the philosophy of consciousness, as a systematic *foreshortening* and *distortion* of a potential always already operative in the communicative practice of everyday life, but only selectively exploited.

Poststructuralists have difficulty accepting Habermas' argument, based on a phenomenological notion of the lifeworld, that particular forms of life, which are heterogeneous and emerge in the plural, are connected in the sense that they exhibit universal structures common to lifeworlds in general. These universal structures, we are told, are only imprinted on particular life forms through the medium of action oriented to mutual understanding. The normative content of modernity, therefore, is to be justified from the rational potential inherent in everyday communicative practice.

In sum, then, Habermas returns to the counterdiscourse of modernity to examine the major crossroads. At the first crossroads, as Thomas McCarthy (1987: xvi) points out, he returns to Hegel to reconsider the notion of ethical life, equipped with the paradigm of mutual understanding, and "to argue that the other of reason invoked by the post-Nietzscheans is not adequately rendered in their 'model of exclusion.' " At the next major crossroads he follows Marx's injunction for philosophy to be both practical and anchored in practice. Yet with the advances of the linguistic turn in philosophy this praxis is to be conceived not in terms of labor but in terms of communicative action, where universal validity claims transcend the local context to make possible the learning that proceeds from rational argumentation.

Yet Habermas' commitment to a universalistic perspective on rationality and ethics became increasingly contestable as the 1980s and 1990s proceeded. Accordingly, Habermas has modified his position from assertions about what is implicit in the speech actions of *all* actions to assertions about the intuition of competent members of *modern* societies. For Habermas, the displacement of humanism is the displacement of the individual knowing subject—the cogito—as the universal source of all authority, morality and power. It is, however, not a complete rejection of humanism *per se* or the Enlightenment impulse. Rather, it is an attempt to understand the subject in the wider linguistic, social and cultural networks of intersubjectivity.

To seek to define the internal teleology of time and the direction in which the history of humanity is moving, Foucault (1984) argues, is essentially a *modern* preoccupation—"modern" in the Kantian sense. The Kantian sense of "modern," Foucault tells us, is derived from the question, *Was ist Aufklärung?* which is posed in terms of the difference "today" introduces with respect to "yesterday." This is not to make any statement about the historical relation between the Enlightenment and the modern era conceived of as a separate and distinct epoch of Western culture.

We are given a clue to Foucault's position in a reading of a crucial but minor text of Kant. Foucault (1984: 21) asks: "What, then, is the event that is called the Aufklärung and that has determined, at least in part, what we are, what we think, and what we do today?" In an ironic inversion, posing the question, "What is modern philosophy?", Foucault answers:

Perhaps we could respond with an echo: modern philosophy is the philosophy that is attempting to answer the question raised so imprudently two centuries ago: *Was ist Aufklärung?*

We are informed that Kant defines Enlightenment in a negative way, as the process that releases us from the status of immaturity. Enlightenment, then, is the moment we come of age in the use of reason, when there is no longer the need to subject ourselves to forms of traditional authority. The notion of critique is also required at exactly this point, for its role is that of defining the conditions under which the use of reason is legitimate in order to determine what can be known, what must be done and what may be hoped. This reading of Kant's text allows Foucault to characterize modernity as an attitude rather than an epoch (or a style) and to assert that the thread connecting us to the Enlightenment is not "faithfulness to doctrinal elements, but rather the permanent reactivation of an attitude—that is, of a philosophical ethos that could be described as a permanent critique of our historical era" (Foucault, 1984: 42).

NOTES

1. Barry Smith (Editor, *The Monist*) instigated the letter which was signed by Hans Albert, David Armstrong, Ruth Barcan Marcus, Keith Campbell, Richard Glauser, Rudolf Haller, Massimo Mugnai, Kevin Mulligan, Lorenzo Pena, Willard van Orman Quine, Wofgang Rod, Edmund Ruggaldier, Karl Schuhmann, Daniel Schulthess, Peter Simons, Rene Thom, Dallas Willard and Jan Wolenski. In a related incident,

Ruth Barcan Marcus, the Halleck Professor of Philosophy at Yale, wrote to the French government (Ministry of Research and Technology) on March 12, 1984 to protest Derrida's nomination to the position of director of the International College of Philosophy, citing Foucault's alleged description of Derrida as practicing "*obscurantisme terrioriste.*" Derrida was teaching at Yale at the time. He remarks upon this affair in a footnote to "Afterword: Toward an Ethic of Discussion" in *Limited Inc* (Derrida, 1988: 158–159) in relation to the exchange with John Searle, who used the same epithet as Marcus in an article published in the *New York Review of Books.* In relation to Searle's usage, Derrida remarks:

I just want to raise the question of what precisely a philosopher is doing when, in a newspaper with a large circulation, he finds himself compelled to cite private and unverifiable insults of another philosopher in order to authorise himself to insult in turn and to practice what in French is called a *jugement d'autorite*, that is, the method and preferred practice of all dogmatism. (p. 158)

He comments on the "Marcus affair" in the same footnote in the following terms:

I have cited these facts in order better to delimit certain concepts: in such cases, we are certainly confronted with chains of repressive practices and with the police in its basest form, on the border between alleged academic freedom, the press, and state power. (p. 159)

2. David Cooper mentions Wittgenstein in relation to Nietzsche. Explaining Nietzsche's philosophy of truth, Cooper (1983a: 69) writes:

For Nietzsche, as for Wittgenstein, concepts do not emerge through paying private attention to inner experience; on the contrary, "inner experience enters our consciousness only after it has found a language the individual understands."

Cooper (1983: 78) likens Nietzsche to Wittgenstein again when he explains that some conceptions are so ingrained that it becomes peculiar to speak of them as beliefs or knowledge at all: rather, they are preconditions for the making of such claims—the "unmoving foundations" of Wittgenstein's language-games. Finally, he speculates on why Nietzsche and Wittgenstein differ over philosophy itself and whether, in Wittgenstein's dictum, it "leaves everything as it is":

It is puzzling, *prima facie*, that the reaction of Wittgenstein and Nietzsche—who clearly thinks many of our ways of talking must be overturned and reconstructed—should be so different, given their remarkable kinship on so many large matters: the rejection of "private languages", denial of the sense of comparing language and reality as wholes, the emphasis on behavioural criteria for psychological concepts, the idea of logical grammer, and so on. (Cooper, 1983: 80)

I have argued for a Nietzschean reading of Wittgenstein, or at the least, the adoption of a historico-cultural approach to Wittgenstein, that made room for the influence of Nietzsche in *fin-de-siècle* Vienna based on the parallels between Wittgenstein and Nietzsche; Viennese modernism, the crisis of identity, and the critique of language and culture initiated by Kraus and Mauthner; the interpretation of Wittgenstein's later philosophy and Jean-François Lyotard's philosophy of the *differend* as philosophical responses to European nihilism; and a philosophy of education developed from these insights (see Peters and Marshall, 1999).

3. Whether Wittgenstein should properly be viewed as an analytic philosopher has occasioned much comment and debate. Janik and Toulmin (1973: 19–21) first raised the heretical idea that the "analytical" Wittgenstein was a Cambridge construction:

By labeling Wittgenstein as a foreigner of odd personal habits, with an extraordinary, phenomenal, and possibly unique, talent for philosophical invention, the English thus defused the impact of his personality and moral passion as completely as they had neutralized Shaw's social and political teachings. (p. 20)

Sluga (1998) in a review of Hacker's (1996) *Wittgenstein's Place in Twentieth-Century Analytic Philosophy*, first questions "what is analytic philosophy?" Then he makes a plea for the importance of the history of analytic philosophy as a genuine philosophically and useful antidote to the ahistoricism of analytic philosophy, before he criticizes the Anglocentrism and nostalgic perspective that characterizes Hacker's account. In particular, Sluga (1998: 109) suggests that Hacker's reductive account

does not take proper note of the array of ideas that Wittgenstein brought with him from his Viennese background, such as his anti-metaphysical positivism, his concern for models and representations, his interest in ordinary language, his minimalist concern with formal structures. . . . By the time he wrote the *Tractatus*, he had also come under the spell of Tolstoy and Nietzsche—a fact not acknowledged by Hacker. (p. 109)

Sluga also notes an emerging new conception of Wittgenstein, which sees him less as a "producer of philosophical masterpieces" and more as "exemplifying a performative and process-oriented understanding of philosophy" (p. 115).

4. Critchley (1997: 348) suggests that it is

the conflation of philosophical tradition with political geography that leads to the ideological stereotyping and distortion that can be found in such labels as "British empiricism", "French rationalism", and "German metaphysics," labels which only seek to widen the gulf between philosophical traditions and block the possibility of dialogue.

He suggests that the locution "Continental philosophy" is a projection of the Anglo-American academy.

Bibliography

The translations of Nietzsche's works on which this collection in the main depends, except where specific texts and editions are cited, are the following:

STANDARD TEXTS AND TRANSLATIONS OF NIETZSCHE'S WORKS

The Antichrist. (1954) Trans. W. Kaufmann. In *The Portable Nietzsche*, ed. W. Kaufmann. New York: Viking Press.

Beyond Good and Evil. (1996) Trans. W. Kaufmann. New York: Viking Press.

The Birth of Tragedy. (1966) Trans. W. Kaufmann. New York: Viking Press. This volume also contains *The Case of Wagner*, trans. W. Kaufmann.

Daybreak: Thoughts on the Prejudices of Morality. (1982) Trans. R. J. Hollingdale. Cambridge: Cambridge University Press.

Ecce Homo. (1992) Trans. R. J. Hollingdale. New York: Penguin Books.

The Gay Science. (1974) Trans. W. Kaufmann. New York: Vintage Books.

Human, All Too Human. (1986) Trans. R. J. Hollingdale. Cambridge: Cambridge University Press. This volume also contains *Assorted Opinions and Maxims*, trans. R. J. Hollingdale, and *The Wanderer and His Shadow*, trans. R. J. Hollingdale.

Nietzsche Contra Wagner. (1954) Trans. W. Kaufmann. In *The Portable Nietzsche*, ed. W. Kaufmann. New York: Viking Press.

On the Genealogy of Morals. (1968) Trans. W. Kaufmann and R. J. Hollingdale. New York: Vintage Books. This volume also contains *Ecce Homo*, trans. W. Kaufmann.

"On Truth and Lies in a Nonmoral Sense." (1979) In *Philosophy and Truth: Selections from Nietzsche's Notebooks of the Early 1970s*, trans. and ed. D. Breazeale. Atlantic Highlands, NJ: Humanities Press.

"The Philosopher: Reflections on the Struggle between Art and Knowledge." (1979) In *Philosophy and Truth: Selections from Nietzsche's Notebooks of the Early 1970s*, trans. and ed. D. Breazeale. Atlantic Highlands, NJ: Humanities Press.

Richard Wagner at Bayreuth. (1983) The fourth of the *Untimely Meditations*, trans. R. J. Hollingdale. Cambridge: Cambridge University Press.

"Schopenhauer as Educator." (1983) In *Untimely Meditations*, trans. R. J. Hollingdale. Cambridge: Cambridge University Press.

Thus Spake Zarathustra. (1954) Trans. W. Kaufmann. In *The Portable Nietzsche*, ed. W. Kaufmann. New York: Viking Press.

Twilight of the Idols. (1954) Trans. W. Kaufmann. In *The Portable Nietzsche*, ed. W. Kaufmann. New York: Viking Press.

"Unfashionable Observations." (1995) In *The Complete Works of Friedrich Nietzsche*, vol. 2, ed. E. Behler. Stanford, CA: Stanford University Press, 1995.

The Will to Power. (1968) Trans. W. Kaufmann and R. J. Hollingdale. New York: Vintage Books.

OTHER NIETZSCHE WORKS AND EDITIONS REFERENCED IN THE TEXT

Beyond Good and Evil (1967) Trans. Helen Zimmern. Edinburgh: T. & A. Constable Ltd.

Beyond Good and Evil. (1990) Trans. R. J. Hollingdale, intro. M. Tanner. New York and London: Penguin Classics.

Beyond Good and Evil. (1992) In *Basic Writings of Nietzsche*, trans. W. Kaufmann. New York: Modern Library.

Beyond Good and Evil: Prelude to a Philosophy of the Future. (1996) New York: Random House.

The Birth of Tragedy and *On the Genealogy of Morals.* (1956) Trans. F. Golfing. New York: Anchor Books, Doubleday.

Daybreak. (1997) Trans. R. J. Hollingdale. Ed. M. Clark and B. Leiter. Cambridge: Cambridge University Press.

Die Fröhliche Wissenchaft. (1980) In *Friedrich Nietzsche: Sämtliche Werke. Kritische Studienausgabe in 15 Bänden, Band 3*, ed. G. Colli and M. Montinari. München: Deutscher Tasherbuch Verlag.

Ecce Homo. (1980) In *Friedrich Nietzsche: Sämtliche Werke. Kritische Studienausgabe in 15 Bänden, Band 6*, ed. G. Colli and M. Montinari. München: Deutscher Tasherbuch Verlag.

Genealogy of Morals. (1992) In *Basic Writings of Nietzsche*, trans. W. Kaufmann. New York: Modern Library.

Gesammelte Werke. Musarionausgabe. 23 vols. (1920–1929) Munich: Musarion Verlag.

Götzendämmerung. (1980) In *Friedrich Nietzsche: Sämtliche Werke. Kritische Studienausgabe in 15 Bänden, Band 6*, ed. G. Colli and M. Montinari. München: Deutscher Tasherbuch Verlag.

Human, All Too Human. (1984) Trans. M. Faber and S. Lehman. Lincoln: University of Nebraska Press.

Human, All Too Human. (1995) In *The Complete Works of Friedrich Nietzsche*, vol. 3, ed. E. Behler. Stanford, CA: Stanford University Press.

Nietzsche-Wagner Correspondence. (1922) Trans. Caroline V. Kerr. Ed. Elizabeth Förster-Nietzsche. London: Duckworth.

On the Future of Our Educational Institutions. (1964) Trans. J. M. Kennedy. In *The Complete Works of Friedrich Nietzsche*, vol. 3, ed. Oscar Levy. New York: Russell & Russell, 1964.

On the Genealogy of Morals. (1989) Trans. and ed. W. Kaufmann and R. J. Hollingdale. New York: Vintage Books.

On the Genealogy of Morals and *Ecce Homo.* (1989) Trans. and ed. W. Kaufmann. New York: Vintage Books. [Orig. 1887 and 1908]

Friedrich Nietzsche: Sämtliche Werke: Kritische Studienausgabe. 15 vols. (1980) Ed. G. Colli and M. Montinari. München: Deutscher Tasherbuch Verlag.

Untimely Meditations. (1997) Trans. R. J. Hollingdale. Cambridge: Cambridge University Press.

OTHER WORKS

Adler, M. (1982) *The Paideia Proposal: An Educational Manifesto.* New York: Collier Books.

Aloni, N. (1989) "The Three Pedagogical Dimensions of Nietzsche's Philosophy." *Educational Theory*, 39(4), 301–306.

Althusser, L. (1976) "Les Appareils idéologiques d'Etat." In *Positions (1964–1975).* Paris: Editions sociales, 67–125.

Altieri, C. (1994). *Subjective Agency: A Theory of First-Person Expressivity and Its Social Implications.* Oxford: Blackwell.

Ansell-Pearson, K. (1994) *An Introduction to Nietzsche as a Political Thinker.* Cambridge: Cambridge University Press.

Arcilla, R. V. (1995). *For the Love of Perfection: Richard Rorty and Liberal Education.* New York: Routledge.

Ascheim, S. (1992) *The Nietzsche Legacy in Germany 1890–1990.* Berkeley: University of California Press.

Aviram, A. (1991) "Nietzsche as Educator." *Journal of Philosophy of Education*, 25(2), 219–234.

Baier, A. (1985) "Theory and Reflective Practices." In *Postures of the Mind.* London: Methuen.

Bataille, G. (1945) *Sur Nietzsche.* Paris: Gallimard. [English translation. *On Nietzsche*, trans. B. Boone. New York: Paragon House, 1992.]

Bataille, G. (1985a) "Nietzsche and the Fascists." In *Visions of Excess: Selected Writings, 1927–1939*, trans. A. Stoekl with C. Lovitt and D. Leslie, ed. and intro. A. Stoekl. Manchester: Manchester University Press, 182–196.

Bataille, G. (1985b) "Nietzschean Chronicle." In *Visions of Excess: Selected Writings, 1927–1939*, trans. A. Stoekl with C. Lovitt and D. Leslie, ed. and intro. by A. Stoekl. Manchester: Manchester University Press, 202–212.

Bataille, G. (1985c) "Propositions." In *Visions of Excess: Selected Writings, 1927–1939*, trans. A. Stoekl with C. Lovitt and D. Leslie, ed. and intro. by A. Stoekl. Manchester: Manchester University Press, 197–201.

Bauman, Z. (1988) "Is There a Postmodern Sociology?" *Theory, Culture & Society*, 5, 217–237.

Baumler, A. (1931) *Nietzsche der Philosoph und Politiker.* Leipzig: Philipp Reclam.

Bearn, G. (1997) *Waking to Wonder: Wittgenstein's Existential Investigations.* Albany: State University of New York Press.

Behler, E. (1991) *Confrontations: Derrida, Heidegger, Nietzsche,* trans. S. Taubeneck. Stanford, CA: Stanford University Press.

Benda, J. (1927) *La Trahison des Clercs.* Paris: B. Grasset.

Benn, S. I. and Peters, R. S. (1959) *Social Principles and the Democratic State.* London: George Allen and Unwin.

Berkowitz, P. (1995) *Nietzsche: The Ethics of an Immoralist.* Cambridge, MA: Harvard University Press.

Besnier, J. (1995) "Bataille, the Emotive Intellectual." In *Bataille: Writing the Sacred,* ed. Carolyn Bailey Gill. London and New York: Routledge.

Bingham, C. (1998) "The Goals of Language, the Language of Goals: Nietzsche's Concern with Rhetoric and Its Educational Implications." *Educational Theory,* 48(2), 229–240.

Blanchot, M. (1987) "Reflections on Nihilism: Crossing of the Line." In *Friedrich Nietzsche,* ed. H. Bloom. New York: Chelsea House, 35–42.

Blondel, E. (1991) *Nietzsche, the Body and Culture: Philosophy as a Philological Genealogy.* Trans. S. Hand. Stanford, CA: Stanford University Press.

Bloom, A. (1987) *The Closing of the American Mind.* New York: Simon and Schuster.

Braidotti, R. (1996) *Patterns of Dissonance.* Cambridge: Polity Press.

Bullock, A., Stallybrass, O., and Trombley, S., eds. (1977) *The Fontana Dictionary of Modern Thought.* London: Fontana Press.

Camus, A. (1991) *The Myth of Sisyphus and Other Essays,* trans. Justin O'Brien. New York: Vintage Books.

Canguilhem, G. (1994) *A Vital Rationalise: Selected Writings from Georges Canguilhem.* ed. F. Delaporte. New York: Zone Books.

Cavarero, A. (1995) *In Spite of Plato: A Feminist Rewriting of Ancient Philosophy.* New York: Routledge.

Clark, M. (1990) *Nietzsche on Truth and Philosophy.* Cambridge and New York: Cambridge University Press.

Colli, G. and Montinari, M. (1980) *Friedrich Nietzsche: Sämtliche Werke. Kritische Studienausgabe in 15 Bänden.* München: Deutscher Tasherbuch Verlag.

Comay, R. (1990) "Redeeming Revenge: Nietzsche, Benjamin, Heidegger, and the Politics of Memory." In *Nietzsche as Postmodernist: Essays Pro and Contra,* ed. C. Koelb. Albany: State University of New York Press.

Connolly, W. E. (1991) *Identity/Difference: Democratic Negotiations of Political Paradox.* Ithaca, NY: Cornell University Press.

Conway, D. W. (1989) "Literature as Life: Nietzsche's Positive Morality." *International Studies in Philosophy,* 21, 41–53.

Conway, D. W. (1995) "Returning to Nature: Nietzsche's Götterdämmerung." In *Nietzsche: A Critical Reader,* ed. Peter R. Sidgwick. Oxford: Blackwell, 31–52.

Conway, D. W. (1997). *Nietzsche's Dangerous Game: Philosophy in the Twilight of the Idols.* Cambridge: Cambridge University Press.

Cooper, D. (1983a) *Authenticity and Learning: Nietzsche's Educational Philosophy.* London: Routledge and Kegan Paul.

Cooper, D. (1983b) "On Reading Nietzsche on Education." *Journal of Philosophy of Education*, 17(1), 119–126.

Copleston, F. C. (1965) *A History of Philosophy*, vol. 7. New York: Image Books.

Cormier, R. (1978) "Silence in Philosophy and Literature." *Philosophy Today*, 22, 301–306.

Critchley, S. (1997) "What Is Continental Philosophy?" *International Journal of Philosophical Studies*, 5(3), 347–365.

Dale, R. (1989) *The State and Education Policy*. Milton Keynes: Open University Press.

Danto, A. (1980) *Nietzsche as Philosopher*. New York: Columbia University Press.

Dasenbrock, R. W. (1989) *Redrawing the Lines: Analytic Philosophy, Deconstruction and Literary Theory*. Minneapolis: University of Minnesota Press.

Dávila, J. (1997) "An Exegesis of the Text *Was ist Aufklärung?* Foucault's Intellectual Testament." In *Foucault: The Legacy*, ed. Clare O'Farrell. Queensland: Queensland University of Technology, 185–191.

De Martelaere, P. (1994) "De al te menselijke wetenschap" [The all too human science]. In *Landschappen van Nietzsche. Kunst, wetenschap, leven en moraal* [Landscapes of Nietzsche. Art, science, life and morality], ed. O. De Bleeckere and E. Oger. Kampen: Kok Agora.

Deleuze, G. (1983) *Nietzsche and Philosophy*, trans. Hugh Tomlinson. London: Athlone Press. [Orig. 1962]

Deleuze, G. (1984) *Difference and Repetition*, trans. Paul Patton. London: Athlone Press.

Deleuze, G. (1995) *Negotiations 1972–1990*. New York: Columbia University Press.

Derrida, J. (1978a) "Violence and Metaphysics." In *Writing and Difference*. Chicago: University of Chicago Press.

Derrida, J. (1978b) *Writing and Difference*. Chicago: University of Chicago Press.

Derrida, J. (1979) *Spurs: Nietzsche's Styles/Eperons Les Styles de Nietzsche*. Chicago: University of Chicago Press.

Derrida, J. (1983) "The Principle of Reason: The University in the Eyes of its Pupils," trans. Catherine Porter and Edward P. Morris. *Diacritics*, 13, 3–20.

Derrida, J. (1985) *The Ear of the Other: Otobiography, Transference, Translation*, trans. Peggy Kamuf and ed. Christie V. McDonald. New York: Schocken.

Derrida, J. (1988) *Limited Inc*. Evanston, IL: Nortwestern University Press.

Derrida, J. (1994) "Nietzsche and the Machine: An Interview with Jacques Derrida by Richard Beardsworth." *Journal of Nietzsche Studies*, 7, 7–66.

Devine, N. (1998) " 'Trompe-l'oeil': A Critical Exploration of Theory Underpinning Public Choice Theory and the Preference for Individual Action." *Access*, 17 (2), 15–25.

Dewey, J. (1935) *Liberalism and Social Action*. New York: Capricorn Books.

Dewey, J. (1938) *Experience and Education*. New York: Collier Books.

Dewey, J. (1944) *Democracy and Education*. New York: The Free Press.

Dewey, J. (1950) *Human Nature and Conduct*. New York: The Modern Library.

Diprose, R. (1989) "Nietzsche, Ethics and Sexual Difference." *Radical Philosophy*, 52, 27–33.

Diprose, R. (1993) "The Pathos of Distance." In *Nietzsche and Political Theory*, ed. Paul Patton. St. Leonards, NSW: Allen and Unwin.

Diprose, R. (1994) *The Bodies of Women*. London and New York: Routledge.

Dreyfus, H. and Rabinow, P. (1982) *Michel Foucault: Beyond Structuralism and Hermeneutics.* Chicago: University of Chicago Press.

D'Souza, D. (1991) *Illiberal Education: The Politics of Race and Sex on Campus.* New York: The Free Press.

Eagleton, T. and Jarmon, D. (1993) *Wittgenstein: The Terry Eagleton Script: The Derek Jarmon Film.* London: British Film Institute.

Foot, P. (1973) "Nietzsche: The Revaluation of Values." In *Nietzsche: A Collection of Critical Essays,* ed. R. Soloman. Notre Dame, IN: University of Notre Dame Press.

Foucault, M. (1977a) "Theatrum Philosophicum." In *Language, Counter-Memory, Practice: Selected Essays and Interviews,* ed. D. Bouchard. Oxford: Blackwell, 165–198.

Foucault, M. (1977b) "Nietzsche, Genealogy, History." In *Language, Counter-Memory, Practice: Selected Essays and Interviews by Michel Foucault,* ed. D. Bouchard. New York: Cornell University Press, 139–164.

Foucault, M. (1984a) *The Foucault Reader,* ed. P. Rabinow. London: Penguin.

Foucault, M. (1984b) "What Is Enlightenment?" In *The Foucault Reader,* ed. P. Rabinow. New York: Pantheon.

Foucault, M. (1986) *The Care of the Self: The History of Sexuality: Vol. 3—An Introduction,* trans R. Hurley. London: Penguin.

Foucault, M. (1988) "Critical Theory/Intellectual History." In *Michel Foucault: Politics, Philosophy, Culture. Interviews and Other Writings 1977–84,* ed. L. J. Kritzman. London and New York: Routledge, 17–46.

Foucault, M. (1990) "Nietzsche, Freud, Marx." In *Transforming the Hermeneutic Context: From Nietzsche to Nancy,* ed. Ormistan and Alan Schrift. New York: State University of New York Press, 59–87.

Foucault, M. (1991) *Discipline and Punish: The Birth of the Prison.* Middlesex: Penguin.

Frazer, N. (1981) "Foucault on Modern Power: Empirical Insights and Normative Confusions." *Praxis International,* 1, 272–287.

Frazer, N. (1983) "Foucault's Body-Language: A Post-Humanist Political Rhetoric?" *Salmagundi,* 61, 55–70.

Gerhardt, V. (1992) "Selbstbegründung. Nietzsches Moral der Individualität." *Nietzsche Studies,* 21, 28–49.

Golomb, J. (1985) "Nietzsche's Early Educational Thought." *Journal of Philosophy of Education,* 19(1), 99–109.

Gordon, H. (1980) "Nietzsche's Zarathustra as Educator." *Journal of Philosophy of Education,* 14(2), 181–192.

Gray, J. (1984) *Hayek on Liberty.* Oxford: Blackwell.

Gray, J. (1986) *Liberalism.* Milton Keynes: Open University Press.

Habermas, J. (1971) *Knowledge and Human Interests,* trans. J. Shapiro. Boston: Beacon Press.

Habermas, J. (1981) "Modernity Versus Postmodernity." *New German Critique,* 22, 3–22.

Habermas, J. (1984) *Theory of Communicative Action,* Vol. 1, *Reason and the Rationalization of Society,* trans. T. McCarthy. Boston: Beacon Press.

Habermas, J. (1987a) *The Philosophical Discourse of Modernity,* trans. F. Lawrence. Cambridge, MA: MIT Press.

Habermas, J. (1987b) *Theory of Communicative Action, Vol. 2, System and Lifeworld: A Critique of Functionalist Reason.* Boston: Beacon Press.

Habermas, J. (1990) "Remarks on the Discussion." *Theory, Culture and Society,* 7, 127–132.

Hacker, P. M. S. (1996) *Wittgenstein's Place in Twentieth-Century Analytic Philosophy.* Oxford: Blackwell.

Haertle, A. (1937) *Nietzsche und der Nationalsozialismos.* Munich: F. Eher Nachfolger.

Harris, K. (1979) *Education and Knowledge: The Structured Misrepresentation of Reality.* London: Routledge and Kegan Paul.

Havas, R. (1995). *Nietzsche's Genealogy. Nihilism and the Will to Knowledge.* Ithaca, NY: Cornell University Press.

Hayman, R. (1980) *Nietzsche: A Critical Life.* New York: Oxford University Press.

Hegel, G. W. F. (1977) *Phenomenology of Spirit,* trans. A .V. Miller. Oxford: Oxford University Press.

Hegel, G. W. F. (1979) *Phenomenology of Spirit.* Oxford: Clarendon Press.

Hegel, G. W. F. (1990) *Encyclopedia of the Philosophical Sciences in Outline and Critical Writings,* ed. E. Behler, and trans. S. Taubeneck. New York: Continuum. [Orig. 1817]

Heidegger, M. (1977) "The Word of Nietzsche: 'God Is Dead'." In *The Question Concerning Technology and Other Essays,* trans. and intro. W. Lovitt. New York: Harper and Row.

Heidegger, M. (1991) *Nietzsche* (Vols. 1, 2, 3, 4), trans. D. Krell. San Francisco: Harper. [Orig. 1961]

Higgins, K. (1986) "Nietzsche's View of Philosophical Style." *International Studies in Philosophy,* 18, 67–81.

Higgins, K. (1988) "Reading Zarathustra." In *Reading Nietzsche,* ed. R. C. Solomon and K. Higgins. New York: Oxford University Press.

Higgins, K. (1990) "Nietzsche and Postmodern Subjectivity." In *Nietzsche as Postmodernist: Essays Pro and Contra,* C. Koelb. ed. Albany: State University of New York Press, 189–216.

Hillesheim, J. (1973) "Nietzsche Agonistes." *Educational Theory,* 23, 343–353.

Hillesheim, J.(1986) "Suffering and Self-Cultivation: The Case of Nietzsche." *Educational Theory,* 36(2), 171–178.

Hillesheim, J. (1990) "Nietzschean Images of Self-overcoming: Response to Rosenow." *Educational Theory,* 40(2), 211–215.

Howie, D. and Peters, M. (1996) "Positioning Theory: Vygotsky, Wittgenstein and Social Constructionist Psychology." *Journal for the Theory of Social Behaviour,* 26(1), 51–64.

Irigaray, L. (1985) *This Sex Which Is Not One.* Ithaca, NY: Cornell University Press.

Irigaray, L. (1991) *Marine Lover of Friedrich Nietzsche.* trans. G. C. Gill. New York: Columbia University Press.

Irigaray, L. (1992) *Elemental Passions.* New York: Routledge.

Irigaray, L. (1993a) *An Ethics of Sexual Difference,* trans. C. Burke and G. Gill. London: Athlone.

Irigaray, L. (1993b) *Sexes and Genealogies.* New York, Chichester, West Sussex: Columbia University Press.

Irigaray, L. (1993c) *Je, Tu, Nous.* New York and London: Routledge.

Irigaray, L. (1994) *Thinking the Difference*. New York and London: Routledge.

Irigaray, L. (1996a) *I Love to You*. New York and London: Routledge.

Jacoby, R. (1987) *The Last Intellectuals*. New York: Basic Books.

Jacoby, R. (1997) "Intellectuals: Inside and Outside the Academy." In *The Postmodern University? Contested Visions of Higher Education in Society*, ed. A. Smith and F. Webster. Buckingham: Society for Research into Higher Education/ Open University Press, 61–71.

Janaway, C. (1989) *Self and Will in Schopenhauer's Philosophy*. Oxford: Oxford University Press.

Janaway, C. (1994) *Schopenhauer*. Oxford and New York: Oxford University Press.

Janik, A. and Toulmin, S. (1973) *Wittgenstein's Vienna*. New York: Simon and Schuster.

Jaspers, K. (1947) *Nietzsche: Einfuhrung in das Verstandnis Seines Philosophierenes*. 2nd ed. Berlin: DeGruyter.

Jenkins, K. (1982) "The Dogma of Nietzsche's Zarathustra." *Journal of Philosophy of Education*, 16(2), 251–254.

Johnson, P. (1996) "Nietzsche's Reception Today." *Radical Philosophy*, 80 (November/December), 24–33.

Johnston, J. S. (1998) "Nietzsche as Educator." *Educational Theory*, 48, 67–83.

Jones, D. (1990) "The Genealogy of the Urban Schoolteacher." In *Foucault and Education: Disciplines and Knowledge*, ed. Stephen Ball. London: Routledge, 57–77.

Kaminsky, J. (1992) "A New History of Educational Philosophy in the United States: A Prologue." *Journal of Education*, 174 (1), 26–33.

Kaufmann, W. (1974) "Translator's Introduction." In *The Gay Science* by F. Nietzsche, trans. W. Kaufmann. New York: Vintage Books, 3–26.

Kaufmann, W. (1976) "Introduction." In *The Portable Nietzsche*, trans. and ed. W. Kaufmann. Harmondsworth: Penguin.

Kaufmann, W. (1989) "Introduction." In F. Nietszche, *On the Genealogy of Morals* and *Ecce Homo*, trans. and ed. W. Kaufmann and R. J. Hollingdale. New York: Vintage Books.

Kaufmann, W. (1990) *Nietzsche: Philosopher, Psychologist, Antichrist*. Princeton, NJ: Princeton University Press.

Kellner, D. (1995) "Intellectuals and New Technologies." *Media, Culture and Society*, 17, 427–448.

Kelsey, J. (1995) *The New Zealand Experiment: A World Model for Structural Adjustment?* Auckland: Auckland University Press.

Kholi, W. (1995) "Educating for Emancipatory Rationality." In *Critical Conversations in Philosophy of Education*, ed. W. Kholi. New York: Routledge.

Kimball, B. (1991) *Tenured Radicals*. New York: HarperPerennial.

Klossowski, P. (1969) *Nietzsche et le Cercle Vicieux*. Paris: Mercure de France.

Koelb, C., ed. (1990) *Nietzsche as Postmodernist: Essays Pro and Contra*. New York: State University of New York Press.

Kofmann, S. (1993) *Nietzsche and Metaphor*, trans. Duncan Large. London: Athlone Press.

Kohli, W. (1995) *Critical Conversations in Philosophy of Education*. New York: Routledge.

Krell, D. F. (1991) "Analysis" to Martin Heidegger's *Nietzsche*, Vol. 2. San Francisco: Harper, 255–276.

Krell, D. F. (1996) *Infectious Nietzsche*. Bloomington and Indianapolis: Indiana University Press.

Kristeva, J. (1987) *Tales of Love*, trans. Leon S. Roudiez. New York: Columbia University Press.

Kroker, A. and Weinstein, M. (1994) "The Hyper-Texted Body, or Nietzsche Gets a Modem." *Ctheory* <http://www.ctheory.com/e-hyper-texted.html>.

Kumar, K. (1997) "The Need for Place." In *The Postmodern University? Contested Visions of Higher Education in Society*, ed. A. Smith and F. Webster. Buckingham: Society for Research into Higher Education/Open University Press, 27–35.

Langsam, H. (1997) "How to Combat Nihilism? Reflections on Nietzsche's Critique of Morality." *History of Philosophy Quarterly*, 14, 235–253.

Large, D. (1993) "Translator's Introduction" to Sarah Kofman, *Nietzsche and Metaphor*. London: Athlone Press, vii–xl.

Larner, W. (1998) "A Means to an End: Neoliberalism and Social Process in New Zealand." *Studies in Political Economy*, 52 (Spring), 7–38.

Lash, S. with R. Boyne (1990) "Communicative Rationality and Desire." In S. Lash, *Sociology of Postmodernism*. London: Routledge.

Leiter, B. (1997) "Nietzsche and the Morality Critics." *Ethics*, 107, 250–285.

Lemert, C. C. (1991) "The Politics of Theory and the Limits of the Academy." In *Intellectuals and Politics: Social Theory in a Changing World*, ed. C. C. Lemert. Newbury Park, CA: Sage Publications, 177–187.

Lenk, H. (1991) "Logik, cheng ming und Interpretationskonstrukte." *Zeitschrift für Philosophische Forschung*, 45, 391–401.

Levinas, E. (1969) *Totality and Infinity*, trans. Alphonso Lingis. Pittsburgh, PA: Duquesne University Press.

Levinas, E. (1981) *Otherwise Than Being or Beyond Essence*, trans. Alphonso Lingis. Hingham, MA: Martinus Nijhoff.

Lingis, A (1977) "The Will to Power." In *The New Nietzsche: Contemporary Styles of Interpretation*, trans. D. B. Allison. Cambridge, MA: MIT Press.

Lotringer, S. (1992) "Furiously Nietzschean." Introduction to G. Bataille, *On Nietzsche*, trans. B. Boone. London: Athlone Press, vii–xv.

Louden, R. (1988) "Can We Be Too Moral?" *Ethics*, 98, 361–380.

Lyotard, J.-F. (1983) "Answering the Question: What Is Postmodernism?" In *Innovation/Renovation: New Perspective on the Humanities*, ed. I. Hassan and S. Hassan. Madison: University of Wisconsin Press, 329–341.

Lyotard, J.-F. (1984) *The Postmodern Condition: A Report on Knowledge*, trans. G. Bennington and B. Massumi. Minneapolis: University of Minnesota Press.

Lyotard, J.-F. (1988) *The Differend: Phrases in Dispute*, trans. Georges Van Den Abbeele. Minneapolis: University of Minnesota Press.

Lyotard, J.-F. (1994) "Nietzsche and the Inhuman: Interview with Jean-François Lyotard by Richard Beardsworth." *Journal of Nietzsche Studies*, 7, 67–130.

MacIntyre, A. (1981) *After Virtue*. Notre Dame, IN: University of Notre Dame Press.

Magnus, B. and Higgins, K., eds. (1996a) "Introduction." In *The Cambridge Companion to Nietzsche*. Cambridge: Cambridge University Press.

Magnus, B. and Higgins, K. (1996b) "Nietzsche's Works and Their Themes." In *The Cambridge Companion to Nietzsche*, ed. B. Magnus and K. Higgins. Cambridge, MA: Cambridge University Press, 21–70.

Magnus, E. (1970) *Heidegger's Metahistory of Philosophy*. The Hague: Martinus Nijhoff, 9–26.

Mahon, M. (1992) *Foucault's Nietzschean Genealogy: Truth, Power and the Subject*. Albany: State University of New York Press.

Marshall, J. (1996a) *Michel Foucault: Personal Autonomy and Education*. The Netherlands: Kluwer Academic Publishers.

Marshall, J. (1996b) "Foucault and Neo-liberalism: Biopower and Busno-Power." In *Philosophy of Education*, ed. Alven Neiman. University of Urbana–Champaign: Philosophy of Education Society:

Marshall, J. (1996c) "The Autonomous Chooser and 'Reforms' in Education." *Studies in Philosophy and Education*, 15, 89–96.

Marshall, J. (1996d) "Liberalism and Neoliberalism." Unpublished paper, University of Auckland.

Marshall, J. (1997) "The New Vocationalism." In *Education Policy in New Zealand: The 1990s and Beyond*, ed. Mark Olssen and Kay Morris Matthews. Palmerston North: Dunmore Press, 304–326.

Martin, G. T. (1989) *From Nietzsche to Wittgenstein: The Problem of Truth and Nihilism in the Modern World*. New York: Peter Lang.

McCarthy, T. (1987) "Introduction." In J. Habermas, *The Philosophical Discourse of Modernity*, trans. F. Lawrence. Cambridge, MA: MIT Press, vii–xvii.

Miller, J. (1998) "The Prophet and the Dandy: Philosophy as a Way of Life in Nietzsche and Foucault." *Social Research*, 65(4), 871–896.

Monk, R. (1996) *Bertrand Russell: The Spirit of Solitude*. London: Jonathon Cape.

Moore, G. E. (1955) "Wittgenstein's Lectures at Cambridge 1930–32." *Mind*, 64, 1–27.

Morris, M. (1998) "Address on Public Culture." University of Auckland, July 2.

Nagel, Thomas. (1986) *The View from Nowhere*. New York: Oxford University Press.

Nehamas, A. (1985) *Nietzsche: Life as Literature*. Cambridge, MA: Harvard University Press.

Nehamas, A. (1996) "Nietzsche, Modernity, Aestheticism." In *The Cambridge Companion to Nietzsche*, ed. B. Magnus and K. Higgins. Cambridge: Cambridge University Press, 223–251.

O'Farrell, C., ed. (1997) *Foucault: The Legacy*. Brisbane: Queensland University of Technology.

Ojakangas, M. (1997) "The Ethics of Singularity in an Era of Complete Nihilism." In *Foucault: The Legacy*, ed. Clare O'Farrell. Brisbane: Queensland University of Technology, 176–184.

Oppel, F. (1993) "Speaking of Immemorial Waters." In *Nietzsche and Political Theory*, ed. P. Patton. St. Leonards, NSW: Allen and Unwin.

Ornery, M., Miller, J., and Ellsworth, E. (1996) "Excessive Moments and the Educational Discourses That Try to Contain Them." *Educational Theory*, 46(1), 71–91.

Patton, P. (1993) "Introduction." In *Nietzsche, Feminism and Political Theory*, ed. P. Patton. London: Routledge.

Peters, M. A. (1996) *Poststructuralism, Politics and Education*. Westport, CT: Bergin & Garvey.

Peters, M. A. (1997) "What Is Poststructuralism? The French Reception of Nietzsche." *Political Theory Newsletter*, 8(2), 39–55.

Peters, M. A. (1998) "Introduction: Naming the Multiple—Poststructuralism and Education." In: *Naming the Multiple: Poststructuralism and Education*, ed. M. Peters. Westport, CT: Bergin & Garvey.

Peters, M. A. and Marshall, J. D. (1996) *Individualism and Community: Education and Social Policy in the Postmodern Condition*. London: Falmer Press.

Peters, M. A. and Marshall, J. D. (1999) "Nietzsche and Wittgenstein: Philosophers of the Future." In *Wittgenstein: Philosophy, Postmodernism, Pedagogy*. Westport, CT: Bergin and Garvey, 33–51.

Peters, R. S. (1966) *Ethics and Education*. London: Unwin University Books.

Pitkin, H. (1972) *Wittgenstein and Justice*. Berkeley: University of California Press.

Podach, E. F. (1930) *Nietzsche's Zusammenbruch*. Heidelberg: N. Kampmann.

Poster, M. (1984) *Foucault, Marxism and History: Mode of Production versus Mode of Information*. Oxford: Polity Press.

Prado, C. G. (1995) *Starting with Foucault: An Introduction to Genealogy*. Boulder, CO: Westview Press.

Pulliam, J. and Van Patten, J. (1995) *A History of Education in America*. Englewood Cliffs, NJ: Prentice-Hall.

Readings, B. (1995) "From Emancipation to Obligation: Sketch for a Heteronomous Politics of Education." In *Education and the Postmodern Condition*, ed. Michael Peters. Westport, CT: Bergin & Garvey, 193–208.

Rethy, R. (1986) "The Metaphysics of Nullity." *Philosophy Research Archives*, 12, 357–386.

Richardson, J. (1997) "Is there a Nietzschean Post-analytic Method?" *International Studies in Philosophy*, 29, 9–36.

Ridley, A. (1998) "A Nietzsche Round-Up." *The Philosophical Quarterly*, 48(191), 235–242.

Rorty, R. (1989) *Contingency, Irony and Solidarity*. Cambridge and New York: Cambridge University Press.

Rosenow, E. (1973) "What Is Free Education? The Educational Significance of Nietzsche's Thought." *Educational Theory*, 354–370.

Rosenow, E. (1986) "Nietzsche's Concept of Education." In *Nietzsche as Affirmative Thinker*, ed., Y. Yovel. Dordrecht: Martinus Nijhoff.

Rosenow, E. (1989) "Nietzsche's Educational Dynamite." *Educational Theory*, 39 (4), 307–316.

Rousseau, J. (1979) *Emile or on Education*, trans. A. Bloom. New York: Basic Books. [Orig. 1764]

Royle, N. (1995) *After Derrida*. Manchester: Manchester University Press.

Russell, B. (1946) The *History of Western Philosophy*. London: George Allen and Unwin.

Russell, B. (1967) *The Autobiography of Bertrand Russell: 1872–1914*. London: George Allen and Unwin.

Salomé, L. (1988) *Nietzsche*. ed., trans., and intro. by S. Mandel. Redding Ridge, CT: Black Swan Books.

Sassone, L. (1996) "Philosophy Across the Curriculum: A Democratic Nietzschean Pedagogy." *Educational Theory*, 46(4), 511–534.

Schacht, R. (1990) "Zarathustra/*Zarathustra* as Educator." In *Nietzsche: A Critical Reader*, ed. P. Sedgwick. Oxford: Blackwell, 222–249.

Schacht, R. (1994) *Nietzsche, Genealogy, Morality: Essays on Nietzsche's The Genealogy of Morals.* London and Berkeley: University of California Press.

Schacht, R. (1995a) *Making Sense of Nietzsche: Reflections Timely and Untimely.* Chicago: University of Illinois Press.

Schact, R. (1995b) "Nietzsche." In *The Oxford Companion to Philosophy*, ed. Ted Honderich. Oxford: Oxford University Press, 619–623.

Schneider, J. (1992) "Nietzsche's basler Vorträge 'Ueber die Zukunft unserer Bildungsanstalten' im lichte seiner Lektüre pädagogischer Schriften." *Nietzsche Studien*, 21, 308–325.

Schopenhauer, A. (1969) *The World as Will and Representation*, Vols. 1 & 2, trans. E. F. J. Payne. New York: Dover.

Schor, N. and Weed, E. eds. (1994) *The Essential Difference*. Bloomington and Indianapolis: Indiana University Press.

Schrift, A. (1990) *Nietzsche and the Question of Interpretation: Between Hermeneutics and Deconstruction*. London: Routledge.

Schrift, A. (1995) *Nietzsche's French Legacy: A Genealogy of Poststructuralism*, London and New York: Routledge.

Schrift, A. (1996) "Nietzsche's French Legacy." In *The Cambridge Companion to Nietzsche*, ed. B. Magnus and K. Higgins. Cambridge: Cambridge University Press, 323–355.

Schroeder, W. (1992) "Nietzschean Philosophers." *International Studies in Philosophy*, 24(2), 112–113.

Schutte, O. (1984) *Beyond Nihilism: Nietzsche without Masks*. Chicago: University of Chicago Press.

Schwab, G. M. (1994) "Mother's Body, Father's Tongue: Mediation and the Symbolic Order." In *Engaging with Irigaray*, ed. Carolyn Burke, Naomi Schor and Margaret Whitford. New York: Columbia University Press.

Sen, A. (1987) *On Ethics and Economics*. Oxford: Blackwell.

Shapiro, G. (1989) *Nietzschean Narratives*. Indianapolis: Indiana University Press.

Shapiro, G. (1991) "Nietzsche and the Future of the University." *Journal of Nietzsche Studies*, 1, 15–28.

Sharp, A. M. (1984) "Nietzsche's View of Sublimation in the Educational Process." *Journal of Educational Thought*, 9(2), 99–106.

Simons, M. (1988) "Montessori, Superman, and Catwoman." *Educational Theory*, 38(3), 341–349.

Slote, M. (1983) *Goods and Virtues*. Oxford: Clarendon.

Sluga, H. (1998) "What Has History to Do with Me? Wittgenstein and Analytic Philosophy." *Inquiry*, 41, 99–121.

Smith, A. and Webster, F. (1997) "Changing Ideas of the University." In *The Postmodern University? Contested Visions of Higher Education in Society*, ed. A. Smith and F. Webster. Buckingham: Society for Research into Higher Education/Open University Press, 1–14.

Smith, G. B. (1996) *Nietzsche, Heidegger and the Transition to Postmodernity*. Chicago: University of Chicago Press.

Solomon, R. C. (1986) "A More Severe Morality: Nietzsche's Affirmative Ethics." In *Nietzsche as Affirmative Thinker*, ed. Y. Yovel. Dordrecht: Martinus Nijhoff, 69–89.

Solomon, R. C. (1996) "Nietzsche *Ad Hominen*: Perspective, Personality and *Resentiment* Revisited." In *The Cambridge Companion to Nietzsche*, ed. B. Magnus and K. M. Higgins. Cambridge and New York: Cambridge University Press, 183–222.

Spivak, G. (1976) "Introduction." To Jacques Derrida, *Of Grammatology*. Baltimore, MD: Johns Hopkins University Press.

Starrett, S. N. (1992) "Nietzsche and MacIntyre: Against Individualism." *International Studies in Philosophy*, 24, 13–20.

Strike, K. (1982) *Educational Policy and the Just Society*. Chicago: University of Illinois Press.

Sykes, C. J. (1988) *Profscam: Professors and the Demise of Higher Education*. Washington, DC: Regnery Gateway.

Taubeneck, S. (1991) "Translator's Afterword: Walter Kaufmann and After." In *Confrontations: Derrida, Heidegger, Nietzsche*, trans. S. Taubeneck and ed. E. Behler. Stanford, CA: Stanford University Press.

Thacker, A. (1997) "Clutter and Glitter: Foucault and the Writing of History." In *Foucault: The Legacy*, ed. C. O'Farrell. Brisbane: Queensland University of Technology, 192–201.

Van Tongeren, P. (1994) "Een moraal voor moralisten (A morality for moralists)." In *Landschappen van Nietzsche. Kunst, wetenschap, leven en moraal (Landscapes of Nietzsche. Art, Science, Life and Morality)*, ed. O. De Bleeckere and E. Oger. Kampen: Kok Agora.

Vasseleu, C. (1993) "Not Drowning, Sailing." In *Nietzsche, Feminism and Political Theory*, ed. Paul Patton. St. Leonards, NSW: Allen and Unwin.

Waller, B. N. (1995) "Authenticity Naturalized." *Behavior and Philosophy*, 23, 21–28.

Warren, M. (1988) *Nietzsche and Political Thought*. Cambridge, MA and London: MIT Press.

Warren, M. (1998) "Political Readings of Nietzsche." *Political Theory*, 26(1), 90–111.

Wellbery, D. (1985) "Postmodernism in Europe: On Recent German Writing." *The Postmodern Moment*, ed. S. Trachtenberg. Westport, CT: Greenwood Press, 229–250.

Whitford, M. (1994) *Engaging with Irigaray*, ed. Carolyn Burke, Nancy Schor and Margaret Whitford. New York: Columbia University Press.

Wicks, R. (1997) "Friedrich Nietzsche." In *The Stanford Encyclopedia of Philosophy*, ed. Edward Zalta and Eric Hammer. Stanford, CA. <http://plato.stanford.edu/archives/win1997/entries/nietzsche/>.

Williams, B. (1993) "Nietzsche's Minimalist Moral Psychology." *European Journal of Philosophy*, 1, 4–11.

Wilshire, B. (1990) *The Moral Collapse of the University*. Albany: State University of New York Press.

Wittgenstein, L. (1953) *Philosophical Investigations*, trans. G. E. M. Anscombe. Oxford: Blackwell.

Wittgenstein, L. (1961) *Notebooks, 1914–1916*. Oxford: Blackwell.

Wittgenstein, L. (1963) *Tractatus-Logico-Philosophicus*, trans. D. F. Pears. London: Routledge and Kegan Paul.

Wittgenstein, L. (1969) *On Certainty*. Oxford: Blackwell.

Wittgenstein, L. (1980) *Culture and Value*, trans. Peter Winch. Chicago: University of Chicago Press.

Wittgenstein, L. (1993) *Philosophical Occasions, 1912–1951*, eds. J. C. Klagge and Alfred Nordmann. Indianapolis, IN: Hacket Publishing Company.

Wittgenstein, L. (1994) *The Wittgenstein Reader*, ed. Anthony Kenny. Oxford: Blackwell.

Wolf, S. (1982) "Moral Saints." *Journal of Philosophy*, 79, 419–439.

Young, J. (1992) *Nietzsche's Philosophy of Art*. Cambridge: Cambridge University Press.

Young. M. F. D. (1971) "An Approach to the Study of Curricula as Socially Organised Knowledge." In *Knowledge and Control*, ed. M. F. D. Young. New York: Collier-Macmillan.

Index

About the Contributors

VALERIE ALLEN teaches Medieval Studies and Philosophy at the John Jay College of Criminal Justice, City University of New York. She previously taught at the University of South Florida and at the University of Stirling, Scotland.

ARES AXIOTIS, formerly a Research Fellow of Clare Hall, Cambridge, and Lecturer in Philosophy at the University of Stirling, Scotland, practices law in New York.

PATRICK FITZSIMONS is Senior Lecturer at James Cook University in Australia. He has published nationally and internationally on wide-ranging topics including education policy, critical social theory, poststructuralist approaches to social policy, globalization, teacher education and human resource issues and the implications of electronically mediated technology. He is currently an associate editor of *Educational Philosophy and Theory*.

PETER FITZSIMONS is a mature post-graduate student at the University of Auckland, where he brings a broad life experience to his current Ph.D. thesis on Nietzsche and Education. His research interest is on perspectivism and ethics, particularly the impact of Nietzsche's thought on formulations of the self in an education system. He is a member of the Friedrich Nietzsche Society and Assistant Editor of *Educational Philosophy and Theory*.

F. RUTH IRWIN is a graduate student in the School of Education at the University of Auckland. Her research interests are the nature of knowledge, subjectivity, and philosophy of mind. Her present focus is on Nietzsche and Heidegger and their interpretation by poststructuralist theorists, particularly Deleuze, Foucault and Lyotard. Her other field of interest is feminist approaches to equity issues in education.

SCOTT JOHNSTON is a doctoral student at the Department of Educational Policy Studies at the University of Illinois at Champaign-Urbana. He has published recently on Nietzsche in *Educational Theory* and is presently completing a thesis on aspects of Nietzsche's educational philosophy.

JAMES MARSHALL is Professor of Education and was the Foundation Dean of the Faculty of Education at the University of Auckland, New Zealand. He is the author or editor of 22 books, including an authored book on Foucault, a co-authored book with Michael Peters on social policy, a co-authored book with Dominique Marshall on punishment of children, and books on Wittgenstein with Paul Smeyers and Michael Peters. He has published widely in international journals in the areas of social theory, policy and education.

BETSAN MARTIN has taught in Te Aratiatia, Maori Education, in the area of ethnic relations. The Treaty of Waitangi, which was signed between the British Crown and Maori Chiefs in Aotearoa/New Zealand in 1840, has been a major area of research and educational focus for Dr. Martin.

MICHAEL PETERS is Professor in the School of Education, University of Auckland, New Zealand. His research interests are in the areas of philosophy and policy studies. He is the author of a number of books, including *Poststucturalism, Politics and Education* (Bergin & Garvey, 1996) and *Wittgenstein: Philosophy, Postmodernism, Pedagogy* with James Marshall (Bergin & Garvey, 1999). He also has edited a number of collections including *Education and the Postmodern Condition* (Bergin & Garvey, 1995), and *Naming the Multiple: Poststructuralism and Education* (Bergin & Garvey, 1998).

STEFAN RAMAEKERS is Research Fellow and Tutor at the Katholieke Universiteit Leuven, Belgium. His M.A. thesis was a study of Annette Baier's critique, inspired by Hume, on the moral, rationalistic tradition. He is currently working on the topic of skepticism for a Ph.D.

PETER ROBERTS is a Senior Lecturer in the School of Education at the University of Auckland in New Zealand. His major areas of scholarship are educational philosophy and higher education policy. His work has appeared in a wide range of international journals, and he has published several books, including *Virtual Technologies and Tertiary Education* (co-edited with Michael Peters, 1998), and *Education, Literacy and Humanization* (forthcoming with Bergin & Garvey).

PAUL SMEYERS is a Professor in the Faculty of Psychology and Educational Sciences, University of Leuven, Belgium, where he teaches philosophy of education and qualitative research methods. He has published widely in Anglo-Saxon and European journals on issues related to a Wittgensteinian Philosophy of Education. With Nigel Blake, Richard Smith and Paul Standish he co-authored *Thinking Again: Education after Postmodernism* (Bergin & Garvey, 1998).

JULIANE VARVARO is a Ph.D. candidate at the University of Illinois at Champaign-Urbana. Her primary research interests are "the care of the self" as well as the role of language and knowledge in the construction of the self. She has continued her interests in ethics through the points of view of modern/postmodern thinkers; she has also begun directing increasing attention to Classical Greek and Christian understandings, as well as to the French philosophical and psychoanalytical philosophers.